# The Sociology of Gender

# The Sociology of Gender

A Brief Introduction

Third Edition

Laura Kramer
*Montclair State University*

New York    Oxford
OXFORD UNIVERSITY PRESS
2011

Oxford University Press, Inc., publishes works that further Oxford University's
objective of excellence in research, scholarship, and education.

Oxford   New York
Auckland   Cape Town   Dar es Salaam   Hong Kong   Karachi
Kuala Lumpur   Madrid   Melbourne   Mexico City   Nairobi
New Delhi   Shanghai   Taipei   Toronto

With offices in
Argentina   Austria   Brazil   Chile   Czech Republic   France   Greece
Guatemala   Hungary   Italy   Japan   Poland   Portugal   Singapore
South Korea   Switzerland   Thailand   Turkey   Ukraine   Vietnam

Copyright © 2011, 2005, 2000 by Oxford University Press, Inc.

Published by Oxford University Press, Inc.
198 Madison Avenue, New York, New York 10016

http://www.oup.com

Oxford is a registered trademark of Oxford University Press

**Library of Congress Cataloging-in-Publication Data**

ISBN: 978-0-19-538928-9

Printed in the United States of America
on acid-free paper

# CONTENTS

In 1976, my friend Laurie Davidson suggested we write a textbook for the new academic phenomenon: a sociology course on "sex roles." That collaboration resulted in *The Sociology of Gender* (Rand McNally 1979). We discussed many topics in that text based on our training in sociology, cobbling together evidence from a discipline with a literature that generally took gender for granted or defined it as an unwanted complication in research design, and we posed a multitude of questions for which no research had yet been conducted to provide or even suggest answers.

By the time I edited *The Sociology of Gender: A Text-Reader* (St. Martin's Press 1991), the area had developed into one of the most intellectually dynamic specializations within sociology. It was daunting to select from among the wealth of possibilities, and to write introductory essays to frame each of the collection's major sections. Don Reisman, my superb editor, helped me face that challenge.

Writing the first edition of *The Sociology of Gender: A Brief Introduction* (Roxbury 2001), I found the inclusion of a gender perspective in the work of many sociologists with other specializations, enormously enlarging the literatures that would help inform the text. In the following years, the further growth in feminist research and theoretical work on gender has been enormous. The dramatic political, social, and economic dynamics of the last few years added to the need for a second, and now a third edition, and the intellectual excitement of creating them. Revision is often tedious and mechanical, but in this case it has been intellectually exciting. Reflecting on the thirty-five years since I first offered a selected topics course on gender (team-taught with Meredith McGuire), I am delighted by what has been accomplished in the scholarship and in the social world that feminist sociologists have helped to bring about.

### CHANGES TO THE THIRD EDITION

The third edition has been revised throughout, making use of the considerable literature published in the last five years, a literature particularly strengthened with scholarship on boys, men, and masculinities, and the body and sexuality. This edition situates the gender system in the rapidly changing political and economic circumstances of the U.S. presidential primary and election of 2008 and the mortgage and credit crises of 2008–2009. Information about gender in the family (e.g., the composition of U.S. households), education (e.g., the distribution of men and women in various fields of study at the bachelor's degree level), the economy (e.g., the distribution of women and men of the largest racial-ethnic groups among the major occupational categories), and the political and legal system (e.g., the sex composition of the U.S. Congress and state legislatures as of 2009) have been updated or added. In addition, the final chapter, "The Changing

Gender System," has been substantially revised. These updates are useful for showing both areas of change and areas of persistent inequality in the social realities of gender.

My students at Montclair State University have made invaluable contributions to this project. They have helped educate me to the many changes in the gender system and provided feedback about my work. Colleagues at Montclair State provided invaluable assistance throughout my career. For this edition, I give particular thanks to Yasemin Besen, Alice Freed, Sally McWilliams, Susan O'Neil, and Janet Ruane. As I tried desperately to keep track of the whirlwind changes in news organizations, and to strategize making sense of available "information," I often wished I could turn for guidance to Ruth Bayard Smith. Librarians are always in a class by themselves. The reference, interlibrary loan, periodicals, and circulation departments at Montclair State's Sprague Library have always been able to meet my challenges.

I benefitted recently from eighteen months at the ADVANCE Program at the National Science Foundation (NSF); people working hard to achieve gender equity in science and engineering (at NSF and elsewhere) added to my appreciation of the complexity of such efforts. I will be eternally grateful to Alice Hogan for this opportunity, and to Carla Howery for helping me to make the most of it. Many kinds of guidance and insight came from Jessie DeAro, Sonia Esperanca, Anne Fischer, Judy Vance, Vanessa Richardson, and the NSF knitters. I increasingly appreciate my tacitly but fundamentally feminist education at (then all-girls) Hunter College High School, with teachers and classmates who presumed we all could do anything if we tried hard enough.

Friends who have helped include Ursula Brylinsky, Laurie Davidson, Betty Ferber, Lisa Frehill, Beth Hutchison, Harriet Klein, Bob Pomerance, Barbara Repetto, Phyllis Rooney, Sally McWilliams and Mary Zimmerman. Margo Sage-El provides a wonderful space, at Watchung Booksellers, for the exploration of ideas, and takes seriously the strangest of questions and requests.

Sherith Pankratz and Whitney Laemmli have shown great confidence in my efforts. They left me to my own devices, but answered questions almost before I asked them. They gathered a useful group of critiques for use as I began the revisions. Thanks to those colleagues: Shawna Cleary, University of Central Oklahoma; Jean Egan, Asnuntuck Community College; Jean Elson, University of New Hampshire; Marilyn Helterline, State University of New York College at Oneonta; Caroll Hodgson, Rowan-Cabarrus Community College; Jennifer A. Johnson, Virginia Commonwealth University; Kathryn Feltey, University of Akron; Diamantino P. Machado, Drexel University; Jane Emery Prather, California State University, Northridge; and Glenna L. Simons, St. Mary-of-the-Woods College. I also received very helpful comments from Lisa Brush of the University of Pittsburgh and Gail Murphy-Geiss of Colorado College.

This text is the product, in some ways, of my life time. My parents and grandparents were feminists, and the first edition of this book was dedicated to them: Aaron and Katherine Kramer, and Anna and Jack Kolodny. My sister, Carol Kramer, was an outstanding feminist social scientist, friend, sister, and aunt; I dedicated the second edition to her. My daughters and our newer family members are more than able to carry on the feminist tradition. Once again I thank Nora and Joanna Gordon and John Douard, and I happily add Jeremy, Aaron, and Gabriel Horowitz to this list.

# The Sociology of Gender

# Introduction

Imagine that you wake up tomorrow and you have become a member of the "opposite" sex. Many things about your day will be unchanged: you will listen to the same music, wear the same clothes to class (whether blue jeans and a bright T-shirt or all black), spend some time at a job or hanging with friends, and enjoy the sunshine or complain about the rain. But many things about your day will be different.

For example, if you have become a woman, you may spend more time getting yourself ready to leave home. If you have become a man, you will probably have to be more careful about not doing anything that seems disrespectful of other males you encounter in public places. Becoming male may lead you to volunteering for the campus escort service, accompanying students who are concerned about walking on campus alone after dark; if you've become female, you may call for an escort. In addition, you may find your family responsibilities have changed. Newly male, you are expected to clear out the trash, or newly female, you are expected to get the dinner started when you return from campus. If you are a male who is expected to cook dinner, it will probably be something easier to prepare than what is on the menu for your female self.

Regardless of the change, you won't drop English composition or American history to meet graduation requirements. But if you have become male, you will be more likely to major in physics or philosophy than you are today, and if you have become female you are more likely to major in psychology or biology. You may work in a local restaurant today; tomorrow, though, the particular job you have in that restaurant may change. If you were female and waited on tables, you may now be washing dishes. If you were male and waited on tables, that restaurant may not be interested in your services at all. If you have become male, you may sit further back in the classroom than you did yesterday, whereas on becoming female, you may find some teachers don't call on you when you raise your hand. If you have become female, you may feel self-conscious when you realize you are the only nonmale working in the computer lab in the engineering building. If you have become male, you may lose the baby-sitting job you have today.

Would these changes in your daily life bother you? Do you assume you'd prefer them, that you would want different things and have different tastes if your sex changed? What if you did not want to go along with these differences? If you objected to such changes in your obligations and responsibilities, privileges and prohibitions, what success would you have? Would your objections be respected, or would it be worth the trouble to object at all? Looking at these questions sociologically helps in understanding the processes that lead us to where we are and affects our chances of changing our circumstances.

Sociologists study the social meanings that groups build around the categories of female and male. We use **sexes** to refer to the categories that most contemporary societies define as physically based, despite the existence of many people whose bodies (genitally or genetically, or both) do not fit neatly into either a female or male category. Even though people increasingly also use the word gender to refer to those physically related categories, sociologists define **gender** as the totality of meanings that are attached to the sexes within a particular social system. More broadly, the **gender system** is a system of meaning and differentiation, linked to the sexes through social arrangements.

Over the last hundred years and more, gender has been dynamic; a variety of the social meanings attached to the sexes have changed. Although the sorting of people into two categories continues, the socially constructed character of gender has become visible. In many ways, gender has become less obvious as a system that influences our lives. In particular, women's opportunities have expanded—from gaining the right to own property, to vote (in the U.S. in 1920, for white women and some women of color, and in the 1960s, for those disenfranchised on the basis of race rather than sex), to enter many occupations and professions previously closed to women, to work night shifts, to wear pants rather than skirts to school, work, and public accommodations, such as restaurants. Men's lives have changed as well—to the greater acceptance of fathers' involvement in the daily care of their children, to sharing the risk of asking someone for a date, to the acceptability of wearing more varied and colorful clothes.

In other ways, the meanings of gender have changed, but not lost, importance in our lives. For example, young women are not expected to be virgins at marriage (Brumberg 1997). Yet the expectations of the amount and the circumstances of young people's sexual activity are strongly differentiated between those for females and those for males, with a harsher judgment passed on young women who have had multiple sexual partners than on young men who have done so. Few men now succeed at work because of physical strength, but many use chemicals in pursuit of the embodiment of cultural notions of masculine size and strength.

Thus, the gender system has changed a great deal. Sociologists of gender focus on the nature of those changes, the forces that lead to them, and the obstacles to change. If we consider that some contemporary realities of the gender system are not fair, then we can learn from past experiences about the ways that struggles for justice have been successful.

## WHAT IS THE SOCIOLOGY OF GENDER?

The sociology of gender is an important aid to developing an accurate picture of the dynamic gender system, its influence on the lives of individuals and groups, and the kinds of human efforts that have led to a reduction of its influence.

Sociology is the study of people in groups; it examines the whole range of social phenomena—from relationships among individuals in the smallest groups to comparisons of whole societies and patterns of sociohistorical developments. In the study of gender, sociologists explore the meanings of maleness and femaleness in social contexts, examining the diversity of gender systems in various cultures and social groups. Sociologists take the view that gender is **socially constructed**; that is, the differences between females and males are not based in some biologically determined truth. For example, in the nineteenth century, affluent white women in the United States were expected to stay at home once their pregnancies were apparent (a period called "confinement") and to be treated as infirm for weeks after delivery. Enslaved women, in contrast, worked until going into labor and resumed work shortly afterward. The impact of pregnancy and childbirth on a woman's physical capacities was constructed differently depending on social categories other than her sex.

Sociologists investigate the significant impacts that social meanings of gender have on individual and collective experience, finding ways that social forces influence even physical differences between sexes. For example, the speed of female and of male runners is affected by opportunities and expectations, rather than being dictated by genetically linked differences. In the first decades after equal access to physical education was extended to girls, and notions of women's inherent limitations were challenged, one women's speed record after another fell, and the gap in speed between male and female champions was reduced. In this sense, social construction refers simply to the social forces that shape differences. If one must put up with being called a "tomboy" for being very active, she may decide not to, and her performance will suffer. If one must put up with being called a "sissy" or a "girl" for not being athletic, he may decide to put extra hours into practicing to develop whatever "natural" ability he might have.

But social construction has a stronger meaning as well; it refers to the social practice of perceiving and defining aspects of people and situations inconsistently, to force our observations to fit our social beliefs. Thus, before the women's movement (which started in the late 1960s), the scoring of vocational tests, taken by people to determine what careers they might best follow, was done with two answer keys—one for females and one for males. Even if your answers were identical to those of someone of the other sex, the vocational advice was different.

For a more dramatic example, the very notion that all humans can be clearly and without argument categorized as female or male is a social construction. Some people have chromosomal patterns associated with one sex, and they have primary (genital) sex characteristics or secondary (e.g., facial hair) sex characteristics, or both, associated with the other. Some people have genitalia that are not clearly what our culture labels either "male" or "female." These variations in people's biological characteristics are more common than our cultural beliefs suggest. Indeed, we are unable to know how common these variations are because we are unable (in the case of chromosomal difference) or unwilling (in the case of forcing those with visible characteristics labeled male and others labeled female into one of the two categories) to see the variability in the population. When a group, such as the International Olympic Committee, has the authority to decide which is the defining characteristic, a person who has thought herself or himself one sex may find she or he suddenly has been labeled as the other.

Sociologists of gender pursue questions about people and **social structure**: the pattern of social relationships and behaviors. They investigate gender in the smallest and most transitory collections of people, such as strangers' conduct in a public place, to the largest and most stable social groups, such as women's social power in agricultural and industrial societies. What makes an inquiry essentially *sociological* is the initial and fundamental expectation that patterns observed in social life, such as discriminatory practices and pay scales, are themselves strongly influenced (if not caused) by social forces. The search for social explanations for patterns in society is common to the various and often contrasting sociological theories that shape research projects.

Although the sociology of gender does address many popular questions, it uses a perspective unusual in the United States, where people tend to focus instead on the personal and psychological. In the pages that follow, the topics may seem familiar, but you may believe, at least initially, that the search for answers is misdirected. For example, many people within and outside of academia are interested in knowing the responsibilities that each spouse has around the house. It is easy to see a widespread pattern of husbands having fewer responsibilities at home than wives, regardless, it seems, of both husbands' and wives' other responsibilities. In accounting for this imbalance, sociologists are especially likely to look at associated factors, such as the differences between husbands' and wives' earnings. In contrast, you may be used to looking only at differences in personality or personal habits and tastes stemming from early childhood experiences.

The important causal role that sociologists expect to find for social forces contrasts sharply with the approaches taken in other social sciences as well as in popular explanations of social phenomena. Sociologists do sometimes focus on small groups, called the **micro-social** level. Even in micro-social studies, however, the sociological perspective differs from the psychological. Sociologists are unlikely to turn to personality or other individual characteristics for fundamental explanations as do psychologists. That is, psychologists more often than sociologists highlight early childhood differences in treatment of the sexes. Psychologists are also much more likely than sociologists to include or even emphasize biological factors in their explanation of gendered patterns.

Thus, sociologists studying how women workers and men workers are distributed into different occupations (such as secretaries and mechanics) will look for causes outside the individual worker. **Opportunity structures**, patterns of easier access to some positions than to others, exist before a person enters the labor market. When considering her or his possibilities, the person usually ignores jobs apparently held only or mainly by members of the other sex. This is especially likely if those jobs have significantly lower rates of pay than jobs held by people of one's own sex. Psychologists may want to know why some people choose jobs culturally defined as gender inappropriate, but sociologists are more interested in the existence and persistence of occupational sex segregation and its consequences for social life.

Sociologists talk about a **marginal** social position, or **status** when we are discussing people whose membership in some group or category is not socially defined as complete, who are instead seen as members of two different categories that in some way contradict one another. For example, a college student who has come back to school after military service is marginal, in that she or he is viewed as different in some fundamental way from those who entered college directly from high school and have continued to attend without any leave of absence. Other students, faculty, and staff may have somewhat different expectations of, and behave differently toward that student. People outside school will probably view the veteran as not a "regular" member of the "adult" world because of the college student status.

Because so many social statuses have gendered expectations attached to them, people may often find themselves, one way or another, feeling marginal to some sphere of their social lives. This affects the way that they perform their roles and the ways that others interact with them, affecting how they are able to perform their roles. They will have to put more energy into establishing their credentials in each position to be treated as a legitimate occupant of it by others. If the veteran is a woman returning to military service, in some ways she will be marginalized; both male veterans and non-veteran females feel that she is somehow not a "regular" member of their own category. If you have read the last sentence believing that times have changed, go to your local post office and look at the forms for registering for the Selective Service. Men must register, and women cannot.

In sum, most sociologists think that when a person's characteristics conform to societal expectations, it is a result of the social contexts of their earlier experiences and current situations and not due to inevitable, biologically determined sex differences. We emphasize the ways that people's surroundings draw out particular behaviors from what is usually a broader repertoire of an individual's behaviors.

Contemporary sociologists view social life itself as gendered: Experiences, opportunities, and burdens are differentially available to males and to females because of social views about maleness and femaleness. The closing off or opening up of opportunities often occurs even for people who do not fit gendered expectations. For example, if nurturance is defined specifically as feminine, men will not have a chance to show that they are sufficiently nurturant to be hired as child care workers. If they do have a chance to show they are nurturant, they may find that higher standards are applied to them, to disprove the gendered expectations. Alternatively, they may be moved quickly into less nurturant administrative jobs, no longer implicitly challenging those gendered expectations.

In other words, social definitions of gender contribute to the social stratification of society and smaller social groups within it. **Social stratification** is the differentiation among people (on the basis of their membership in categories socially defined as significant) and the accompanying differences in their access to scarce resources and in the obligations they bear. To varying degrees, sociologists of gender focus on the ways in which particular combinations of gender, race and ethnicity, and social class are socially defined as justifying unequal social treatment.

Sociologists also view individuals' behavior as leading to changes in the social world. We study individuals' **agency**, or active approach to finding ways to participate in, adapt to, or change their circumstances. Although agency may be limited to creating means to survive within difficult social arrangements, it sometimes produces changes in the environment. Individually or together, people may affect their immediate (micro-social) surroundings. Human history is filled with stories of people changing the patterns in their societies or even globally. These national, multinational, and international levels are **macro-social**. Currently, many people in the United States are participating in activities aimed at ending the international sexual tourism trade, which involves the prostitution of ever younger women and girls. This struggle includes people around the world who pressure governmental bodies to condemn child prostitution and to adopt programs that put muscle behind the condemnations.

Clearly, there is a **middle level** of social life, between units as big as nations and as small as a sociology class. Much of our micro-social life takes place within such middle-level settings as colleges, workplaces, and churches. When individuals actively attempt to change or to sustain existing arrangements, it is the middle level that may be most crucial for their focus. For example, if a married couple chooses to share equally in the care of their infant, their ability to do so will depend on being able to arrange suitable schedules at their workplaces and to earn prorated pay rather than taking a steep cut in earnings because of a change to part-time worker status. So the micro-social decision making about how the birth of the child may change the marriage is really not just about the couple. Indeed, they will have to work around the demands of their employers. In a time of high unemployment, the partner with a job is unlikely to leave to care for the newborn. Even if employers are legally required to provide flexibility in scheduling, concerns about losing one's job may keep the new parent from requesting that flexibility. In other words, the macro-social level influences both the middle-level and micro-social possibilities. Using the concepts of these three levels helps sociologists to zero in on a particular question, but the three levels are actually always simultaneously important in understanding social life.

Thus, sociologists have a fundamental and broad assumption of the primacy of social factors in explaining many aspects of people's lives. We agree on the impact of **socialization**, or the process of learning the rules of the social group or culture to which we belong or hope to belong, and learning to define ourselves and others within that setting. We also agree on the impact of **social control**, the term for the myriad rewards (such as expensive wedding presents) and punishments (such as the fictional scarlet letter that Nathaniel Hawthorne's heroine was forced to wear for having had an adulterous relationship). Similarly, sociologists agree on the importance of social structure and of **culture**, a people's established beliefs and practices, their design for living. Nevertheless, sociologists have widely divergent ideas about the *best* ways to explain the social world. We do not always agree on the importance of each idea or its relative importance, such as social structure compared with culture, or socialization compared with social control.

This text, however, tends to emphasize the importance of social structural factors and social control, partly to counterbalance most students' greater familiarity with the prevalent belief in the United States that personality and the individual are the most important sources of difference in one's life experience.

## SOCIAL INSTITUTIONS AND SOCIAL CHANGE

The study of social institutions has a central place in the sociology of gender. A **social institution** is a constellation of activities and ideas that addresses a major area of human need in a particular society. For instance, several basic human needs are addressed primarily and consistently in the institution of the family: sexual activity, reproduction, and the physical care of and early socialization of children. Virtually all people in the United States spend their earliest years in family contexts in which they are exposed to the significant cultural meanings of gender and receive their first and most intense lessons in gender relations on the micro-social scale. The specific relations may vary, but they typically fall within a recognizable range of acceptable behavior. These relations are broadly patterned in our culture even though they are acted out by individuals with unique personalities. Members of culturally diverse subgroups are similarly influenced by forces beyond the personalities of their intimates and themselves. When adults seek intimacy, parenthood, or practical living arrangements in which costs and labor are shared, their choices are limited by the patterns of family and household arrangements of the larger culture and by the particular variants of their immediate social environment. Obviously, the economic situation of a family also affects the alternatives available to its members.

Institutions are characteristically slow to change; major innovations are not easily integrated into institutions. As many activists have learned, new beliefs must eventually be supported by changes within institutionalized arrangements. Without such a process, holders of the new beliefs will remain on the social margin. For example, if a man who takes a paternity leave is subsequently penalized when personnel decisions are made, only those most highly committed to active parenting will consider taking a paternity leave. In contrast, if a father's use of leave is seen as a normal event, and his performance evaluation is not hurt by it, more men will take advantage of leave programs.

Once institutionalized changes occur, they facilitate the spread of new ideas and behaviors beyond their initial institutional context. For example, when a work organization develops and promulgates guidelines for dealing with allegations of sexual harassment, many individuals will start to think about the nature of male–female interaction in new ways beyond that specific organization. Even if they remain unconvinced that certain acts are harassing, what was previously unexamined becomes open to consideration. Thus, social change at the grass roots may sometimes be prodded by institutional changes. Institutions change at an uneven pace, with periods of little change and periods of rapid change. For instance, in 1991 President George Bush nominated Clarence Thomas to serve as a Supreme Court justice. During the constitutionally required Senate confirmation hearings, reports emerged that Judge Thomas had sexually harassed an attorney on his staff, Anita Hill. The confirmation hearings were televised live for three days, and the nation was caught up in a public debate over the meaning of sexual harassment. Without producing consensus about the problem, and with a senatorial decision to confirm Judge Thomas, the hearings nonetheless changed the ways in which individuals and work organizations regard the topic of sexual harassment.

More generally, the social implications of being female or male have changed rapidly during the last half-century. Even for women with young children, working outside the home has become expected. Indeed, with the welfare reform legislation of

1996, the U.S. government embraced a definition of motherhood in which wage-earning activity is more important than child care; previously, Aid to Families with Dependent Children provided a "safety net" for people unable to support their minor children themselves. Now, in both one- and two-parent families, if parents are able-bodied they are expected to work outside the home to support their children regardless of the children's ages, the inadequacies of alternative child care arrangements, and the inability to provide adequately for their children with the wages they are paid. Even when unemployment rates are high, both men and women are expected to participate in the labor force (the **labor force participation rate** is the proportion of people, in a specified category, who are either employed or actively seeking work).

Men's labor force participation has declined slightly over the last several decades, but is still **normative**; that is, it follows a social rule, or **norm,** for behavior. Despite media portrayals of househusband characters, the real "stay-at-home" father remains rare. He is almost always in the labor force and just working out of his home.

The kinds of work that women and men do, though still quite segregated, have been at least symbolically integrated (for example, the first woman to serve as the U.S. Attorney General was appointed in 1993). In some occupations, such as the legal profession, integration is more than token. Nonetheless, the comparable numbers of women and men in an occupation do not assure full equality; for instance, women attorneys remain very underrepresented in higher-status positions, specialties, and organizations.

Although it is now normative for women to work, it remains socially questionable for a woman to have a high-powered job that involves long absences from her children. If there has been any change in this area, it is toward expecting fathers to join mothers in greater involvement in the lives of their growing children. However, a man whose career keeps him away is considered to be merely in an unfortunate situation, but is not expected to move into a male equivalent of what is called the **mommy track**—a career ladder with limited prospects because the loyalties of women on it are presumed to be greater to family than to job. Some men who participate actively in family care have discovered themselves on a "daddy" track, encountering some career limitations, although less extreme than those documented for the mommy track. During the 2008 presidential campaign, Sarah Palin (the Republican candidate for vice president) was pressed to defend her ability to be a good parent, if she were elected, in a way that male candidates do not experience.

How much has changed? How do we know, stepping back from media portrayals and pop journalism? Throughout this text, we will see how sociologists and other social scientists have used systematically collected observations and critical thinking to address these questions.

## THE DEVELOPMENT OF FEMINIST SCHOLARSHIP

**Feminism** is the view that women are oppressed in significant ways and that this oppression should be ended. Because of the wide variation in other beliefs that accompany this view, it is more accurate to refer to "feminisms" when discussing the belief systems of feminists. In every period of activism, feminists have energetically and intensely debated appropriate strategies, important goals, and their underlying assumptions about the sources of gender differentiation and of sexism. Even in quieter times, some of those who believe that women's oppression should be eliminated have worked for change.

Feminist analyses can also be thought of as falling along a continuum of perspectives on differences between women and men. At the **difference** end, feminists "focus on sexual and procreative oppression and . . . valorize women's procreative, sexual, and nurturance proclivities." This position calls for gender equity despite its fundamentally different characterizations of males and females. The difference perspective in feminism is oddly familiar—it is like the very common belief that males and females are fundamentally different, but that most male characteristics are superior to female ones. At the other end of the continuum, **equality** (as sameness) feminists base their advocacy of equitable treatment of people on a challenge to the social construction of the sexes as fundamentally different. The difference position makes the mistake of "treating all women as mothers (or as motherly) which we clearly are not" (Lorber 1989, 158). On the other hand, the equality position provides no intellectual approach to those still-significant differences common, if not universal, in a variety of aspects of women's and men's lives. Gender scholarship needs to be alert to the traps of the extreme positions on the continuum.

Though feminist views have been publicly expressed from time to time for hundreds of years (see Mary Wollstonecraft 1787), the first "wave," or period of feminist social activism in the United States, began in the mid-nineteenth century with the Seneca Falls Women's Rights Convention. That struggle focused primarily (but not exclusively) on equal legal rights for women, particularly the right to vote. Once women had the vote, activists believed, they could tackle other areas of legal injustice. The struggle for national suffrage lasted until 1920, when the Nineteenth Amendment to the United States Constitution was ratified. Both equality and difference feminism had adherents during this period. Difference feminists argued that the horrors of war would be less likely if women—nurturing rather than combative by nature—had the vote. Equality feminists actively pursued economic rights such as the right of a widow to own the family farm that had been in her husband's name.

---

"I myself have never known what feminism is. I only know that people call me a feminist whenever I express sentiments that differentiate me from a doormat."
—Rebecca West, 1913

---

Even though the "first wave" refers to the entire period between the Seneca Falls meeting and the achievement of suffrage in 1920, it actually included periods of greater and lesser activism (Springer 2002). Like all metaphors, the idea of feminist activism as occurring in "waves" has drawn attention to some kinds of activities and rendered others invisible. African American women struggled against sexism and racism (the systems of prejudicial beliefs and discriminatory behaviors toward people because of their race or because of their sex) even before the abolitionist movement, which is generally credited with giving rise to the first wave. And between the first and second waves, African American women's organizations continued to struggle against ongoing **racism** and **sexism**.

Feminist activism decreased after the achievement of the vote, as some supporters saw their goal achieved and as others' differing goals for further progress led to a splintering of movement organizations. The first wave included the active participation of women of color, immigrant women, and women of various social class positions. The pursuit of rights for women of color was sometimes set aside by white leaders, who argued that taking on race privilege at the same time as gender privilege would increase resistance from those opposing (white) women's suffrage. White planners of a famous suffragist parade on President Wilson's inauguration day (1916) told African American suffragists they would have to march separately from whites, although not all complied with this order.

The women's movement, or the "second wave" of feminist activism, started in the late 1960s and remained intense during the 1970s (see Chapter Seven for more detail about the development of both the first and second waves). As a result of the activism during that period, people have come to look at the social world in profoundly different ways. Social conditions, such as sexual harassment, marital rape, and domestic violence, that are now considered serious problems were invisible fifty years ago. These conditions existed previously, but the social perception of them and the insistence that society confronts rather than denies them are both developments of the late twentieth century.

Current views of the second wave generally lack awareness of the many conflicts and challenges among second-wave feminists holding varied intellectual positions and political goals (Armstrong 2002; Snyder 2008). This is consistent with other histories of social movements: The positions that end up triumphing over their competitors are present in historical accounts, and other positions become invisible. Current views also erase the racial/ethnic and social class diversity within the second wave. It is typically constructed as exclusively white and middle class. This makes invisible a wide variety of women who participated in caucuses within male-run organizations, who participated in organizations formed and led by women of color, and who sometimes collaborated in and even led groups with majority white participation (Evans 2003; Gilmore 2008). Women of color who spoke and worked against sexist practices within their community often faced charges of race disloyalty, a charge with greater penalties when brought against women than men (Cole and Guy-Sheftall 2003, 99). Echoing the 1916 experience of racist behavior by white women, African American men refused to let any women leaders be speakers at the enormous civil rights demonstration in Washington (August 1963) at which Martin Luther King, Jr., made his famous "I Have a Dream" speech.

Although important feminist scholarship was accomplished between the periods of intense political activism (for example, Simone de Beauvoir's *The Second Sex*, first published in France in 1949, and Betty Friedan's *The Feminine Mystique*, in 1963), the huge growth in self-consciously feminist scholarship was both produced by and influential in the women's movement. As academic feminism flourished, many scholars found themselves simultaneously interested in a critical theoretical and research stance and in achieving success within the traditionally structured, male-dominated professoriate. Activists and scholars were found along the full length of the "equality–difference" continuum. Difference feminists were most often white and middle class, privileged to ignore the real differences among women of varied social class and racial-ethnic positions. This led to an emphasis on problems, such as rape and domestic abuse, shared by most women and different from those of men. They paid little attention to problems that did not affect them, such as discriminatory management and labor union practices that kept women out of dangerous but relatively well-paid blue-collar work. Equality feminists, more diverse in composition, were more likely to be interested in achieving equity with men, for example, in the payment of social security benefits and the premiums charged for life insurance policies.

During the 1990s, some young feminists started calling themselves the "third wave," referring to their generation as distinct from those who participated in the "second wave." Feminists who grew up during the 1980s and 1990s were exposed to backlash against the women's movement. By this time, many took the achievements and issues of the movement for granted. Yet, the third wave has moved its focus to new challenges opened up by the greater freedoms achieved by the second wave. For example, questions about combining home and work lives are now different for these women, who have a greater range of career opportunities. If one is on a real career track, leaving work to fulfill home responsibilities can seriously damage future opportunities. On the other hand, to maintain a career and develop a partnership, or to parent, or to do all of these, is not viable unless one is a superwoman. Third-wave feminists have also grown up hearing about the importance of differences among women, particularly women of different racial-ethnic identities, social class positions, and sexuality. Solidarity among feminists of different generations has often been elusive in part because younger women were unaware of the wide range of feminist views and actions of preceding generations (Evans 2003; Radford-Hill 2002; Snyder 2008). During the Democratic party's primary race (2007–2008), many young women were struck by media treatment of Hilary Clinton that appeared to take her candidacy less seriously and that was disrespectful of her in distinctive ways. This experience brought many women of different generations together in an unexpected way, even those who did not support Clinton's candidacy.

Cultural symbols that had one clear meaning in the 1970s have very different, often multiple meanings now. For example, although Madonna's explicit sexuality could be interpreted as catering to the **commodification** of women (i.e., turning women's bodies into objects of economic value), it is generally interpreted as the embracing of the sexual freedom that women fought to achieve in the 1960s and 1970s (*The Righteous Babes* 1998). Sometimes social rules are assumptions about sexuality. This example, subjected to intense discussion, illustrates the simultaneous use of traditional images of the objects of heterosexual male desire with a challenge to it. Increasingly, feminist scholars look at practices in which women appear to both conform to and challenge social arrangements they find oppressive in groups or communities to which they are loyal. Making sense of such apparently contradictory positions, and others that may be less obvious, is one facet of contemporary feminist scholarship.

Violence in the home (e.g., wife battering, child abuse, and marital rape) and sexual harassment in the workplace have been focuses of growing intellectual and political activity since the early 1970s. Other problems have more recently gained public attention and are increasingly recognized as serious and widespread; "date rape" is one such topic that is actually not a new phenomenon at all. However, studying newly visible problems requires more than becoming aware of their existence, and many scholars argue that other ways of looking at the world are required for achieving a nonsexist understanding of it.

Itself a product of the 1970s wave of the women's movement, the sociology of gender is a major area of feminist scholarship, with active building of feminist theory and lively debate about what is required for a methodology to be feminist. Because of the centrality of social change to feminist belief, it is not surprising that feminist scholarship is forthright about the legitimacy of addressing politically important questions in the pursuit of knowledge. It is not always the case that the sociology of gender is conducted from a feminist perspective, but this text is firmly situated in the feminist tradition.

Early in the study of gender, attention was paid mainly to the ways sexism limited females' lives. As in the popular culture, the social constraints on boys' and men's lives were rarely considered problematic. In part, this inattention reflected the view that behaviors usually considered out of bounds for men (such as the public expression of emotions other than anger) were unimportant or even undesirable because these were associated with women. Limits on men were an integral part of the justification for men's superior position in the stratification system. For example, men are less free than women to show feelings of panic or helplessness; but women have been excluded from certain positions because of this very freedom. It constructs women as unreliable—they might panic or act helpless. However, some people now reject this notion and believe that women can serve well even in positions such as combat soldiers. Perhaps with the basis of women's exclusion being eroded, men's emotional toughness may be less useful in justifying their dominance, and they may be freer to appear emotionally vulnerable. Indeed, some men have noted that this is an effective way to present themselves when they want to appear attractive to women!

In the 1970s, ideas of what equality would mean typically highlighted the expansion of women's freedom. Instead of women gaining some of the freedoms of men, there are areas in which the growing equality of the sexes is associated with men's loss of freedom. For example, men are expected to meet increasingly unrealistic standards for appearance, and are a rapidly growing clientele for cosmetic surgery. The study of men *as* men is a flourishing interdisciplinary area within the social sciences and humanities, with scholarship appearing in journals such as *Gender & Society* and *Men and Masculinities*. It reflects in part the increased recognition of cultural values other than economic and political power. For example, there is a growing acknowledgment of men's increasing involvement in parenting and, thus, a growing interest in learning more about that involvement. The sociology of sport has been another particularly fruitful area of research on masculinities and feminities and their ongoing negotiation.

## LEADING PERSPECTIVES

Feminist theorizing and feminist analysis are now being done by sociologists working outside the study of gender itself. Feminist analysis is making important contributions to other sociological specialities and to other disciplines (see England 1999; Ferree, Hess, and Lorber 1999; see also numerous review essays in *Signs*, Summer 2005). For example, child psychologists had long studied the effects of "maternal deprivation," which referred to children whose mothers spent the day at workplaces and to children whose mothers had died or were otherwise permanently absent. When the question was reframed to consider the effects of "maternal absence," researchers were more likely to see neutral or positive influences on children as well as negative ones.

A wide range of perspectives can be called feminist even though media references to feminists and feminism typically assume that all feminists think the same way (for an excellent introduction see Lorber 2001b; Gimenez 2004). In three decades of active feminist scholarship, numerous scholars have tried to categorize the major feminist perspectives. This is somewhat ironic because much feminist work actually criticizes the use of categories and types, for prematurely closing off inquiry.

Nonetheless, many of us have a preference that we usually follow. Every scholarly perspective (whether or not it is feminist) is concerned with somewhat different sets of questions about the social world, and each gives rise to hypothesized answers that emphasize different aspects of the social world. Even when scholars address similar issues, if they use different perspectives they tend to look for different causes. For example, many researchers are interested in the current phenomenon of young women's eating problems, but differ in where they look for both causes and solutions. Some authors explicitly identify the perspective from which they work, but many actually use more than one perspective. Of course, scholars starting from the same perspective do not always agree on all questions.

One common categorization of feminist perspectives dominant in the sociology of gender during the 1970s and 1980s includes *liberal feminist, socialist feminist,* and *radical feminist* approaches. In the United States, *multiracial feminism, postmodern* and *poststructural feminisms,* and *global feminism* have more recently grown in popularity among sociologists. Some perspectives complement one another while focusing on different questions, but others actually have contradictory premises. Nonetheless, each provides us with useful insights. Rather than viewing the lack of agreement on a single perspective (and even a lack of agreement on how to categorize the variety of viewpoints) as symptomatic of a problem in feminist studies, such a variety of perspectives indicates the robustness of the field. In the following pages, I describe the perspectives you will encounter in this text. **Liberal feminism** is rarely encountered among contemporary researchers in the sociology of gender; its relatively narrow approach is seen as outmoded. Rather than focusing on the underlying stratification of U.S. society, it emphasizes "leveling the playing field" between females and males (see Lorber 2001b). But it does not challenge the scarcity that would remain (and be inequitably experienced) if women stopped being denied a chance to play on that field simply because they are women. Nonetheless, liberal feminism remains important for people interested in the presence and extent of sexism in the treatment of individuals who are otherwise in relatively privileged categories.

More than any other perspective, this text takes a **multiracial feminist perspective.** This approach is **intersectional,** in that it highlights the simultaneous impact of race, class, gender, and sexuality in formulating questions and looking for answers about gender. For example, we cannot understand the situations and experiences of African American women by simply adding up what we know about the situations of some "average" woman and some "average" African American person. An African American woman may suffer more or less than the sum of the discriminatory treatments experienced by the "average" member of these two categories separately (Crenshaw 1989), and understanding her experiences will be further clarified by paying attention at the same time to her social class position and her sexuality. Although looking at multiple dimensions at the same time yields a more complete and accurate understanding of social reality, such research presents complex challenges to researchers (McCall 2005).

Multiracial feminism makes the important point that race and class are relevant in research about white, middle-class, and heterosexual women. Their lives are influenced by divisions based on race, class, and sexuality, typically to their advantage (Smith 1999). To ignore that influence is to give a partial and distorted explanation for their situation (Frankenberg 1993). Similarly, studying people of both sexes adds to the understanding of each, because gender is relational. The social meanings attached to femaleness or maleness depend, that is, on the meanings attached to the other sex and gender.

The multiracial approach tends to look for causes of gender-related problems in macro-social and middle-level arenas. It emphasizes the importance of social structure in shaping the inequalities in opportunities and obstacles. These structural factors are associated with some combination of cultural beliefs about race, sex, age, sexuality, and economic position. This complexity adds to the accuracy this view provides (Daniels 2008). At the same time, it is difficult to pay attention simultaneously to all dimensions of difference. Sociological tradition values the development of generalizations and working toward the development of abstract theories that explain many observations of the social world. However, the emphasis on difference can slow down progress toward generalization and theory building.

Particularly with the move toward intersectionality, sociologists increasingly use a framework that takes the *multiplicity* of femininities and masculinities as given (see, for example, Pascoe 2007; Broughton 2008). **Doing gender**, or trying to act womanly or manly, has different meanings depending on one's location in the social structure (Connell 1995; Connell and Messerschmidt 2005). For example, a working-class man may establish his masculinity by his physical strength or his physical bravery (e.g., fire fighting), while an upper-middle-class man is able to establish his masculinity by providing a very comfortable home and other material assets to his family. Although physical strength and bravery are dominant as measures of masculinity in youth, economic achievement is the highest indicator of adult manliness. Indeed, a very wealthy middle-aged man who is not physically attractive or strong may marry a trophy wife—a younger and attractive woman who symbolizes his achievements.

Nonetheless, in the absence of opportunities to achieve economic success, that most prestigious and powerful version of manliness, there are alternatives available to men. Those born into settings with no visible hope of economic success may not think of their versions of masculinity as second best. However, that is the assessment of the larger culture.

Thinking about eating problems, Thompson (1992) used a multiracial feminist perspective. She argued that eating problems, rather than "disorders," is a more accurate term. It does not locate the source of the trouble in the individual, as disorder implies. Indeed, she argued that eating problems may stem from rational choices (such as the choice to become less attractive to lower the chances of being sexually victimized). She challenged the race- and class-limited explanation of eating disorders that focuses attention solely on the "cult of thinness." For example, she discussed eating as one of the few affordable and reliable sources of enjoyment in some women's lives and suggested that overeating may be a choice, rather than a compulsion.

More recently, Hesse-Biber (2007) described an increased interest in thinness among young, occupationally successful African American and Latina women. She suggested that white, middle-class ideas about body shape are spreading, shared along class lines. Clearly, an intersectional approach will develop a more accurate picture of the extent and kinds of eating problems in contemporary U.S. society. Such accuracy will help design more effective solutions to the variety of eating problems.

Socialist feminism and racial and ethnic studies were the leading influences in the development of multiracial feminism. The **socialist feminist** view weighs **patriarchy** (the social domination by males over females) and **capitalism** (the economic system of private ownership of production, with the paramount value of maximizing profit) as equally important forces in explaining inequalities in society. By examining differences among men (in their access to power and other resources), we are better able to explain the different ways in which men exploit women. Thus, economic stratification among men as well as women is viewed as an essential part of the contemporary system of patriarchy. Feminists who were socialists developed this position in reaction to the secondary position most socialist theorists traditionally assigned to gender in their explanations of social life (England 1999).

Socialist feminists draw attention to the ways patriarchal beliefs divide groups that might otherwise unite to unseat the economically powerful through coalition. The socialist feminist is interested in the economically disadvantaged of both sexes and all races, in people of color of both sexes and all economic positions, and in women of all races and economic positions. Socialist feminists would not disagree with a multiracial feminist view, but as a matter of practice have emphasized social class over racial-ethnic differences in seeking explanations of inequality. Thus, socialist feminists emphasize the interest that people in power have in maintaining the status quo. They focus on the social relations of power (especially economic power) that enable men to control women (Sokoloff 1980, 154). A socialist feminist approach to current eating problems might focus on the enormous commercial investment that companies have in creating and maintaining women's obsession with size, shape, and muscle tone (see Brumberg 1997).

Although multiracial feminism is the major perspective taken in this text, in some discussions I employ ideas associated with radical feminism. **Radical feminists** view gender as the crucial dimension dividing people. They focus on how males dominate women through a system of supporting beliefs and social structures. Power differences among women, and the role of other dimensions of difference, such as class and race, are not central to a radical feminist analysis. Although narrow, this perspective can provide a useful analysis by generalizing about women's experiences where such generalizations are appropriate. For example, a radical feminist approach to eating problems might look at the ways in which women are oppressed by patriarchal standards of appearance. In addition, a radical feminist approach would highlight the greater demand for resources of time, energy, and money required for women to meet standards of appearance required for occupational or social success. Although a multiracial feminist might argue that there are important differences among women in the appearance expectations related to jobs, any explanation of body problems in the United States will be more robust if it recognizes the relatively greater emphasis on women's appearance compared with men's.

One of the most recent developments is the growth of **global feminism**, which puts at the center of its analysis the study of gender across national and regional boundaries. It challenges many presumptions of Western feminists, sometimes simply by making visible what those (particularly in the United States) have ignored. For example, the intertwined character of the current global economy has generally received attention only when it disadvantages the economic arrangements in the United States. Global feminists draw attention to the dependence of affluent U.S. families on the grossly underpaid labor of workers from other countries, whether in the United States (Hondagneu-Sotelo 2001) or in their home or in other countries where their cheap labor produces goods for export. Global feminists also reject the dismissal as sexist of non-Western cultures' patriarchal belief systems, instead calling for and conducting analyses of the complexities of practices and beliefs previously often only superficially examined by Western feminists. Scholars also investigate the effect of economic globalization on people in relatively privileged positions. For example, a new version of "business masculinity" has developed among some managers who have become vulnerable to the export of their positions by transnational corporate employers (Connell and Wood 2005).

Finally, in some sections of the text, I take a view that might be considered *postmodern* or *poststructural feminism*. Although it is not a central perspective in the sociology of gender, **postmodern feminism** makes some unique contributions to our understanding of women and men in contemporary society. At the core of postmodernism is the drive to unsettle or destabilize existing assumptions about how the world works. Postmodern thinkers emphasize the temporary and local nature of reality. Because they view life as socially constructed, they see it as ever changing, often profoundly. In our context, postmodernism has been important in questioning the categories we use, as U.S. sociologists, as feminist social scientists, or more generally as participants in contemporary American society and culture (Lorber 1999). Perhaps the most challenging is the position that even the two sexes are categories that are socially created, rather than existing biologically (see, for example, Stoltenberg 1990). **Poststructuralism** also rejects the possibility of somehow discovering a set of "underlying rules, codes, and systems that govern social phenomena" (Petersen 2003, 55), but differs from postmodernism in its emphasis on the distribution of power in a society to explain the forms that social constructions take. Taking this perspective, we can look at how those who lack power make use of cultural forms to express their resistance to hegemonic arrangements or constructions. Ironically, the poststructuralist simultaneously highlights the significance of (presumably real) power differences and the social-political-economic system of society, while espousing the socially constructed nature of cultural forms, ideas, and roles.

This emphasis on social construction is productive, making it easier for us to "break frame," "step out of the box," or overcome assumptions that have kept us from seeing aspects of the world that don't fit our expectations. The importance of this contribution cannot be overstated. However, the postmodern and poststructural approaches dispute the possibility of valid generalization, and generalization is an essential feature of contemporary sociology.

In sum, each perspective highlights fruitful areas of inquiry, but by itself it would draw an incomplete picture. Thus, liberal feminism's examination of the ways in which the culture is brought home to individuals through socialization helps solve the puzzle of people's behaving in ways that apparently contradict their self-interest, and helps explain the mechanism by which changes in institutions are often followed by changes in individuals' worldviews. Radical feminism's focus on the shared experiences of women helps make sense of employment discrimination based on assumptions of biologically inevitable physical weakness or emotional vulnerability. Multiracial feminism brings attention to the conflicting interests among women by insisting we look simultaneously at their variation in class, racial-ethnic, and sexual identities. Finally, a poststructural approach directs our attention to the ongoing construction of meaning in people's daily lives and the need to explore those meanings rather than imposing our own.

### FEMINIST METHODS OF INQUIRY

Conceptualizing questions, choosing subject matter for study, defining the basic strategy of a research project—all are influenced, even if unconsciously, by the values and worldview of the researcher. Until the feminist activism of the 1960s and 1970s, social research was blind to the importance of gender. Men dominated the social organization of scholarship, and for men gender was not problematic. Like privileged racial or social class groups, people in the more privileged sex category are unlikely to see the multiplicity of ways that being male makes a difference in how they are treated in the social world (McIntosh 1988).

Many studies included only male respondents; it was simpler to limit the sample to only one sex, and men were assumed to be the sex to study. An early strategy to improve scholarship, nicknamed "add women and stir," brought women into the topic to be studied, but did not rethink assumptions about the topic that were rooted in its male-focused research tradition. This limited approach has been rejected as inadequate. Instead, investigative strategies and their theoretical bases have to be rethought. As long as research questions were designed with a single "normal" experience in mind (usually that of a middle-class white man), central issues were likewise ignored.

In the first decades of research on wife battering, most studies focused on the kinds of individuals involved in battering and the relationships in which battering occurs, searching for explanations in individual characteristics without reference to the larger social, political, and economic environment. Instead, as Fine (1989) argued, a feminist approach to studying wife battering would include questions about cultural and social influences. What aspects of the larger environment actually foster battering, what aspects simply take it for granted, and what aspects work to reduce domestic violence against women?

Even when researchers focus on topics including women and women's interests, the manner of thinking about central ideas needs attention. For example, when Sacks (1988) studied the drive for unionization at the Duke Medical Center, she identified leadership activities that were different among women than among men. Being the spokesperson in large meetings or the representative to outsiders is central to the male norm for leadership. If being defined as a leader were based only on being a spokesperson, the significant daily contributions of women leaders would be ignored. Instead, Sacks broadened the definition of leadership to include the importance of developing and maintaining group commitment.

How people create conceptual categories affects our thinking about observations related to those categories. Imagine that apples and oranges had been categorized only as appanges (or oraples) and that researchers, visiting different orchards (or groves), described many contradictory features (best climate for growing the fruit, appearance of the fruit, in/edible character of the skin). If someone introduced the distinction between apples and oranges, however, many of the apparent contradictions would disappear. Though variations would remain within each of the new categories (such as the color of apples), much more can be clearly and consistently described and understood because the division "works"—it fits the observations. For example, Johnson (1995) developed a distinction between different types of domestic violence—"patriarchal terrorism" and "common couple violence." By thinking of individual episodes of violence as one or the other of these types, he made sense of previously contradictory sets of research findings, most important, major differences in the extent to which these acts are gendered (as discussed in Chapter Four). You might have noticed the use of quotation marks in the first sentence of this chapter, in the phrase "opposite" sex. This was done to warn against casually assuming males and females are extremely different on all dimensions. Regularly encountering this phrase may itself encourage us to make (or continue to make) this assumption.

Feminist scholars have argued that basic ethnographic research should always come before survey research in gathering evidence to address a research question (see Naples 2003). Surveys, and quantitative analyses of their results, are the dominant methodological form in contemporary sociology. Ethnography is the use of some combination of observation and participation by the researcher(s) in the social context being studied. Ethnography develops a textured and complex understanding of the site in which the research is conducted. Of course, in conducting ethnographic research, individuals are most effective if they are thoughtful about how others in the research setting are likely to perceive them (see, for example, Davison 2007). Generalization to a larger population is possible from large surveys, and not from ethnographic research, but the ethnographer can inform the survey researcher about the deeper meaning of phenomena on which her survey may focus. Thus, before developing quantitative research designs (e.g., surveys), we must first broaden our understanding of their range of meanings for all the people involved in the phenomena. For example, before we can do a large survey of undergraduates to find explanations of gender differences in majors, we need to speak in depth with some students to develop the survey questions themselves. We may assume women avoid mechanical engineering because of a misperception that they would get greasy doing it; but through ethnographic work, we might find out that professors in mechanical engineering are more likely than, for example, professors in chemical engineering to assume that theirs just isn't a field for women. The ethnographic work in a few engineering schools could lead to a survey of a broader range of engineering faculty and students. Sprague and Zimmerman (1989) argue that an effective feminist methodology will require a reconstruction of methods to include an integration of aspects of both quantitative and qualitative approaches.

Regardless of their position in the ongoing debate about the particular methods that are consistent with feminist inquiry, most people accept that researchers should make their assumptions explicit so that others may be alert to possible distortions. This view of knowledge has contributed significantly to progress toward more valid approximations

## Central Variations in Approaching the Study of Gender

Despite the popular social construction of feminism and of women's studies, there are many variations in the assumptions and the approaches taken by feminist social scientists. Some dimensions along which feminist scholarship varies are represented by the following questions. In addition to illustrating the variation among social scientists, these questions allow each of us to reflect on the assumptions on which we base our own ideas as we participate in everyday conversations, make decisions about how to behave or assess others' behavior, and consider what we want the organizations and governments around us to do. As you review each question, think of possible answers along a continuum, rather than as an either/or, such as a strong **"yes"** or **"no,"** or an intractable **"all"** or **"none."**

1. What are the significant impacts of the gender system on individual lives? For people considering life choices that don't conform, what are the costs?
2. What are the significant causes of, or influences on, the gender system? What is the relative importance of biology, personality, social group memberships, nationality, historical moment, economics, and politics?
3. How central are race-ethnicity, class, and sexuality to the way one thinks about gendered patterns or the gender system?
4. How much and what kinds of attention are paid to boys and men when we shape the questions to be examined and look for answers to those questions?
5. What counts as evidence?
6. To what extent are these ideas of ours based on knowledge of communities, regions, or countries other than our own? ✦

of truth through intellectual effort. Discussion of **epistemology** (or ways of knowing) is traditionally a matter for philosophers. Since the late 1980s, feminist epistemology has been an increasingly important area where scholars of disciplines across the humanities and the social sciences draw on one another's work (see, for example, Sprague and Kobrynowicz 1999).

### TECHNOLOGY AND SOCIAL CHANGE

For much of the twentieth century, U.S. sociology emphasized a view and explanation of social reality as stable; researchers in this discipline tacked on questions of how change occurs almost as an afterthought. The shift to change-oriented analysis, which began to gather steam in the 1970s, is particularly well-suited to the study of gender. Because of changes both in the status of women and men in many arenas and in the ways in which scholars have approached gender (in the development of theories, the re-creation of methodologies, and the selection of research questions), the field has grown and changed remarkably within its relatively short existence. A view of social life as *normally* dynamic rather than static is integrated throughout this volume; in the final chapter, we focus particularly on social change and the future.

An important impetus for changing gender relations comes from developments in technology. For example, lack of control over the timing of pregnancies often undermined both employers' and individual women's willingness to invest resources in job training. The development of increasingly reliable contraception removed a major obstacle to women's employment possibilities (Goldin and Katz 2000). But, the development of the Internet and the availability of violent pornography remind us that technological changes are not always liberating (Gossett and Byrne 2002).

Although it is widely recognized that technologies, and developments in them, affect social arrangements, we generally ignore the enormous importance of social arrangements in shaping the directions and implementation of technological innovation. Thus, research into the development of new contraceptive technologies continues to assume that women are primarily responsible for contraception and that their biology, rather than men's, should be tinkered with (Oudshoorn 2003). The victims in Web-circulated violent pornography are disproportionately women of color, particularly women who appear to be Asian, reflecting dominant cultural beliefs about the variation in sexual attractiveness and availability (Gossett and Byrne 2002).

The design of new technologies is typically intended to be consistent with cultural norms regarding gender, race, class, and age. However, unintended consequences of new technologies sometimes lead to changes in the culturally dominant forms of masculinity and femininity and to changes in distribution of power in the system of gender. For example, the reliability of the birth-control pill allows single women to be sexually active without depending on a male partner's cooperation with the use of a condom.

Even where no change in the gender hierarchy results from a particular technological change, this innovation may well have implications for the everyday realities of gendered roles. Thus, the microwave oven (based on a technology initially designed decades before) was developed and became a household "necessity" only in the 1970s, when more and more women were working outside the home. Nonetheless, planning meals (even those to be cooked or reheated in the microwave) remained largely the woman's responsibility. Indeed, when the microwave enabled a greater variety of meals to be prepared with relatively little effort (compared with the premicrowave era), those responsible for household shopping and menu planning were expected to provide for the individual likes and dislikes of each family member. The shopping and menu planning may have become more complex, counterbalancing any time gained by using the microwave oven. Thus, we see that technological innovations are themselves social products, rather than objectively inevitable developments; they are influenced by the gender system as well as influencing it.

Similarly, mechanization decreased the importance of physical strength in men's labor, although it was not intended as a means of interfering with gender arrangements. Physical strength is now largely irrelevant in most jobs, and working-class men have to turn elsewhere to establish their masculinity. You will encounter other instances of the "chicken and egg" relationship between gender systems and technologies in this book.

## LOOKING AHEAD

You started the chapter with a "thought experiment" about the impact on your life if tomorrow you switched your sex. Much of your challenge would involve changing how you present yourself (through symbols and language) and how you interpret others' words and appearance. As you move through the following chapters, keep this experiment in mind. In the next chapters, you will examine culture (Chapter Two), and how people learn about it and work to maintain or change it in their own lives (Chapter Three).

Most of the implications of your "switching" would depend on how the social institutions in which you participate are themselves gendered. In Chapter Four, we look at the institution of the family as a social structure and as the primary setting of our socially intimate relationships. This is followed by examinations of three other major social institutions: education (Chapter Five), the economy (Chapter Six), and the political and legal systems (Chapter Seven).

Finally, this book will focus on social changes both intentionally and unintentionally affecting gender relations and gender systems (Chapter Eight). This last chapter will help you to think about what the outcome of that experiment might be if you repeated it in 2035 and what might happen between now and then to create a new outcome.

### DISCUSSION QUESTIONS

1. The chapter began with a thought experiment in which you woke up as a person of the other sex. Now imagine that you wake up as a person of that sex, but it is 2035. Do you expect the implications of this "sex change" to be less broad, or about the same (or even more important)? Why do you think so? Consider the same questions for the year 1970.
2. One of the traditional ways in which sociologists learn about the world is by observing it as they participate in it. Which of your ideas about how the world works do you think you might reconsider if you observed it as a person of another sex, racial-ethnic group, and social class?
3. At this point, what do you think are some of the most interesting (or puzzling, or disturbing) patterns of gender in contemporary life? Which of the feminist perspectives described in this chapter seems best suited to pursing these topics, and why do you think so? ✦

# CHAPTER 2

# Culture and Ideology

The culture of a people is their established beliefs and practices. It serves as a design for living, transmitted from one generation to the next and usually slow to change. The view of the world taken for granted in a culture includes ideas of what must inevitably be, what is most attractive or unattractive, and what is moral and immoral. Even for a "nonconformist," culture influences individual choices, if only because one anticipates having to cope with the reactions of others. Nevertheless, culture is neither all-determining nor always consistent. As a design for living, a culture must be general enough to apply to diverse situations in a modern society. This often allows individuals a range of culturally acceptable behaviors from which to choose. A culture may include ideas that are actually contradictory, and the internal contradictions within a culture may be reflected by contradictions in individuals' and in groups' behaviors.

The common idea of a culture is also an oversimplification when a "people" (such as the people of the United States) is composed of immigrants or long-term visitors from various other places or when varied alterations in the "design for living" are introduced and variously adopted among some of the "people" of the society. Thus, individuals may choose from various competing cultural ideas as well as choose how to interpret some broadly conceived aspect of a particular design for living. For example, even though immigrants and their children retain some aspects of their original culture, they also learn U.S. culture. The U.S. culture is enriched by the multiplicity of other cultures from which immigrants have come; but for the most part, American culture shapes the way of life of immigrants' descendants.

The definition of "a design for living" implies a consensus about the content of a culture. In the mid-1990s, and again in recent years, the media have regularly discussed ongoing "culture wars" (see, for example, Toner 2004). Although particular issues, such as same-sex marriage, are certainly topics of real controversy, the social construction of "war" distracts people from the wide-ranging cultural content that is held in common by the vast majority of people in the United States. Much press coverage after September 11 focused on ways in which being attacked had made people aware of all that is shared in the culture. Similarly, when the economy took a swift and sharp downturn in 2008, some commentators declared the culture wars ended.

Further, the use of the term *culture* implies that until recently, cultural consensus has prevailed. Yet at frequent periods in U.S. history, the coexistence of divergent designs has been the focus of public discussion and concern. During the late 1960s, for example, there was dissensus about premarital sex, the use of marijuana, and the war in Vietnam. In the "roaring [19]20s" the "new woman" wore her hair and her skirt short, smoked in public, and in other ways appeared to reject the design for living followed by her mother and grandmother. During the live broadcast of the Super Bowl halftime show in 2004, the costume of recording figure Janet Jackson was opened to reveal one of her breasts. A furor resulted, with debates about the cause of the nudity (Was it planned? Was it accidental?) and about the moral health of the United States in general and the entertainment industry in particular (Stanley 2004). As discussed in Chapter One, the repeated reference to "culture wars" might be viewed as socially constructed. On the one hand, the use of the phrase by the media is a way to build audience interest. On the other, it is a way to create a sense of urgency to help attract members to and to strengthen allegiance to groups for whom the cultural shifts over more than forty years have been unacceptable. Despite those declaring the culture wars were over during the 2008–2009 economic crisis, others pointed to a steep growth in gun sales and suggested it might indicate a growing militance among social conservatives threatened by the Democratic victories.

This chapter provides an overview of the cultural *content* regarding gender and the cultural *vehicles* that transmit the content. Although it keeps in mind the current multiple and often contradictory gender-related cultural content, it features the currently dominant views and the most serious competitors with those views. We will look at the messages about gender found in language and media and consider to what extent people actually absorb cultural messages about gender. Similarly, the social institution of religion encompasses a wide range of messages about gender. It exemplifies the ongoing struggle to redefine the relative authority of females and males. Science and social science are cultural practices themselves, and we will look at culture's impact on scientific work about sex and gender. The practice of medicine, an applied science, is a powerful area of social life in which gendered messages are communicated.

Even though culture is usually slow to change, there are periods of rapid change. The chapter closes with a focus on the processes of cultural change, highlighting the relationships between social structure and culture to explain why cultural content develops in some ways and not others.

IDEOLOGIES OF GENDER

All cultures have accorded sex and gender a central place in explanations of how the world is and should be. Not all have agreed on how to categorize the sexes or on their social meanings (Nanda 2000). However, most significantly, every culture of which researchers know has been patriarchal to some degree. In some cultures, certain women's positions may have a great deal of authority (for example, grandmother or midwife). Further, there are numerous instances of groups in which individual women achieve exceptional authority. Such an arrangement has never been the cultural ideal, however. Often women have authority only in the absence of men, and when men become available (for example, when they return from war) they again occupy the positions of authority.

The ideas, norms, and even the *things* created and used as part of a people's way of life carry implicit and explicit significance for females and males in a society. For example, the acceptable language, posture, dress, and tasks for one sex are often different from those for the other. To be viewed as **gender appropriate,** one must follow the norms applicable to one's sex. Biological differences between the sexes comprise a universally popular, essentialist explanation for their social differentiation. However, the behaviors labeled as masculine and feminine actually vary from one culture to another, and within a culture they vary over time, supporting the view that gender is socially constructed.

In some cultures, a task may be seen as appropriate for women, and men may be completely excluded from its performance. Other cultures may assign the same task only to men. The *importance* and *flexibility* of these socially constructed notions of what is gender appropriate vary as well. Thus, there may be a third group of cultures in which that same task is usually associated with members of only one sex, but in which it is not unknown for members of the other sex to take part. Finally, in some cultures, that particular task may be equally likely to be performed by a man or by a woman. Likewise, one culture may vary over a long period of time in its norms about what is gender appropriate. For example, in the United States delivering a baby was originally "women's work"; it became "men's work" and is now performed by both women and men. Other jobs, like federal judge, were closed to women entirely and are still disproportionately held by men.

There has also been a great range in the degree of male dominance itself: in its breadth (the range of activities affected) and its depth (the degree of social inequality based on sex). In some cultures, women have had avenues to authority in particular spheres, although achieving this authority has been harder for women than men. In others, the subjugation of women has been virtually total, with no area of social activity in which women could gain authority. Being a man has been a necessary, though far from sufficient, requirement for gaining authority in these more restrictive patriarchies. Cultures have also varied in the degree of inequality among the social categories—those with authority and those without it. For example, contemporary women in the United States experience far less sexist oppression than do women in societies in which women are viewed as the chattel of their fathers, husbands, or other male kin (Ridd and Calloway 1987). However, in the United States, gender continues to be salient in all kinds of aspects of people's lives, from the ways they are expected to dress and walk to the ways they expect to earn a living. Women are now a large proportion of the military and have seen combat. Nonetheless, only men must (and only men may) register with the Selective Service System. If "a national emergency requires rapid expansion of the Armed Forces," only males will be in the registry to be called to service involuntarily (U.S. Selective Service System, undated). Thus, though the particular meanings of gender have varied dramatically over time, the breadth of gender's influence in U.S. society continues to be far greater than the impact of most other characteristics we use to categorize people.

The patriarchal essence of a culture is rarely baldly stated; rather, it is understood as natural and inevitable. Powerful groups dominate, in part, by creating and perpetuating a set of cultural beliefs and practices that legitimate their power. This **hegemony**, or domination, is usually invisible. The dominant ideology of a culture includes narratives that legitimate the patriarchy of the system along with other characteristics of the society's organization. Patriarchal ideologies have varied, with diverse and sometimes mutually contradictory approaches, but religious and scientific doctrine have typically played leading roles in legitimating men's dominance. Most legitimations of patriarchal arrangements depend on **essentialist** ideas about women and men, ideas that hold that many gender differences are actually biologically based. Those members of subordinated groups who are skeptical of some cultural messages may be endangered if they publicize their alternative views, or simply laughed off by members of dominant groups. For example, if women are believed to be naturally monogamous, those who prefer multiple partners will be punished (formally or informally) for making their preferences known.

Differences in the hegemonic beliefs about gender appear not only between cultures, but also within a culture at different times. Even so, it is possible to sketch the most common and fundamental content of traditional U.S. patriarchal ideology. Perhaps the most basic theme is the belief in men's superiority, which is used to justify men's authority over women. Some of the important alleged differences often used to argue men's superiority include a superior male intellect, men's freedom from rule by emotions or intuition, and greater physical strength. People who contradict the stereotypic differences are likely to be labeled as "less than" a man or a woman—and very often to be labeled homosexual. Conversely, anyone who identifies as not heterosexual (whether as homosexual, bisexual, or transgendered) will be judged as less than a "real" man or woman.

In patriarchal ideologies, men and men's characteristics are considered "normal." Any ways in which women are not like men are claimed to show that women are inferior to men. Even when a woman's characteristic is taken as superior to a man's (for example, her presumed superiority as a nurturer), this asset disqualifies her from the most highly regarded positions in social life (she can't be relied on to fire an incompetent subordinate or to lead people in battle). Consequently, in areas of life in which men and women regularly participate, but are seen as typically different, standard arrangements are tailored to men's (presumed) characteristics, rather than women's. For example, jobs may require mandatory overtime hours or rotating shifts, or both; these are feasible for people with freedom from child care responsibilities, but not for people primarily responsible for child care. That is, being free to go to or stay at work when needed is considered "normal" and having to juggle work and family is not.

Some traditional belief systems maintain that women are as valuable as are men, but the activities that men are expected to participate in have more authority and often more prestige than the activities to which women are restricted. Commonly, in a strongly patriarchal culture, differences between the sexes are used to justify the restriction of political positions to men and the assignment of everyday authority over children to women. Aside from rhetoric, other signs indicate that authority over children is not particularly prestigious, but political service is. Furthermore, should there be any question about child rearing, male family members may have the authority to overrule women.

The genders are typically defined in opposition to one another, with a (simple) binary, or oppositional, system of characteristics. So, too, gender ideology has traditionally looked at the category "women" as itself containing oppositional types, either pure or evil. The former are thought to need protection from men's aggressive sexuality, and the latter are thought to take advantage of it through calculated seduction. The vulnerability of pure women to men and of men to temptresses is based on the belief in men's uncontrollably strong, biological sexual drive. Women (who may be evil) must, therefore, be controlled to prevent their taking advantage of men's vulnerability to these urges, and to protect them (if they are pure) from men's acting on those urges.

In 2002, Florida enacted a law requiring that any woman offering a child for adoption place her name and address and information on all possible biological fathers of the child in the newspaper. A public outcry and court challenges followed, partly because women who were victims of sexual assault were included in the requirement. Though the government justified this legislation as preventing future disruptions of adoption arrangements by men claiming paternity rights, the law clearly punished sexually active women through public shaming (Kristof 2002). Ultimately the law was repealed.

The victimization of real women is often explained by their presumptive evil. For example, the immoral behavior of prostitutes was suggested as the motivation for their murder by a serial killer during the late 1980s. Furthermore, when violence is done to any woman, it is routine in the popular interpretation of the act to question whether she was actually, if not obviously, an evil woman who brought the violence upon herself (Caputi 1989). In a 2009 Human Rights Watch report on the extraordinary backlog in the testing of rape kits, this problem was connected to the frequent challenge to the credibility of rape victims that is not often raised to victims of other crimes (cited in Kristof 2009).

### SITUATING GENDER-BASED IDEOLOGY WITHIN CULTURE

Historical periods differ markedly along many significant dimensions. They vary in what are seen as the most authoritative sources of knowledge (for example, church, state, or institutions of scientific knowledge). Periods also vary in their systems of material subsistence (for example, hunting and gathering, agricultural, and industrial societies), and in the organization of ownership (individual, household, clan, cooperative, or corporate). Each of these dimensions has been correlated with different degrees of male domination. Finally, systems of government—fiefdoms, monarchies, colonizers, democracies—have been related to differences in gender systems. As Connell (1995) argues, even while patriarchy is found across profoundly different types of social organization, the dominant versions of masculinity and of femininity within the existing ranges are defined by the economic and politically dominant forces at the time. For example, as a colonizing society needed its population to dominate the colonized, physical strength and aggressiveness were highly prized. Two hundred years later, when most of the population of the former colony works in large-scale organizations, physical aggressiveness is less desirable. Lower status men may still use physical strength to define themselves as masculine, but that definition is no longer dominant, or hegemonic, among the variety of definitions in that culture's repertoire. In this case, a man may believe himself more masculine because he is physically stronger than another, more economically successful man. However, people in the larger society will not agree.

The doctrine of **separate spheres** was a historically powerful ideology of gender. A central part of the teachings of Western religions, this doctrine stated that males and females should dominate in different kinds of social activities because of purportedly essential differences in their biological and psychological natures. The doctrine of separate spheres took on a new meaning with industrialization, as men and women literally spent their working days in different places. Before industrialization, work and family life were conducted in the same location, and family members worked together even when their tasks were assigned on the basis of sex. The belief in separate spheres justified relegating women to the home and assigning men to economic work outside it. At the same time, it preserved men's authority in the family, despite the physical segregation of the sexes.

Even some arguments for the enfranchisement of women were based on the construction that males and females have essentially different natures and on the doctrine of separate spheres. For example, it was said that if women could vote, their special devotion to the home would ensure an injection of a more humane, family-oriented, life-embracing voice into the electorate and eliminate drinking, brawling, and other forms of deviance. This argument was bolstered by the highly visible contributions of women in morally focused movements of the time, such as abolitionism and prison reform.

The doctrine of separate spheres exemplifies the complexity of cultural beliefs about sex and gender at any given historical moment. Though the "woman's place is in the home" ideology reigned, there were nonetheless categories of women who typically worked outside the home. Immigrant women, women of color, and other working-class women were never expected to behave in accordance with the doctrine. The intersection of social class, racial-ethnic, and gender hierarchies narrowed the range of people to whom the doctrine was expected to apply. Indeed, the ability of privileged women to act in conformity with the doctrine depended in large part on the availability of other women to work in the homes and businesses of the affluent. For example, white women used slave or cheap African American or immigrant labor to care for their children and do their housework. The "Mammy" was the stereotyped African American woman who took loving care of white children. Analogous to the virgin or Madonna symbol, the Mammy was asexual and trustworthy. She differed, however, from the white symbol by abandoning her own family to faithfully serve whites. The Mammy contrasted with Jezebel, named for the sexually manipulative biblical character. Jezebel was the symbolic, sexually predatory African American woman whose nature provoked white men's sexual approaches (Mullings 1997). Thus, the common sexual exploitation of African American women by white men was redefined to blame the women.

The dominant version of masculinity was unattainable by large numbers of men in the United States. In the public sphere, immigrants, Native Americans, African Americans, and Chicanos were essentially powerless in their relations with and compared with more privileged men. Even within their own families, the authority relations were patriarchal, although often to a lesser degree than in the homes of the privileged (Lorber 1994). In sum, at any historical moment the belief system of patriarchy is part of a more complex ideology that justifies the existing stratification system, with its intersecting social categories and accompanying class and racial-ethnic inequalities.

Just as ideas about gender are dynamic, so are ideas about race and social class and about the intersection of the three dimensions. For example, Brodkin (1998) described the shifting social definitions of Jewish men and women as being "not quite white" (early in the twentieth century). They were accepted as fully white after World War II, but with their Jewish identity kept private, if not actually hidden. Most recently, many Jews have moved to a more open acknowledgment of Jewish identity—and a revitalized challenge to their whiteness from members of some extremist white Christian groups. The cultural images of Jewish femininity and masculinity have also shifted (e.g., the stereotype of the Jewish American Princess is an invention of the late twentieth century).

### CONTEMPORARY IDEOLOGIES OF GENDER

Current masculinities and femininities are in a state of flux, as the range of possibilities for properly performing them are rapidly changing due to economic and social conditions and as military service is increasingly visible and respected. The varied prescriptions for gender performance in many ways reflect some traditional elements and show the influences of long-occurring and recent social changes. Among contemporary arguments about women's proper place, only rarely does the assumption of separate spheres appear. Even where it does appear, it has evolved. For example, in some white hate groups, women may simultaneously be responsible for family and family-like relationships, but actively participate in public representations of their groups. Totally rejecting a public–private dichotomy, some women skinheads are among the most aggressive members of their hate groups (Blee 2004). Across U.S. society, a worldview that was extremely powerful only three or four generations ago is now regarded by most members of our culture as so old-fashioned that it is completely irrelevant.

For some time, the idealized man in the United States has been emotionally and economically independent, physically powerful, protective of women and children, and emotionally inexpressive with a strong, heterosexual appetite. Traditional visions of femininity prescribed a nurturant, intuitive, vulnerable, asexual, dependent person. Feminist activism during the "second wave" resulted in a recognition of the actual multiplicity of femininities that had long been practiced and in an acknowledgment that adult women were more heterogeneous in personality, as well. However, views of masculinity were less affected. Indeed, well after the onset of feminism's second wave, David and Brannon (1976) suggested that men's long-standing normative characteristics (independence, physical power, protector of women and children, and a strong, heterosexual appetite) were still encountered in four culturally dominant versions of masculinity. The "No Sissy Stuff" version emphasizes manliness as the opposite of assumedly feminine qualities, especially openness and vulnerability. "The Big Wheel" is the successful, achieving man. "The Sturdy Oak" is strong, self-confident, and independent. The "Give 'Em Hell" man is aggressive, violent, and daring.

A growing perception that the hegemonic version was typically unavailable to men of color has added to some younger men's challenge to visions of masculinity like The

Many schools, YMCAs, and other public buildings constructed early in the twentieth century routed people through different entrances, indicating their physical separation once inside.
Photographs of Hillside School, Montclair, New Jersey, taken by the author.

Big Wheel and The Sturdy Oak. For those men who perceive economic achievement as within their reach, emotional expressiveness and nurturance may have become somewhat more acceptable, but for those who perceive themselves less able to achieve economically than their fathers were, No Sissy Stuff or Give 'Em Hell have gained in appeal. The growing use of body-building steroids among boys can be interpreted as an embracing of the No Sissy Stuff masculinity (Egan 2002).

Several social movements (e.g., white hate groups, Ferber and Kimmel 2004; the Promise Keepers, Kimmel 1997) have attracted members from men who perceive their traditional ways of life under attack. However, members of hate groups refashion traditional views of masculinity in complex ways, not simply enacting some binary view of men as either tough guys or wimps (Dobratz and Shanks-Meile 2004).

Themes in the very popular *The Simpsons* and *South Park* satirize all the traditional themes of masculinity in the context of the economic and political disempowering (or continued disempowerment) of most men (Gardiner 2000). Although disdaining Big Wheels and Sturdy Oaks, these representations offer no alternative, ridicule-free models. Representations of women are also hostile, often in traditionally sexist ways.

Labeling a person as homosexual has been used to punish people who deviate from the dominant gender rules. The label is powerful only in a context where homosexuality and bisexuality do not fit traditional versions of masculinity and femininity. **Homophobia**, the fear and hatred of homosexuality and homosexuals, is not found in every culture. There are societies in which homosexuality is not subject to the strongly negative reactions that have been common in the United States. One explanation offered for the existence of homophobia suggests that homosexuality threatens the beliefs that justify patriarchy. If the idealized model that justifies male dominance is fundamentally inaccurate regarding sexual preference, then the whole model and the bases for male dominance in the society are thrown into question. The reaction to the AIDS epidemic was shaped in part by the cultural power of homophobia. Indeed, homophobia appeared to be declining slightly before the epidemic was strongly identified with gay men in the early 1980s.

Homophobia has become increasingly visible as violent crimes against gay men and, to a lesser extent, lesbians have gained local and national attention. Another explanation for "gay bashing" has gained credibility, as a pattern seems to emerge of gay bashing by men who are unable to achieve economically—the currently hegemonic definition of masculinity. Men who are economically marginal cannot establish their masculinity as either a Big Wheel or a Sturdy Oak. Gay bashers are enforcing one definition of masculinity (No Sissy Stuff) by performing another (Give 'Em Hell). Frustration with economic marginalization may also be directed against men of color, and women, because of the belief that they have led to white men's economic woes (Fine et al. 1997). Immigrants may be victimized because they are seen as taking jobs away, or as representing countries whose imports to the United States have led to the closing of U.S. factories.

With the push toward same-sex marriage in the late twentieth century, hostility toward homosexual marriage intensified. At the same time, acceptance is common for civil unions between same-sex couples. Many people who report opposition to the marriage of a same-sex couple have expressed respect for such couples' right to live together with most of the same legal regulation and protection that marriage offers. The furor over same-sex marriage is a good example of the multiplicity of interpretations that people can offer of the same social phenomenon. We need to think through what methods of conducting research will actually help us decide which of these interpretations may be accurate.

Although changes in women's roles have been more widely accepted than changes in men's, there remains a lack of consensus on what femininity does mean. For example, is it gender appropriate for the mother of young children to work outside the home when she does not "need" to? Is it gender appropriate for a wife to earn more money than her husband? Based on an intensive study of married "working parents," Hochschild (1988) identified three types of marital role ideologies: the traditional, the egalitarian, and the transitional. The traditional wife has less power than her husband and identifies with her activities at home rather than in her job. The egalitarian ideology actually prescribes that spouses should be equally powerful at home, and that they should be equally invested in their jobs. There were different versions of the egalitarian view, with different ideals for the degree to which people should be invested in their home lives and in their jobs. Most of the people who were interviewed for Hochschild's study, however, had some form of a transitional ideology. These ideologies represent some point along the continuum from the old (traditional) ideology to the new (egalitarian) ideology. In the transition, the wife's identity involves her work at home and on the job, and the husband's identity is based more on his job than his wife's is on hers. The transitional ideologies varied in particulars, such as the degree of investment of the husband in family matters.

Hochschild's interviews are more than twenty years old. By her name for the "transitional ideologies," Hochschild implied that they were characteristic of a particular historical period. In the mid-1990s, Blair-Loy's (2001) interviews with women who were finance executives (a male-dominated field) revealed an ongoing concern about combining work and family commitments. Comparing women of different generations showed that older women tended to accept the model of commitment to work as precluding appropriate levels of commitment to family expected of mothers. Younger women redefined "the role of wife and mother as an often absent general contractor who subcontracts domestic responsibilities to others while maintaining a demanding career" (p. 687). This allowed them simultaneously to be devoted to work and to family, although continuing to be uneasy about the new definition of their role.

This finding illustrates how qualities that seemed obviously to be mutually exclusive, or in opposition, before or during the women's movement no longer adequately describe cultural approaches to gender. One need not be either a good nurturer or a good wage earner; one can redefine one or both of these so that it becomes possible to succeed at each. Cheerleading represents another illustration of the unpredictability of change and the coexistence of characteristics that would previously have been defined as inconsistent. Cheerleaders' performances are now highly sexualized, with clothing and music that might otherwise be forbidden in their schools. Simultaneously they represent "ideal girlhood" (Adams and Bettis 2003).

Equality of the sexes will not arrive simply as the result of the gradual broadening of definitions of acceptable behavior and division of power. Lorber (1989) and others have argued, instead, that the continuing power of patriarchal ideology limits just how far gender inequality can be reduced. And research on families whose members want to live in a nonsexist way shows that the gendered arrangement of the larger world in which they exist limits their ability to be gender blind at home (Risman 1998).

There is a decrease in the range of ways that biological differences between the sexes are seen as pertinent to how men and women live; for example, pregnancy is no longer considered a reason for a woman to stay at home and out of public sight. For some in the United States, there is also a decrease in how much we think that gender differences are dictated by biology. Thus, the significant decrease in the difference in speed records of male and female runners has made people aware of the historical role of social expectations on women's athletic achievement. Nonetheless, beliefs in difference continue to be strong and to serve patriarchy. When a particular belief is authoritatively established to be wrong, an adjustment to patriarchal ideology may be made that allows the belief system to remain strong. This flexibility is reflected in the double standard illustrated in Table 2.1. Perhaps most troubling of all is the persistent assumption (not universal, but widely recognizable) that a certain trait is more highly valued by virtue of being associated with males in contrast to females. In other words, as long as beliefs in male superiority and male-as-normal are taken for granted (even by those who do not share these notions, but acknowledge their prevalence), the content of any particular sex difference can be questioned without undoing the basis of patriarchy. For example, if a previously male-dominated occupation becomes sex-integrated or female-dominated, it does not raise female status, but lowers the prestige of the occupation (for example, attorneys or accountants).

An important aspect of the current ideology of gender in the United States is the belief that gender inequality is no longer an important problem, widely held among

**Table 2.1 How One's Qualities Are Interpreted Depends on Who and What One Is**

| If a Person is | Call Her: | Call Him: |
|---|---|---|
| Supportive | Bright | Yes-Man |
| Intelligent | Helpful | Smart |
| Innovative | Pushy | Original |
| Insistent | Hysterical | Persistent |
| Tough | Impossible | Go-Getter |
| Cute and Timid | A Sweetheart | A Fairy |

Source: Adapted from Media Women—New York. 1970. "How to Name a Baby–A Vocabulary Guide for Working Women." In *Sisterhood Is Powerful*, edited by Robin Morgan. New York: Vintage Books, 526–527. ✦

whites, particularly, but not only, men. This belief is produced by three related dynamics, according to Rhode (1997). First, it results from what people perceive directly and the kind of information they receive through education and the mass media. Second, there is a common idea that any perceived gender differences are not unjust: "People often rationalize women's inequality as the result of women's own choices and capabilities" (p. 3). Finally, individuals may see themselves as free of responsibility for any injustices they do perceive, as well as free of responsibility to participate in undoing those injustices. In contrast to these views regarding gender in/equality, African Americans (both men and women) are more likely to see gender inequalities as persisting and as an appropriate target for social activism (Kane 2000).

## WHAT ABOUT RACE AND ETHNICITY?

At the same time that people in the United States are part of one culture, in some ways we also participate in **subcultures**, or designs for living, sets of beliefs, and practices that are transmitted from one generation to another within a subgroup of the population, usually defined by membership in a particular racial, ethnic, immigrant, or sectarian religious group. People whose group membership offers a distinctively different design for living from the dominant culture are sometimes bicultural, belonging to and participating in both cultures. For example, you may speak your grandparents' native language when you talk to them and English when you are at work or school. Others may be conversant in the dominant culture, but not feel a part of it.

Although immigrants, and their children, retain some aspects of their original culture, they also learn U.S. culture. The U.S. culture is in some ways enriched by, but is on the whole largely unshaped by, the cultures immigrants bring with them. As immigrants' children learn the ways of U.S. culture, they may feel marginal with regard to both their ancestors' culture and U.S. culture. Because cultures do vary in many ways in the design for *gendered* living, immigrants' children must negotiate between very different rules for their own lives (Pyke and Johnson 2003). Sometimes older immigrants' disapproval of U.S. gender enactments and the hegemonic culture's disapproval of the immigrants' culture lead to negative self-concepts in the younger generation. Alternatively, they sometimes actively construct a positive meaning for the ways in which they differ from the hegemonic gender practices, disdaining those who adhere to hegemonic femininity (Espiritu 2001).

Generalizations about people in one or another racial-ethnic group or nationality are common. We often explain everyday life by referring to individuals' backgrounds. Indeed, throughout this text you will find statements about the relationships between racial-ethnic identity and gendered beliefs and behavior. It is important to be aware, though, of the limitations of such ideas and the need for caution in looking at race, ethnicity, or nationality as a simple cultural dimension that will explain all the diversity in how individuals and groups live gender in the contemporary United States. Such differences are not always due to culture. They may be due instead to differences in the economic situation of racial-ethnic subgroups, to the regions in which they are located (and related differences in economic opportunities), and to the recency of their immigration to the United States.

Furthermore, generalizations about members of one racial-ethnic group often mask the variations within that group. We commonly refer to a few racial-ethnic categories (i.e., African American, Asian American, European American, Latino, and Native American). However, each of these categories actually includes a variety of ethnic groups, whose economic and cultural situations vary greatly (Zavella 1991). Persons *outside* one of these categories, for example, all *non*–Asian Americans, are usually comfortable with broad generalizations about the people within that category. Thus, a common stereotype exists that Asian Americans are economically and educationally more successful than other racial-ethnic groups. In fact, there are significant differences in achievement, for example between Japanese Americans and Filipino Americans. Likewise, Cuban Americans and Puerto Ricans have very different average family incomes. The category "African American" includes both persons descended from many generations in the United States and those who are the children of immigrants from Africa or the Caribbean; these subgroups are also quite different from one another. Though often used interchangeably, "Middle Eastern," "Muslim," and "Arab" refer to three different categories of people; within each category is a wide cultural range. The category of "white," whose members are often ignored as having any racial-ethnic identity, includes people of European or Latin American descent, or both, and is heterogeneous on other dimensions as well.

In recent years, some individuals with multiple racial-ethnic heritage have pushed for recognition of their multiracial identity. Others identify themselves as a member of a particular group while acknowledging the complexity of their backgrounds. Thus President Barack Obama, the child of an African and a European American, identifies himself as an African American.

## LANGUAGE AND THE TRANSMISSION OF CULTURE

Language is the primary vehicle for the construction and transmission of culture; through language, people learn the values, beliefs, and socially defined "facts" or view of reality of their culture. The power of sharing a culture is implicit in the ease with which we usually understand the verbal and nonverbal communications of others as well as their actions and opinions, even when we do not agree with them. We are amused by fantasies in which creatures from another planet (such as those starring in *Third Rock From the Sun*) speak our language literally but fail to understand what we really mean. These characters remind us how much we take our mutual understanding for granted.

Ideas about gender are conveyed in part through the linkage of specific words to one sex or the other, implicitly or explicitly stating what is culturally defined as male or female. By analyzing the particular words used to describe women only or men only, we can discover the hegemonic views of what inheres in masculinity and femininity (Kramer and Freed 1991). Men are much more often described with words that connote competence in highly valued spheres (for example, the word *mastery* means "competence" and is derived from a masculine noun) and with words that connote the presence and sometimes the abuse of power. (How would one describe a female *brute*?) Although being a *nerd* is not hegemonically masculine, it does connote having a high level of technical expertise. Self-identified (male) nerds consider the term masculine; they reserve the term for themselves (Kendall 2000). Women are more often described with words associated with nurturance, softness, and a manipulative sexuality. For example, a *tease* almost certainly refers to a woman. A *sissy* is a boy who is like a girl; in this instance, femininity is obviously negative because it is used to insult a male.

From the eighteenth century until the feminist activism of the 1960s and 1970s, the English language treated sex-indefinite (that is, unspecified) nouns as male (Bodine 1975). Using a masculine pronoun to designate a person whose sex is unknown or to refer to the human species as a whole as male implies that males provide the standard by which "normal" is defined (Miller and Swift 1995).

Another example of maleness being regarded as the norm and femaleness being treated as unusual or invisible is the practice of specifying if the particular individual about whom one speaks is female, as in *woman* judge, but omitting any gender marker if the individual is a man. Many people assume that a judge is a man, and most would be startled to hear the phrase *man* judge. Likewise a *nurse* is assumed to be female; we hear *male nurse* but never *female nurse*. It appears that increasingly popular gender-neutral terms such as *spokesperson* and *police officer* are applied to women more than men, who are often still *spokesmen* and *policemen* (Pauwels 1998). If it is used only for females, however, the term is not actually gender neutral. Those who read or hear it still assume it refers to a female.

Many people believe that the sexist connotations of words are simply vestiges of outdated patriarchal ideology, neither accurately reflecting nor influencing contemporary life. In contrast, researchers have shown that language does influence the thinking and behavior of at least some people (Miller and Swift 1995; Pauwels 1998). Words like *sexism* and new usages that have developed as a result of feminist activism now provide a way for people to think about the gender bias in language and the gender system in general.

When a particular component of sexist language is eliminated or a feminist term is coined, it does not necessarily change the underlying social system. For example, even when *girl* is not used to represent an adult female, an enormous number of alternative expressions still communicate the lesser authority of females compared with males. Without a concurrent weakening of belief in male authority, eliminating particular word usages will be inconsequential (e.g., Cameron 1998). The term *Ms.* was created to remove a woman's marital status from the term by which she is addressed, which was viewed as sexist (why should her marital status be relevant, when a man's is not?). Instead, in the United States it is ambiguous, more or less equivalent to Miss, and sometimes chosen to indicate that a woman is divorced.

Do gendered themes in language actually influence people's ideas? Although language has an influence on us, it is certainly not all-determining. Often messages are interpreted differently among audiences. For example, does *guy* in "you guys" refer to males, or is this a gender-neutral term? The gendered content of language is inconsistent in its impact on people (Pauwels 1998). In a classic study, students were instructed to select illustrations for a textbook on the basis of its table of contents (Schneider and Hacker 1973). One version used the word *people* and the other used the word *man*. The researchers found that students with the *man* table of contents were significantly more likely than the other group to select illustrations with only men. Nonetheless, some students even in this group selected sex-integrated illustrations. This finding illustrates the reality of cultural vehicles: We do not always interpret them in the same way. Just as some people who tell an ethnic- or racially-based joke argue that it is not intended to be insulting, people who use words such as *sissy* argue that those who object are overly sensitive. But research that shows the multiple ways in which people interpret language supports the need to take more care with word choice. With increased usage of gender-neutral language, fewer people will complain that it seems artificial. Indeed, written English in the United States has changed a great deal (particularly in newspapers, textbooks in the social sciences and humanities, and government materials), with the reduction or elimination of many practices criticized as sexist. There appears to be much less change in the use of informal and spoken English (Pauwels 1998). For example, an adult woman is rarely referred to as a girl in public, written materials, but *girl* continues to be used to stand for women in conversation and informal public speech.

In addition to regarding language as a socializing agent, we might look on conversational behavior for indications of how speakers have been socialized into gendered behaviors and identities. Despite widespread assumptions to the contrary, most presumed differences in the language use of women and men turn out to be insignificant, inconsistent, or different than expected when they are systematically investigated (Freed 1995; Cameron 2008). For example, on average, women do not speak more than men, despite the many jokes that assume the contrary (James and Drakich 1993). The persistence of belief in linguistic sex differences is discussed further in the "knowledge professionals" section, later in this chapter. As we shall see, one of the factors that perpetuates beliefs in male–female difference is continued reporting in the mass media of sex differences in linguistic behavior despite the rapidly amassing social science evidence to the contrary.

## MASS MEDIA AND THE TRANSMISSION OF CULTURE
The mass media—including television, radio, the movies, music, music videos, and the Internet—also serve as significant transmitters of cultural ideas about gender (Walters 1999). Their influence is felt both through entertainment-oriented materials and in presentations of news information and analysis. Media organizations, aiming at profit making, are unlikely to risk audience disapproval and loss of sponsorship by taking

unconventional positions. In the same way that institutional cooking often avoids herbs and spices because it seeks to satisfy the broadest range of tastes, the commercial media make "safe" decisions in shaping content and messages. Changing aspects of culture are reflected in media presentations only if they are demanded by the audience, although that audience has no easily available means to make such demands, or when these changes are clearly and strongly backed by evidence drawn from studies of the market. For the most part, the media present a worldview that conforms to the status quo, which includes patriarchal beliefs.

Where there is lack of consensus, content distorts reality to avoid controversy. Thus, a disproportionate number of family-centered situation comedies do not have both parents present. The producers avoid depicting a married couple relationship that might alienate some segment of its audience. Domestic arrangements that might be too traditional for some viewers could be too egalitarian for others; the problem is side-stepped by eliminating the married couple as the basic situation comedy unit. The single-parent households on television in recent seasons tend to be evenly split between male-headed and female-headed families (Lee 2003), while single-parent households in the United States are now actually more than 80 percent female headed.

Early in the women's movement, researchers were pressed to document their claims of media distortions. Feminists were accused of exaggerating the degree to which groups were underrepresented and stereotyped. Systematically collected evidence established clear patterns of the overrepresentation of some categories of people (e.g., young people, white males) and the underrepresentation of others (e.g., African American women, Asian Americans, and older women of all ethnicities). People were also stereotyped; for example, old women appeared almost exclusively as victims.

This patterned underrepresentation of people of color, white women, and older women persists. In the 2007–2008 television season, a sample drawn of one episode from every broadcast network series found that 57 percent of all characters were male (Lauzen 2008). Though there has been some fluctuation each year, the disproportion remains significant. Both sexes are younger on television than in the U.S. population itself, and women are younger than men. For example, 26 percent of women characters were forty years or older, compared to 36 percent of men characters. Television viewers are more likely to be told the marital status of women than of men and more likely to be told a man's occupation than a woman's (Lauzen 2003).

Entertainment is a product of organizations, and media organizations vary in their progress toward more equitable representation of people. For example, with 51 percent of its main characters female, the CW network contrasted in 2007–2008 with the Fox network low of 35 percent female (Lauzen 2008). Fox had a period of airing shows starring or featuring black characters, but reverted to depicting a largely white world after a change in corporate leadership (Smith-Shomade 2002). Proportions of men and women represented in each major racial-ethnic group tends to be similar. However, European Americans and African Americans are overrepresented and Latinos are underrepresented compared to the U.S. population.

Decision makers in advertising remain disproportionately white and male (Bendick and Egan 2009). This helps to explain the continued underrepresentation of women and people of color in both commercials and programs. Corporate interest in profits may lead to more older women characters, as older women have increased movie attendance recently and often select the movie when they go out with a male partner (Holson 2004).

Nonetheless, films with strong female protagonists are often labeled "chick flicks." In another example of "male as normal," action movies, such as the *Terminator* series, are simply movies—not, as they might be called, "dick flicks."

Films and shows that have women involved behind the camera usually also have a somewhat higher representation of women on screen. This may reflect the highest executives' interest in equity, or it may show the influence of women who are hired as writers, producers, or creators; both levels may influence the greater presence of female characters. However, there is a continued underrepresentation of women behind the scenes (Lauzen 2009). In 2008, women were only 16 percent of the directors, writers, editors, and cinematographers on the top 250 U.S. films of 2008, based on gross U.S. earnings. Almost one quarter of these films had no women at all in any of these jobs; none of the films had only women in these jobs.

The representation of women and men of color has tended to feature extremes rather than a realistic range of people. Women and men of color are often shown enacting or reflecting masculinities and femininities different from the hegemonic white variants. For example, a survey of violent pornographic Web sites (Gossett and Byrne 2002) discovered that female objects of pornography were far more likely to be Asian or Asian American than would be expected. They suggest that this reflects the hegemonic U.S. construction of Asian women as exotic and passive. Bruce Lee's movies have been interpreted as offering an alternative masculinity, especially for Asian and Asian American men, who have historically been constructed in the United States as incapable of hegemonic masculinity (Chan 2000).

African American men are typically either celebrities or frightening. African American women tend to be matriarchs (the stern mothers to their own children that Mammies were when they went home from the white families), "welfare queens," or verbally aggressive women (too much "attitude")—the latter being a common character on racially integrated situation comedies (Mullings 1997) and a recent competitor on the Donald Trump "reality" show, *The Apprentice*. With the threat of a boycott of network programming, led by the National Association for the Advancement of Colored People (NAACP), the major networks pledged in 2000 to involve people of color in every program. When Fox premiered *Malcolm in the Middle*, the network was still producing a preponderance of the programming with characters of color. The title character, a young genius, is an otherwise normal (white) boy, with several brothers. Malcolm's best friend in his class for super-bright students is an eyeglasses-wearing, wheelchair-using African American boy, simultaneously violating many common stereotypes.

Traditional heroes, such as Rambo, Indiana Jones, and James Bond, now share the limelight of television and movies with men that Garfinkel (1985) called antiheroes. For example, Homer Simpson is overweight, is economically marginal, and usually laments his lack of an active sex life. He is certainly masculine in recognizable ways, including having some managerial responsibilities at work, owning a home, and enjoying hanging out with his friends. Although traditional male heroes abound on contemporary police and courtroom dramas, more complex male characters are also depicted. Their appearances suggest that the media industry believes that audience ideas about gender have changed. Nonetheless, it seems that characters in these roles perform them in gendered ways. Although women are increasingly among the police officers in action movies, the gendering of role performance persists (King 2008). Women are less likely than men to fight, or to be confrontational. In contrast, men more than women are involved in corruption. Women are disproportionately rookies; this may reflect both the emphasis on youth as more essential to female than to male attractiveness, as well as the tendency to represent women as less powerful than men.

As cable (or satellite) television and Internet access to video programming permit the growing targeting of a show's audience, gender images may be more segregated, with shows trying to reflect their desired viewers' beliefs, rather than introducing some viewers to the newer beliefs that other viewers have adopted. Audiences of mass media increasingly consume within a "cocoon" that provides them with a reflection of their preexisting worldview instead of exposure to others.

Novelist Susan Isaacs suggests (1999) that television, movies, and fiction feature a growing proportion of "wimpettes" and a shrinking number of "brave dames." She defines the wimpette philosophy: the beliefs that men are really little boys, men are strong and women are weak, and a man is the source of one's identity. She says that wimpettes use indirection and subterfuge, have low ethical standards, and betray women friends; a wimpette does not take responsibility for her actions (1999). Brave dames are resilient, are competent, have high ethical standards, stand up to injustice (they are "passionate about something besides passion"), and are *true* friends (Isaacs 1999, 12). Other cultural critics argue that the messages about gender in contemporary "pop" culture are mixed, even contradictory (for example, Zeisler 2008). Interest in contradiction probably fueled the huge appeal of Susan Boyle, the middle-aged, unfashionable Scottish singer whose performance on a British television talent show made her an international YouTube star in 2009.

Although recent versions of fairy tales and Disney movies have featured female characters who are strong and independent, they continue to incorporate female attractiveness as a fundamental characteristic (Grauerholz and Baker-Sperry 2003). Fairy tales mention female attractiveness more often than male attractiveness and those stories with an attractive female hero are more often republished than ones in which the female's appearance is not highlighted. So, too, television characters must be attractive even if they are strong, independent women who perform feminism although they do not generally use the term. The ensemble of friends in *Sex and the City* represented a range of femininities, all focused on (hetero)sexual relationships but with strong bonds and careers. Current or recent shows with such characters include *CSI, Law and Order: SVU, Scrubs, The Mentalist, Cold Case, Bones, NCIS,* and *House.*

Strong women who are not constructed as young and attractive are central characters on *Law and Order* and *The Simpsons,* as well as some of the shows with young and attractive strong women.

Hip-hop, the African American music form, rose to dominance in the 1980s. It boldly confronts racist patterns in the society generally and the criminal justice system in particular. Hip-hop artists communicate widely varied representations of men and women and their relationships. Though hip-hop is often discussed as a homogeneous form, attention reveals a range of themes, both in lyrics and in the video representations of people (and parts of people). Some (such as those known as "gangsta rap") are undeniably misogynist and homophobic, but others (such as some songs of NaS, Chuck D., and Queen Latifah) are unambiguously positive about strong women and the importance of positive relationships between the sexes. Because of hip-hop's importance as a vehicle for protesting the oppression of blacks (especially men), to criticize it is sometimes interpreted as race disloyalty (see Cole and Guy-Sheftall 2003), despite its frequently outrageous demeaning of black women. Further, hip-hop artists sometimes dismiss the significance of violence and misogynistic language and images as trivial, not literal. Instead, they assert it is simply the way people actually talk in young, urban, black neighborhoods. One analysis found that most lyrics in its large sample in fact did not degrade women (Weitzer and Kubrin 2009); however, the songs in this sample generally lacked popular positive representations of women.

In some music videos, movies, and television shows (such as *Xena the Warrior Princess*, or *Buffy the Vampire Slayer*), a highly sexualized brave dame character helps attract a broad audience. Interpretations of such characters conflict: Some cultural critics see these characters as actively using their own sexuality to resist the hegemonic view of females as weak or passive. Others see the characters as having to treat their bodies as commodities, with visual access to them rented or sold—regardless of the message they may simultaneously be able to communicate about their own strength. Still other critics suggest that women performers are exercising their independence by controlling their own sexuality within the video (Emerson 2002).

The media communicate ideas about feminism itself. Most recently, mainstream media have embraced the notion of *postfeminism*. Four major themes commonly appear in coverage about contemporary views of gender: There has been a dramatic decrease in women's support for the women's movement; some women are increasingly antifeminist; some women view the movement as irrelevant; and, finally, some disavow a feminist identity although they agree with the central goals of feminism (Hall and Rodriguez 2003). These themes are not supported in survey data gathered regularly over the years during which the themes have grown dominant in media (Anderson et al. 2009). This fundamental misrepresentation of women's attitudes toward feminism is consistent with earlier media failures to provide audiences with accurate, complex descriptions of the women's movement.

Feminism was portrayed as a civil rights movement during the period of intense feminist activism with its focus on passage of the Equal Rights Amendment to the U.S. Constitution (ultimately, an unsuccessful effort). In subsequent years, however, the media have not developed a coherent framework for presenting news about feminist concerns (Huddy 1997). Because family arrangements are assumed to be the product of only the particular individuals in any one family (see Chapter Four), media do not focus on feminist concerns about family arrangements. Concerns about economic inequities are not the focus of media coverage of feminism for the same reason that they are little reported otherwise—they challenge hegemonic beliefs in the moral superiority and self-correcting nature of capitalism. This leaves feminism to be presented, now and then, in simplistic terms (like news stories more generally, in the current trend to make news into entertainment).

Within entertainment television and film, some women characters can be identified as feminists, although they are rarely explicitly called that. Instead, they are identifiable by their regular insistence, for example, on gender-neutral language in response to the regular use of sexist language by one of their coworkers. These women are working on the problems in their lives as individuals; if they are good at it, they will eliminate those problems. There is no suggestion that their problems are due to social patterns and need to be collectively addressed to actually be solved (Dow 1996). Even when some problem of a character (either ongoing or appearing in only one episode) could be related to a feminist worldview, such connections are never explicitly made. Thus, a working woman struggles to do her job well and to have a happy and equitable home life, but she takes each problem as it arises and never refers to the possibility of working with others to change the arrangements that make balancing work and home lives so challenging. Although the audience may hear that someone was delayed because of a child care problem, no one complains about the lack of day care in her workplace.

### THE IMPACT OF THE MASS MEDIA

After documenting the existence and extent of gendered patterns in media presentations, feminist researchers moved to the question of the impact of these expressions. Do movie depictions of very thin women in heroic roles imply that women must be very thin to be beautiful or heroic? Does the absence of Asian American men on television news programs mean that they are insignificant members of society, or is it just a "random" pattern (Fong-Torres 1986)? Do the media's implicit messages shape people's expectations or behaviors? If so, they represent ways in which the culture is delivered to the individual no matter with whom that individual has face-to-face contact. If language and the media influence people, then they are, by definition, instruments of socialization.

As we know from public discussions of violence, one extreme position holds that media depictions are a leading cause of our culture's violence; others argue that there is no real evidence of such media impact. Certainly most people watch violence without becoming violent. What do we know about the influence of media and of language on people's ideas and behaviors related to gender? Instead of these dualistic positions (in which either violence makes all viewers violent, or it doesn't make any violent), research has shown that media have an influence on at least some people. For example, people who have already been unusually aggressive compared with their peers are likely to become even more so when they view violent programming.

People without an aggressive personal history do not typically become more aggressive because they view violent programming. However, higher levels of exposure to violence tend to desensitize viewers to violence. That is, we find violence less disturbing even if we would not consider engaging in it ourselves. Similar disputes arise about the influence of media stars who smoke on camera, and of the unusually thin bodies of fashion models in advertisements. In the 1992 presidential campaign, Republican vice-presidential candidate Dan Quayle accused the popular title character on *Murphy Brown* of undermining American family values by having a child out of wedlock. A study of college students found that women's exposure to magazines and television shows that focused on thinness, fitness, and personal appearance was related to women's eating problems, concern with thinness, and dissatisfaction with body image (Harrison and Cantor 1997). The researchers found that even when the magazines or shows were initially chosen because of women's exceptional concerns about body image, the women's concerns became greater after reading and viewing these media. Women who listen to feminist rock music report drawing strength from the messages of the songs that are important to them as they deal with the challenges of their own lives

(Savage 2003). Research among African American college students suggests that hip-hop constructions of the character of gender relations have influenced students' views of what those relations actually are like (reported in Cole and Guy-Sheftall 2003).

The setting in which people consume media affects the kind of influence a presentation may have. Thus, parents are urged to watch television with their children to teach them to think critically about its content. Thinking critically about media content is also more likely among viewers whose experiences contradict the show's content than among viewers who are otherwise ignorant of the subject being depicted. Preadolescent girls, for example, have been found to be actively involved in thinking critically about what they view, particularly those aspects of programs that they consider most salient to themselves (Fingerson 1999).

More generally, the very same show will be seen very differently depending on the background of the viewer and the context of the viewing. In a study of women's viewing of television movies about abortion, pro-choice middle-class and pro-choice working-class women interpreted the plots quite differently. Their class positions were related to how they explained what circumstances had led to the pregnancy and what the pregnant woman's options for the future would be if she did not choose abortion. Middle-class viewers sympathized with a poor woman who chose abortion for financial reasons. In contrast, the pro-choice working-class viewers were critical of financial problems as a reason for abortion. They objected to the portrayal of poor women as victims, unable to create alternative solutions if money was the only barrier to carrying out the pregnancy.

Class positions were much less important for anti-abortion women's interpretations of the plot. Instead, their views were largely shaped by a more general sense of being in serious disagreement with many popular cultural beliefs about sexuality and family life (Cole and Press 1999). Similarly, audiences may disagree about whether a specific character is a strong dame or a wimpette. For example, Isaacs (1999) classifies Ally McBeal as a wimpette, but other feminist critics argued that she was a strong (even if highly idiosyncratic) dame. When people viewed Chyna, of the World Wrestling Federation, they may have focused on her remarkable strength. If they watched her over several years (before her 2001 departure), they may have noticed instead that she changed from a "monstrous woman" to a "sex kitten" (Heinecken 2004).

No matter how ambiguous the meanings or how critically the audience reflects on the messages, the media have another kind of influence. They affect audiences by what they do not show. The absence of alternative representations denies people a source of realistic ideas about groups with whom they have no direct contact (Delgado and Stefancic 1995). In other words, even if skeptical viewers react against the ways the media present the world, those viewers receive little constructive input as they seek alternative perspectives. Finally, even when cultural consumers actively communicate their desire for more realistic portrayals, cultural producers may ignore those communications because of multiple organizational pressures. For example, editors of magazines for teenage girls explain their failure to provide more realistic images of girls by pointing to various obstacles from photographers, advertisers, and apparel manufacturers (Milkie 2002).

The recent growth in rapidly circulating amateur videos (particularly through YouTube) has made alternative versions of doing or undoing gender available to many millions of people. In the future, in competing for audiences, the mainstream cultural producers may become more inclusive in the images or perspectives they present.

### RELIGION AND GENDER

The three major monotheistic religions—Christianity, Judaism, and Islam—have traditionally been deeply patriarchal in their teachings. Indeed, the formerly powerful doctrine of separate spheres had its roots in religious teachings. Religion continues to influence and reflect cultural beliefs and practices. Though the Constitution of the United States calls for a separation of church and state, Christianity has been a crucial force in shaping U.S. social life.

Within Judaism, Islam, and Christianity, there is wide variation in the content and interpretations of teachings regarding gender and in the ways in which they limit or shape religious participation depending on one's sex. Since the resurgence of feminist activism in the late 1960s, many religious groups have moved toward the idea of greater equality in their teachings (Sered 1999). Some religious leadership positions previously limited to men have opened up to women since the 1970s: Women have served as religious leaders in many Protestant denominations and non-Orthodox Jewish congregations. Nonetheless, some report that clergywomen's behavior is monitored far more closely than clergymen's (see McKenzie, in Cole and Guy-Sheftall 2003). In those religious organizations that limit women's leadership roles, theological doctrine is sometimes explicitly cited as the rationale (e.g., Roman Catholicism). In addition, continuation of a male-only leadership is sometimes explained by a belief in gendered abilities to lead in worship services (Adams 2007).

The fundamentalist branches of Christianity, Judaism, and Islam continue to embrace an explicitly patriarchal position, taking a very similar shape (in the separate spheres tradition) across the three religions (Ahmed 1993). Indeed, each relies on its gender-related discourse to reiterate the religion's political and social identity. But within each religion there are conflicting standpoints about who or what is the authoritative source of the sacred message, and who are authoritative translators or interpreters of the sacred message.

Rejection of homosexuality is common among those religions that are most patriarchal in their doctrine. Denominations with congregations ranging widely along a theologically conservative–liberal continuum are currently experiencing internal strife, as openly lesbian (e.g., the United Methodist Church in 2004) and gay (e.g., the Episcopal Church) religious leaders are acknowledged and accepted by their church hierarchies.

Language is used to reinforce claims of authority. For example, some Orthodox Jews describe themselves as "observant." By their terminology, Jews who *observe* any other version of Judaism are not observant Jews. Some born-again Christians reserve the label "Christian" for those who are born again. In informal usage, some Protestants reserve the term "Christian" for Protestants. The centrality of Jesus Christ to Roman Catholics and Eastern Orthodox believers is made invisible by such Protestant speakers. Some Muslim feminist scholars from Iran argue that an Islamist (a believer in a particular strand of Islam) cannot call herself a feminist, deeming Islamist interpretations to be essentially sexist (Moghadam 2002).

The power of language has been clear to feminist believers who have actively worked within various religions to review translations of holy texts, to see if gendered language was chosen by translators where original texts had neutral language. Some religious organizations have adopted new versions of religious texts and songs that incorporate gender neutral language. Others have moved away from strongly patriarchal language, but without embracing the goal of a gender-neutral liturgy.

Reformists in all three monotheistic religions—not just Christianity—argue that gender oppression is "against their religion" (though this does not usually include a clear definition of what constitutes gender oppression, nor any acknowledgment that it already exists and is practiced within the respective religious institutions). For example, during the feminist activism of the nineteenth century, some Christian leaders argued that women's second-class legal status violated Christian teachings. Meanwhile, other church leaders found ways to justify women's status inequality on the basis of the Bible. A similar discussion is going on today in Islam (MacFarquhar 2003).

The Muslim faith is typically represented in U.S. media as extremely oppressive of women. There are wide variations in the teachings and practice of Islam within and among the many countries in which it is followed, but media representations in the United States rarely depict this variability and instead highlight practices that are most different from our own. Practices, such as the wearing of a head covering, which strike many non-Muslims as depriving women of equal rights, are not viewed that way by many of those who follow the practice. For example, Muslim women wearing head coverings may be leading lives that are otherwise quite nontraditional; in Oman, veil-wearing women have high-ranking positions in the banking and information technology industries (*Not Without My Veil* 1993). Women who wear head coverings in public may instead view U.S. women as oppressed by the amount of time, attention, and money they devote to appearance. Muslim women who wear looser clothing also consider U.S. women as oppressed by the demand that they reveal their bodies, after which women are judged according to narrowly defined (and perhaps unattainable) standards of physical beauty. Though Muslim women who reject veiling may see it as oppressive, they do not necessarily condemn others who follow the practice. Veiling in the United States may be chosen as a public expression of pride in one's religious identity. Some Muslim women explain that they wear the veil as a protection for themselves, believing as they do in men's strong sex drive and women's vulnerability (Read and Bartkowski 2000).

Religious institutions have much cultural, economic, and political power. Within many religions, groups struggle to retain or to change the beliefs about the social world that are manifest in the religion's doctrine and hierarchy. Much is to be gained or lost from a shift in a church's official position. In 1999, the Southern Baptist Convention issued a policy statement reaffirming its position that the father is the head of the family. As the U.S. church with the largest membership, its affirmation of a non-egalitarian family form made headlines. The Convention made it clear to all that the view of the family is not simply a ritualistic adherence to older teachings, but a strongly supported view for contemporary life. This affirmation probably strengthened the allegiance of traditional church members. However, it also probably weakened the loyalty of some church members who had previously chosen to overlook the traditional teachings.

The number of people in various religious organizations does not indicate the number of people who agree with all facets of its teachings and social arrangements. Despite popular representations of fundamentalist and evangelical Christians as hostile toward feminism, there is actually a wide range of views toward feminism within this population (Gallagher 2004).

Women and men who disagree strongly with some aspect(s) of their religion may resist from within the religion. They may reach an accommodation by emphasizing the aspects of their religion with which they are in accord and dismissing the others—not changing their divergent views, but defining them as peripheral to their religious identification. They may resist through formal organization (for example, the reproductive rights group Catholics for a Free Choice), by absenting themselves from particular practices with which they disagree, or by attending services less often than in the past. They may leave one congregation for another with a leader or members whose views they perceive as more similar to their own. People with a deep-seated loyalty to their religion often remain despite disagreeing strongly with some aspects of its belief system or its social practices.

People who appear to be challenging some aspect of their religion may actively construct an interpretation of their own beliefs and actions that is consistent with its teachings. For example, by attending a public college (rather than a church-related institution), Mormon women might be viewed as resisting religious teachings about the family-centered role of women. Rather than defining themselves as opposing church teachings, however, they may emphasize ways in which their pursuit of education will enhance their performance as mothers (Mihelich and Storrs 2003). Nonetheless, by pursuing higher education and (usually) deferring marriage and child bearing, they are also enacting a version of femininity that pushes the limits of Mormon conventions.

### KNOWLEDGE PROFESSIONALS

Although we are taught to view the findings of science as universally and objectively true, scientists cannot free themselves completely from cultural influences when they frame the questions that they decide are important and when they interpret the findings of their research. A common example of this phenomenon is the use of an evolutionary, Darwinian narrative (regardless of flaws in logic and evidence) to frame discussions of differences between men's and women's sexual behaviors (McCaughey 2007).

In the twentieth century, scientific findings came to be viewed with the reverence formerly limited to religious pronouncements (see Tavris 1992). Thus, nonspecialists often suspend critical judgment when they hear the conclusions of highly specialized experts. Furthermore, nonspecialists tend not to recognize that even properly researched findings are often arguable among scientists. Finally, laypersons are informed about scientific findings selectively, related to the hierarchy of power and prestige among scientists and scientific organizations and the lack of media investment in the labor-intensive job of researching and writing clearly about complex scientific topics (Nelkin 1987).

Science is itself a social institution, and it has not been immune to the influences of social forces on its production of knowledge. Indeed, as science has gained power in shaping the beliefs of Americans it has often contributed to the continuing legitimation of the nonegalitarian aspects of a society founded on an actively egalitarian rhetoric. The study of "sex differences" is an outstanding example of biases and distortions in scientific research in the last hundred years.

When social scientists speak of sex differences, they are speaking of traits that are usually associated more with one sex than with the other in the population as a whole. For example, height is a characteristic in which males *as a group* differ from females *as a group*; the average height of adult males is greater than the average height of adult females. However, many individual females are taller than many individual males. The difference in heights between the sexes is a group, not an individual, difference. In the absence of other information, however, it would be wise to bet that an unknown male is taller than an unknown female. In a large sample, we would probably not lose money on this bet, but we might very well lose if we had only a few pairs of people to bet on. Nonetheless, in discussions of sex differences, people tend to assume clear-cut differences (such as the presence or absence of female or male genitalia), rather than tendencies (such as the patterned relationship between sex and height). Indeed, the common phrase "the opposite sex" builds in an assumption that differences are stark and contrasting.

Scholars as well as members of the public disagree about which characteristics actually are distributed differently among males and females. Underlying flaws are chronic in research seeking to establish the existence of sex differences in personality (Epstein 1999). That is, numerous taken-for-granted ideas about women and men do not hold up with the certainty and absolute truth with which they are popularized by the mass media and in everyday life. Much contemporary writing on gender distinctions, or the description of the boundaries that supposedly separate men and women's characteristics, fails to notice and account for the changes that people experience as they go through the life course and take on roles in social settings calling for different behavior (Epstein 1999).

As sociolinguists broadened their attention to include differences, such as one's ethnicity, income level, or social class, the intersection at which an individual is located was also expanded (Henley 1995). Linguists increasingly study how language practices vary on the basis of the individual's multiple group memberships as well as the activities in which a person engages. The characteristics of the other people in an interaction also affect how an individual will speak at any particular moment (see, for example, Bergvall, Bing, and Freed 1996; Hall and Bucholtz 1995). Scholars have reassessed and reinterpreted previously documented differences in women's and men's linguistic behavior. Thus, the pattern of men's interrupting women more than women's interrupting men does not simply signify a difference in their socialization into a particular set of manners. Instead, it can reflect men's greater power in the particular group being studied. Both men and women interrupt more or less depending on their relative position in a group and on the norms about interruption of that group. Men can be more polite, and women less polite, when the balance of power in the talking group changes. Men, who are caricatured as unable to listen, must do so with care if they are interacting with a supervisor, customer, or client. In sum, the literature increasingly supports an explanation of gendered patterns of speech and conversation that reflect the contexts in which people are speaking.

Despite the growing body of evidence negating the difference perspective on linguistic and other individual behaviors, journalists continue to report about sex differences as if they were real, well documented, and important (Liberman 2006). Freed (2003) found for the 1990s that hundreds or thousands of articles in professional and popular publications (depending on the periodical index used) discussed either sex or gender differences.

The work of knowledge professionals sometimes reveals the assumption that "male is normal": When females, as a group, differ from males, they are regarded as exceptional although they are often a majority of the population. In a case of questioning this assumption, labor economist Audrey Freedman (1989) critiqued a *Harvard Business Review* article on the costs of employing women as managers. Freedman pointed out the costs to productivity of employing men. Compared with women, men have higher rates of drug and alcotiol addiction, lowering productivity and raising employers' insurance costs. Men also have a "greater inclination to engage in destructive struggles for control" leading to expensive corporate takeover battles (Freedman 1989). Experts consider these costs normal, however, as long as the actions of the males are considered the norm.

When scholars in other disciplines assume the validity of writings on sex differences, the biased production of knowledge extends its influence further. For example, Gilligan's thesis (1982) on basic differences in moral development between males and females was widely reported in the popular press without discussion of the critiques from feminist and other social scientists. Unaware of theoretical and empirical challenges to Gilligan's "difference" thesis, many feminist scholars in the humanities have used Gilligan's ideas without question in their own work.

Early feminist critiques of science used a liberal perspective, focused on the obstacles to women's full involvement in scientific development. A radical perspective has long been common among feminist analysts of science, highlighting the impact of patriarchal ideology on scientific thought; with a difference approach, these views suggest the sexes have fundamentally different "ways of knowing." By limiting women's involvement in science, the potential contributions of any such distinctively female approaches are lost. Commonly invoked dimensions of difference include women's more wholistic view and men's greater interest in invasive treatment strategies. Ironically, while faulting scientists for being unaware of sexist biases in their work and their workplace, most feminist critics have overlooked the need for multidimensional critiques, argued by multiracial feminist and socialist feminist critics of science (Hammonds and Subramaniam 2003; Collins 1999). Slowly there has been a growing attention to class, race and ethnicity, and other dimensions of difference. With the rise of global feminism, there has also been increasing attention to biases in the approaches to medical research about and service provided in other countries (Altman 2004a).

Rather than positing two positions (male and female) from which the world might be explored, feminist philosophers and scientists argue that knowledge is best developed by people in a multiplicity of social positions. One's **standpoint**, or the position from which one observes and experiences the world, opens a particular window on reality (Harding 1987). By broadening participation in the development of knowledge to include people from previously excluded standpoints, knowledge can be enhanced. Although feminism is rarely credited with any contribution to the sciences, they have begun to benefit from the increased participation of people of varied standpoints and people sensitized to such issues through feminist science studies (Schiebinger 2003).

### BIOLOGICAL AND MEDICAL SCIENCE

The possible cultural biases affecting bio-medical scientists and medical practitioners have drawn broader critical attention because of their more obvious effect on people's lives. Expert thinking narrowed by patriarchal assumptions may produce erroneous work, even failing to conceptualize, much less address, important questions. Feminists have identified problems in the framing of issues, the establishment of priorities, and the strategies chosen for studying and overcoming health challenges (Clarke and Olesen 1999). For example, the framing of cluster headache as generally a man's problem shaped medical researchers' approach to the problem in ways that may have interfered with developing an accurate understanding of the problem (Kempner 2006).

Western ideas about gender influenced scientists' visualizations of the relationships between the human egg and sperm (Martin 1991). Casting the behavior of each in traditional views of gender-appropriate behavior, scientists describe the egg as passive and the sperm as active. The egg's fragility is emphasized, although it lives longer than sperm do. The verbs used to describe the movement of sperm toward the egg also show the influence of gender on scientific imagery. Although scientists might maintain that these language choices are merely metaphors, the metaphors incline the expert to think about certain kinds of actions and not others, depending on the gendered character of the discussion. This creates obstacles to imagining other ways of thinking about the egg and the sperm, and so may impede the progress of scientific thinking about conception.

The existence of intersexual individuals shows the inaccuracy of our culture's belief in the existence of two sex categories, as well as the medical profession's participation in that belief. In the binary or oppositional thinking common to Western cultures, reality is divided into "black" or "white." Just as there is no variation in white or in black, it is believed that there is no variation among normal women or normal men.

People who are not within the range of normal (e.g., those infants having an unusually small birth-size penis) are seen as abnormal. Variation in itself is considered abnormal (Fausto-Sterling 1999). Intersexuality is treated as a condition requiring surgery. The condition is diagnosed because the deviation *might* develop (when the child goes through puberty) into an inability to have standard heterosexual intercourse or to protect the infant from future ridicule. Medical professionals leave little room for family members' views about surgical intervention very soon after birth (Preves 2002). Rather than considering, for example, that such genitalia will nonetheless permit sexual pleasure, surgeons may risk damage to the salient nerves to transform the infant's appearance to be unambiguously female. Thus, an unusually small penis at birth may be prevented from developing into an inadequate penis as defined by cultural ideas of proper length, rather than allowed the potential for pleasure.

In addition to those people born with genitalia that do not fit the norm for one of the two sexes, the use of genetic testing has made us aware of additional individuals who are neither clearly female nor male. When testing was initiated to insure that athletes were not fraudulently competing against people of the other sex in world competitions, one or two athletes were discovered at each major gathering to have chromosomal sex identities different from their apparently clear-cut genital category (Kolata 1992). It is impossible to report the prevalence of this combination of the genitalia of one category and the chromosomes of another, because chromosomal testing is not widespread. It is also impossible to report the prevalence of observable combinations of male and female characteristics, because the stigma attached discourages people from revealing them.

Radical feminists drew attention early to the willingness of scientists and physicians to take risks with women's bodies that they would not pursue with men's. For example, women's use of hormone replacement therapy (H.R.T.) was associated for more than sixty years with increased rates of certain cancers, yet such reports were ignored or discounted as pharmaceutical companies encouraged physicians to make the use of H.R.T. a normal part of the preventive medical care for menopausal women (Seaman 2003). In contrast, research on a "male pill" for contraceptive purposes was limited for decades because of the effect of the gender system on thinking about physiology as well as about the interpersonal dynamics between heterosexual intimates (Oudshoom 2003). Recent scholarship has drawn attention to ways in which masculinity has been or is being medicalized (Rosenfeld and Faircloth 2006).

The use of H.R.T., despite its dangers, is related to the hegemony of the male professional standpoint. Menopause is increasingly constructed as a medical condition, rather than a normal physiological experience (Woods 1999). Just as a small percentage of women have serious difficulties with menopause, small percentages of people have serious difficulties while passing through other normal physiological stages, without the stages themselves being medicalized. For example, the outbreak of severe acne occurs to some people in puberty, but puberty is not constructed as a medical condition.

Interviews with menopausal women revealed that they were unprepared by their physicians for positive experiences of menopause, including, for some, increased sexual pleasure (Winterich 2003). Although increasing proportions of gynecologists are women, they often are affected by their professional socialization as well as the standpoint of their relative youth. Older patients sometimes perceive that their doctors are more interested in their obstetric work than in the gynecological care of no-longer-fertile women. The disconnection between physicians' expectations of the important topics for middle-aged women and the actual concerns of their patients creates a serious gap in the medical advisory needs of women in this age group. Feminist social scientists, too, have tended to ignore age as an important dimension of the gender system (Calasanti and Slevin 2006).

CULTURE, SOCIAL STRUCTURE, AND CULTURAL CHANGE

We can sketch two commonly held, contrasting assumptions of cultural change, often implicit in news accounts, encountered in informal discussions among "ordinary" people, or explicitly articulated by social scientists. One view takes change as moving in one direction, away from past patterns (whether for better or for worse); the other views change like the pendulum of a clock, swinging to one extreme and then to the other, passing through moderate points along the way. As we examine the dynamic aspects of gender in culture, we should remember the need for caution. Changing patterns over a short period of time may merely reflect fashion, or the short-lived impact of a particular event.

Egalitarianism has gradually become viewed as applicable to more and more people regardless of social categories. Patriarchy contradicts the fundamental value of egalitarianism that has long been held in American culture. In the past, equal treatment was seen as the norm for people in the same social category (for example, categories defined by race, age, ownership of property, or citizenship), but membership in groups defined as "fundamentally different" (like comparing apples and oranges) implicitly removed any obligation to treat people from different groups as equal to one another.

Despite the growing pressure for universal treatment and the integration of spheres, however, a patriarchal worldview and a patriarchal society survive with adaptations, if not intact. How can we explain this, even in the presence of assaults from the periodic waves of feminist activism? Why has it continued to be not only tolerable, but also appropriate, for one group to be dominated by members of another group?

There are two contrasting theoretical approaches to understanding the endurance of patriarchal ideology. One view emphasizes culture's power and its resistance to change. The other view of patriarchy's endurance emphasizes the influence of social structural arrangements on the content of culture. These standpoints are not in conflict and, indeed, combine to paint a picture of the interdependence of cultural and structural patterns. This interdependence also helps explain changes over time and the direction they take.

Sociologists emphasizing culture explore how and to what extent cultural components, such as language and systems of knowledge and belief, influence individual behavior and social patterns. For example, the questions that scientists and technologists pursue, and that funders of research underwrite, tend to serve the needs of more highly valued members of society and more highly valued activities in society. Decisions by scientists and technologists and analyses by those charged with the public's welfare have sometimes been shaped by scientifically, epidemiologically, and economically unsound biases. Thus, the problems of sufferers of rheumatoid arthritis (overwhelmingly female and elderly) have been underfunded, relative to the societal costs of this chronic disease. Similarly, the slow responses of both governmental and nongovernmental agencies to the AIDS epidemic have long been interpreted as shaped by homophobic beliefs (for example, see Altman 1987; Payne and Risch 1984).

In contrast, some analysts of contemporary society focus on how economically and politically dominant groups use their power to create, promote, and maintain a worldview to support the existing distribution of power. Using this focus, whoever makes

Rosie the Riveter was a major cultural creation of World War II. Topped with the slogan "We Can Do It," the original poster was used to encourage women to take on "men's work" as military production increased and many male workers left for the military. Rosie's image has been a popular icon since that time. The revision here illustrates the process of cultural change in which a traditional symbol is morphed into an icon for a contemporary purpose. Here Rosie represents one position in the ongoing cultural conflict about reproductive rights. Rosie has also been used in advertisements for commercial products.
© 2010 by Micah Ian Wright and AntiWarPosters.com.

decisions about medical funding is likely to fund illnesses from which they themselves suffer, or to which they feel vulnerable, rather than funding other illnesses. In a classical discussion of this position, Frankfort (1972) contrasted the surgically cautious approach to health problems in the male reproductive system compared with a surgically radical approach to "female" problems. For example, the removal of the whole breast used to be the standard procedure when a cancer was detected in it. In response to the influence of female physicians and women's health activists, surgeons developed and increasingly used lumpectomy (removal of the tumor and a limited area around it) rather than the more extreme mastectomy.

From this view, funding priorities will be changed when underserved groups work (alone or in coalition) to show their power. Indeed, activism among people with breast cancer has led to a disproportionately high rate of funding for this disease (relative to its impact on the population). In reaction to the matter-of-fact decision by some medical insurers to subsidize the costs of Viagra (for erectile dysfunction), activists worked to gain expanded coverage for female contraceptives, long the leading prescription category exempted from coverage by insurers. The insurers didn't need to understand the "woman's" view; they needed only to see that they would encounter significant problems, at least of public relations and perhaps of regulation, if they did not make their policies more equitable.

As the examples here show, hegemony includes maintaining the aspects of the culture that serve powerful interests. However, it also involves changing the cultural aspects that challenge prevailing interests. If the interests of the dominant groups change, therefore, cultural change is likely to follow. For example, during World War II the labor force participation of married women was essential to the war effort and to the owners of companies in war-related industries. As vividly documented in the film *The Life and Times of Rosie the Riveter* (1987), a media campaign was launched that helped bring many women into paid employment. Many others who were already employed in traditional women's jobs were ready to take advantage of the more rewarding jobs in war production. The definition of a woman's place changed quickly as economic and political incentives changed. Long-standing cultural beliefs proved to be less powerful in dictating women's behavior than might have been expected. Conversely, as the veterans returned home and were demobilized and unemployed, media campaigns about the essential full-time homemaking role for women proved inadequate to convince many women to resume their prewar activities and voluntarily make jobs available to resuming veterans. Instead, formal obstacles to women's continued participation were necessary to remove them from the labor pool, thus minimizing male unemployment and anticipated social unrest.

If cultural ideas of femininity had been enough to determine behavior, then the media reminders of women's "proper place" would have changed employment patterns, and the patterns of blanket firings and sex-based hirings would have been unnecessary. Likewise, curtailed government support resulted in the closing of daycare centers that had opened during the war, despite continued demand from their clientele. Thus, the usually slow rate of cultural change may indicate the resistance of powerful groups to structural change more than proving some inherent resistance to change in culture itself.

Cultural change may also come about because of changes in the distribution of power in the society. Dissatisfied members of the society may mobilize to gain power to bring about the cultural (and social structural) changes they seek—as the experience with the rapid change in the level of funding for breast cancer research illustrates. The impact of the women's movement of the late 1960s and 1970s is discussed in Chapter Seven, the chapter on politics and the legal system. The growth in hate groups is also attributed to dissatisfaction with power shifts, as many working-class white men have lost economic stability and the ability to achieve hegemonic masculinity through providing for their family (Ferber and Kimmel 2004).

A focus on cultural causes and a focus on social structural causes are each productive in understanding social reality; many social scientists use both perspectives in their work. For example, understanding the current state of the AIDS crisis requires both recognition of the homophobia in scientific and governmental institutions (Treichler 1988) as well as recognition of the extremely well-organized gay and lesbian response that has led to the recruitment of substantial support from nonhomophobic hetero-sexuals (Altman 1987).

In either perspective, the power of culture is significant: a coherent view of the world and a blueprint for living enmesh members of a culture, making it difficult to imagine alternative explanations and prescriptions and difficult for individuals with a different vision to integrate into the social world. The dominant worldview is trans-mitted by vehicles ranging from explicit patterns of verbal and nonverbal commu-nication to institutionalized belief systems communicated through organized systems of religion and knowledge (with accompanying rewards and punishments for con-formity or deviance). In addition, social structural patterns implicitly reflect cultural beliefs.

Science would seemingly be another source of new or modified ideas because it leads to the extension of our knowledge. Some scientists are motivated to draw away from the dominant models and assumptions of their disciplines and to investigate alternative descriptions and explanations of the phenomena they study. However, not all scientific findings are equally likely to be reported to the public. Scientific findings that do not support the complex web of beliefs that society holds about gender are less likely to be reported, or to influence the "background" in news reports, than findings that fit media professionals' ideas (Nelkin 1987). Thus, the changing knowledge related to gender is not generally diffused to members of the culture. This reflects the increasingly powerful role of the media in the process of changing cultural beliefs and knowledge.

The failure to report conclusions that undermine the justifications of patriarchy is not simply a matter of inattentiveness on the part of those who accept patriarchal descriptions of reality. The power to decide what will be reported or portrayed in the mass media belongs to the leaders of media organizations, who are rarely critical of the existing distributions of power in the society. Women who attain decision-making positions in this arena do not usually rush to remove patriarchal patterns in their medium's messages. In fact, they rarely have sufficient power to protect themselves from criticism or from more serious punishment from superiors. Further, women who have succeeded by the "rules of the game" are likely to see them as working well enough.

Although popular ideas can shift or become more diverse without the leadership of mass media organizations, once the media incorporate a newer image of what is "normal," the more traditional segments of the audience are likely to be influenced as well. The electronic media reach an enormous audience (the basis for the occasional description of the world as a global village), so even though other kinds of organizations or groups may initiate cultural change, the changes will spread much more rapidly once the media acknowledge them. The belief that the public passively takes in media messages is, however, clearly false. This point was made in the earlier discussion of audience reactions to movies about women with unwanted pregnancies, in which viewers interpreted the messages differently and with varied skepticism (Cole and Press 1999).

Cultural change occurs at greatly differing speeds in various institutions and among different groups in our population. It is not possible when new content is introduced to know if it is a fad, a clear move to permanent change, or a swing in one direction that will sooner or later be followed by a swing in the other direction. After more than forty years since the beginning of the women's movement, it is clear that many cultural views about gender have changed for the long term.

Men's views about women's proper roles in society have changed at different rates, reflecting the diversity of experience and location of American men. Attitudes among men toward women at home and at work are remarkably varied, both among and within some central social categories of men. For example, men with daughters are more likely to be concerned about equality of opportunity for females than are men with sons only. Furthermore, women's views about gender have changed more than men's (Warner and Steel 1999). Thus, the complexity of patterns of attitudes and attitude change requires taking a very cautious posture in predicting future cultural views of gender.

## SUMMARY

Culture, or a people's design for living, influences behaviors, opportunities, and responsibilities in situations from the everyday to the exceptional. Beliefs of a culture have strong effects on the life of the individual. Even biological differences between the sexes (such as relative average size, strength, and speed) are susceptible to the influences of culture. This is well illustrated by the changing beliefs and changing abilities of male and female participants in sports traditionally restricted to members of the other sex.

Ideologies of gender justify patterns of gender stratification in a particular culture. Despite our belief in the objectivity and curiosity of scientists, as members of a culture they are prone to deviate from the standards of their profession. However, many people fail to question "scientific" assumptions of gender ideology if they are framed in biological terms. For example, it is rarely reported that documented sex differences are often produced not by innate differences, but by the different social treatment of females and males. If they are viewed as natural, then most people believe there is no reason to try to change social arrangements to facilitate broadening opportunities for the sexes.

Views about gender are interwoven with beliefs about other social categories, producing a complex ideological system, rather than separate sets of rules applied to all members of each sex. Primarily, the family-based household and educational institutions share in the transmission of ideology and culture. The next chapters explore these important socialization agents, as well as ways in which people in small group interactions may "undo" gender.

Ideologies do change, and the interdependence of culture and social structure is an important premise in the sociology of gender. In Chapters Four to Seven on social institutions, we will turn to the gendering of social life as a product of the interaction of culture and the family, education, the economy, and the political system.

## DISCUSSION QUESTIONS

1. Describe two or three generalizations in the chapter that you think are inaccurate. How would you propose, in each case, developing a more accurate generalization than the one here? Do you think that you and the author may have different belief systems that lead you to different generalizations?

2. Think about the ways you talk in front of old friends of yours, and with your family members, and with teachers. List some of the words you might use in one setting that you would not use in another. Now imagine that the people you are talking to are of your sex, then imagine they are of the other sex. What differences, if any, would be likely to appear in your speech?

3. Consider some ways in which people you know, of different generations or different racial, religious, national, or regional backgrounds, seem to have different ideas about the capacities, responsibilities, and even the weaknesses of boys and girls, women and men. ✦

# CHAPTER 3

# Learning and Doing Gender

We now turn to a micro-social focus on gender, examining individuals' development of gender and sexual identities and their learning to recognize and perform gender in social groups. Though people do gender while learning it, the chapter focuses first on the process of gender socialization, moving afterward to gender enactments or contestations in social interaction. While biological explanations of gendered behavior remain popular (see Angier 1999), they are most fundamentally challenged by the wide variety of gendered meanings and experiences among different societies and cultures and among people positioned differently in the social intersections of social class, racial-ethnic identities, and other social positions within the same country.

Gender learning has analytically distinct products: the formation of a **gender identity**, by which people view themselves as *masculine* or *feminine*, and the learning of sex-specific roles (e.g., father) and gendered versions of otherwise sex-neutral roles (e.g., student). It also includes learning gendered rules that apply to most roles we will perform or encounter, as we talk, manage our appearance, and otherwise signal to others that we are feminine or masculine.

Socially shaped experiences that are based on social definitions of femininities and masculinities become important in creating and shaping differences between females and males that are often assumed to be biologically based (Brody 1999). Throughout this chapter, keep in mind the too-common tendency to think of people as "programmed," rather than socialized. Socialization is a complicated and partial process, including contradictory messages. Individual agency has a role in people's decisions about which messages to respect and which to ignore or react against, and in the forms such reactions take. If socialization determined everything about us, social change would not be as common as it actually is in social life.

People do gender, following complex rules about acting masculine of feminine, whether at home, school, or work, or as a stranger moving through a public space (West and Zimmerman 1987). People are also doing gender when focused on challenging the dominant rules (Schippers 2000). It is in social interaction that existing versions of gender are most often reproduced, renegotiated, or resisted. The chapter concludes with a discussion of the ways in which people's bodies are used to do gender, through activities aimed at managing attractiveness or health-related goals.

## SOCIALIZATION

**Socialization** is the process of learning the rules of the social group or culture to which we belong or hope to belong, and learning to define ourselves and others within that setting. Most norms specify a range of acceptable behaviors, rather than one narrowly defined possibility. Through socialization, we often internalize, or accept as correct, the rules and definitions of the socializing group.

Sometimes as part of our socialization into a subordinated group, we learn that the rules of the dominant group must be followed even when our subordinated group questions those rules. Whether or not this information is internalized, we learn that there are external pressures to conform. We come to know the rules for getting around without getting into trouble and learn to believe those rules to be unavoidable at worst or desirable at best. We develop ideas about what values are so important that it may be worth getting into trouble if pursuing them requires breaking rules. Social and cultural ideas and practices regarding gender are central to both the intertwined processes of the development of the self and socialization about one's social environments.

The particular content of socialization may be applicable to most or all situations (e.g., prescribing how women should sit in public and what kinds of language men should avoid), or it may apply only to certain social positions, such as firefighter or aunt. It varies among geographical regions as well as differing depending on our other socially significant characteristics (e.g., racial, ethnic, and income group; urban, suburban, or rural residence of origin; religion; age; and birth order) that are also associated with expectations for behavior. These aspects of an individual's place in the social world combine to produce highly complex variations of gender identity and gendered performance.

As we saw in the preceding chapter, culture contains material that is inconsistent and material that is so broad it allows multiple interpretations and enactments. To say that a person is socialized, then, does not mean she is brainwashed. There may be wide latitude for the exercise of personal agency in the choice of which rules to follow and which values to emphasize. Indeed, precisely because of one's internalization of some cultural values (e.g., the belief in equality and individual freedom), one may violate cultural norms. When working to gain the vote, women who chained themselves to the White House fence violated norms of proper behavior to pursue fundamental cultural values.

## SOCIALIZATION AS SOCIAL CONTROL

Socialization into the acceptance of different opportunity structures, rights, rewards, and limitations for men and for women works to the benefit of those who gain from current arrangements. If people are socialized to accept or at least to take for granted as inevitable that their biological sex will be related to life chances, then there is no need to enforce conformity. For example, as long as people take for granted that combat is only for men, many other arrangements justified by the belief in men's greater toughness are seen as correct. Likewise, socializing women into believing that they have inherently superior intuitive and empathic abilities helps to maintain the classical division of child care in the home, and the assignment of women to nurturing occupations outside the home "makes sense."

In sum, socialization serves as an efficient way to impose values, norms, and expectations on the individual. Internalization of the values of a system through the socialization process is a powerful way to perpetuate that system. It is perhaps the most effective method of social control because the individual regulates and polices her or his own behavior. This self-policing may be based on the individual's belief that these rules are appropriate or that these rules must be followed to avoid punishment. Although people do sometimes violate norms they believe in, presumably they are much less likely to do so than to violate rules in which they do not believe.

In becoming socialized, we learn the ways in which the social world is gendered beyond the roles we ourselves perform. We may find ourselves serving as agents of social control, either enforcing or questioning the ways that people in other social positions perform gender. Sometimes the simple indication of surprise at someone's performance will be interpreted as a challenge to it, and so we may be seen as enforcing rules with which we don't particularly agree. Thus, if another parent in a playground comments on how strong a little girl is, her parents may interpret that as implying she lacks femininity, rather than taking it as the compliment that was intended.

## THE SCHEMA MODEL, SIGNIFICANT OTHERS, AND INDIVIDUAL DEVELOPMENT

Contemporary theories of development and socialization have three characteristics in common: They emphasize that children are "active agents who are influenced by and influence others," they increasingly integrate a lifelong perspective, and they appreciate the significance of physical, societal, and sociocultural contexts in which development and socialization occur (Corsaro and Fingerson 2003, 130–131).

**Schema theory**, drawing on earlier theories, depicts children as active seekers of coherent explanations of their social worlds (Albert and Porter 1988). Actively and with attention to their surroundings, children develop two schema, or frameworks, one about each gender. Schema are normally evolving, open to change as the person is exposed to different or more complex aspects of reality. Proponents of this theory hypothesize that the schema for one's own gender is more complex and more detailed than the schema for the other gender. Recent research using the schema approach suggests that a person's schema includes not only knowledge and stereotypes, but also feelings and values (Stockard 1999, 219).

Schema theory has several promising aspects. First, it provides a simple framework with which to explain changes in behavior and attitudes over the life course. Second, its conception of schema as complex and multidimensional helps explain people's ability to hold multiple definitions of femininities and masculinities simultaneously. This is consistent with the multiracial feminist perspective. In addition, the dynamic character of schema builds in the potential that gender will decrease in importance. Just as being a lawyer no longer means doing a "man's job," exercising authority in a mixed-sex interaction may come to be irrelevant to the fact that one is a girl or woman.

The content of these schema, and other aspects of learning gender, are influenced by the significant others who surround the child. **Significant others** are people with whom the child has frequent and regular contact, who have control over rewards and punishments for the child, and who have some image of what the child should become. In addition to being told about gender, the child actively observes how significant others do gender, drawing conclusions from those observations as well as the others' stated gender beliefs. Parents and other household members are the first significant others in a child's life; the child is also a significant other to them. Both children and their primary caretakers are affected by the gendered dynamics of their small group (Brody 1999).

Significant others affect children's development in several ways. The attitudes and behaviors of significant others will influence the particular messages about gender that are communicated, including what gender involves and how dominant it is in determining desirable behavior. Research comparing the gender attitudes of mothers of very young children with the attitudes of those children at the age of 18 found the mothers' attitudes had a strong influence on their children's views of the appropriate division of household labor (Cunningham 2001).

Significant others also influence children with the limits they set, the expectations they communicate, and the pattern of situations that lead to rewards or punishments. Significant others differ in their expectations and preferences about the gendering of children's behavior, leading them to behave differently in influential ways. For example, researchers have found a tendency of mothers to let boy babies crawl or walk farther away than they let girl babies before calling or bringing them closer by. This subtle, but persistent, difference in treatment is linked to boys developing a more adventurous, risk-taking style than girls, which is popularly seen as an inborn sex difference. In research based primarily on whites, fathers and grandfathers have consistently been more interested in children behaving in a gender-appropriate manner than mothers and grandmothers have been. Further, men tend to define *gender appropriate* more traditionally than women do (Brody 1999).

Beyond the ways in which the significant others treat the child, the child will also draw conclusions on the basis of how the significant others themselves do gender. Thus, in Cunningham's (2001) research on 18-year-olds' views of the ideal division of labor in the family, he found that they were influenced by the actual division of labor followed in their home during adolescence. For example, a girl whose mother never does any household repairs is unlikely to take a shop or woodworking class, even if the mother suggests she do so. On the other hand, if her grandfather encourages her to be his helper as he does repair work, she may develop an interest in fixing things and choose the course herself. Because significant others do not necessarily agree with one another, in either attitudes or actions, the individual has an active part in choosing how to behave.

## GENDER IN CHILDHOOD

Although we are socialized throughout our lives, the early years have the most enduring impact. One of the first elements of gender learning is the development of **sex identity**, one's self-perception of being a girl or a boy and the sense that this femaleness or maleness is a permanent trait. Learning the very notion "sex" is a prerequisite for grasping that many role performances may, or sometimes must, be tailored to one's sex. Intersexual infants, born with ambiguous genitalia, present an unusual but instructive example of the power of social labeling. Research on such children has found that when the sex label assigned at birth is consistently applied during the child's early years, that sex remains a permanent self-identity. Even in the cases in which subsequent physiological development objectively identifies the child as a member of the other sex, the early childhood socialization has an enduring impact.

The messages children get about gender reflect variations among different population groups. For example, researchers have found less interest in hegemonic gender distinctions among African American fathers and grandfathers in U.S. society (Hill and Sprague 1999). This is consistent with the relatively egalitarian traditions among African American couples, who typically share major responsibilities more equitably than white couples do. Immigrants' children learn about the gender system in the old as well as the new country (for essays on a range of ethnic family patterns, see Benokraitis and Shaw-Taylor 2001). The longer that members (or generations) of a family live in the United States, however, the fewer the patterns from their previous culture will figure in daily life, being replaced more or less completely by dominant U.S. patterns. The current way of life in the child's home is most important in socialization and continues to be influenced by religion, region, and social class.

In addition to people with whom they have direct contact, children are influenced by cultural products, such as toys, story books, and electronic media, that present accounts of gender. The influence of significant others may be constrained by hegemonic notions of gender-appropriate toys, taken for granted throughout the culture and reinforced through marketing and packaging (see Table 3.1). Children exercise some agency, making choices

**Table 3.1 Toys That Teach.** In 2000, the Mattel Corporation's products included two computers. The Barbie model was designed for use by girls, and the Hot Wheels model was designed for use by boys. These models were not, however, simply different in appearance. They had important differences in the software that they provided.

| **Only Barbie has:** | **Only Hot Wheels has:** | **Both models have:** |
|---|---|---|
| Fashion Designer | A human anatomy & 3D visualization program | An encyclopedia |
| Detective Barbie | Cluefinders Math 9-12 | A 3D World Atlas |
| Miscellaneous Barbie | Compton's Complete Reference Collection | Math Workshop |
| programs* | Kid Pix Studio | Typing Tutorial |
| | Logical Journey of the Zoombinis (a thinking | National Geographic: The |
| | game) | 90s |
| | | Writing and Creativity |
| | | Center |

*According to Mattel, the popular Barbie software did not leave enough space on the Barbie model computer to include all the educational software on the Hot Wheels model.
**Source:** Adapted from Headlam, Bruce. 2000. "Barbie PC: Fashion Over Logic." *New York Times*, January 20, G4. ✦

of whether or how to use toys and other objects they incorporate into their play, but marketing techniques target ever-younger age groups (Schlosser 2000). Market research explores the particular gendered preferences of increasingly young children. This then affects the marketing of products, including advertising, packaging, and displaying in sex-labeled sections of stores (Barnes 2009). The research is based on assumptions that these differences exist and are widely shared, but the subsequent marketing approach contributes to enforcing the gender-linking of these preferences.

As we saw in Chapter Two, corporations and organizations vary in their approach to gender. Toy companies do not all develop the same range of products, and toy stores do not all identify some sections as displaying toys for boys and others as displaying toys for girls (which makes it less likely that those toys will be given to children of the other sex, regardless of their preferences). For example, although female action figures in the Ranger product line are less tough than their male counterparts, they are integral members of the group. In contrast, females in the G.I. Joe product line are clearly only marginal group members (Inness 2004).

Children work to shape their surroundings, and starting at an early age they exhibit a sense of agency in their interactions with older family members, peers, and others (Corsaro and Fingerson 2003). Children witness different and inconsistently gendered role performances, which they may imitate or critique. They make sense out of contradictory messages. For example, if a small boy is dressed as a football player for Halloween, he will probably encounter many smiling adults who comment on what a big boy he is, what a little "man" he is, or perhaps how strong he looks (if he is wearing pads). He may also encounter someone who is critical of the football costume, saying football players are stupid or use steroids and cheat. He may seek some explanation (after all, adults are not usually critical of small children's costumes) of the comment, but he is unlikely to seriously question the excellence of his costume. And he may, in the future, avoid the person who made the comment.

Children may respond to the messages they encounter and to the structuring of their experiences by developing certain potentials and inhibiting other abilities. A child may seek to overcome a deficiency (such as muscular weakness in a boy) because others define it as gender inappropriate. If the same deficiency is defined as gender appropriate, the child may make no effort to overcome it and in fact may be proud of it. Girls may use their supposed weakness as an excuse to avoid certain jobs around the house. On the other hand, potentials that are seen as sex-inappropriate, such as a good throwing arm in a girl and physical grace in a boy, may not be developed and may eventually be lost.

As children expand their experiences beyond the home, they are faced with a widening range of gendered role performances and ideas about gender. Children actively acquire information about the sexes and about hegemonic notions of femininity and masculinity, including the different role performances expected from females and males in apparently sex-neutral positions (such as student or grandchild). Popular children's films communicate **heteronormativity**, which "structures social life so that heterosexuality is always assumed, expected, ordinary, and privileged" (Martin and Kazyak 2009; 316). They also regularly portray male characters looking at the bodies of females (as objects separated from the persons that they are); scholars call this phenomenon the "male gaze"; others might call it "ogling."

As children age, teachers and friends take on greater importance as socialization agents. Teachers reward or punish behavior that conforms to or deviates from their own expectations of gendered role performances. School children learn that their reactions to perceived injustices must be gender appropriate: boys should not cry, and girls should not punch. Norms also apply to the intersection of statuses: For example, interrupting the teacher may be more acceptable for white boys than for girls or for boys of color. Of course, for the status of pupil there is also a large range of behavioral norms unrelated to gender. For example, no one should tell tales to the teacher, but everyone may inquire politely and rationally about the teacher's assignment. In Chapter Five, we turn to the educational institution and examine its impacts on students of all ages.

Recently, increased attention has been directed to the power of peer influence even before adolescence (Corsaro and Fingerson 2003; Harris 1998). Close friendships appear to be most influential, but because children tend to be close to people much like themselves, it is not easy to determine to what extent they are influenced by their friends and to what extent they have chosen their friends because they already approve of their characteristics. Peers who are not close friends also have an impact on children's developing ideas about gender, contributing to their worldview (Moore 2001). Boys and girls enact identities that are simultaneously influenced by gender, class, and race-ethnicity. For example, aggressive physicality, including but not limited to athletic prowess, is central even in small boys' informal dominance over other children, particularly in poor and working-class communities. Middle-class boys are somewhat less likely than lower- and working-class boys to pursue this path to masculinity, instead pursuing a form of masculinity that becomes hegemonic in adulthood—masculinity based on some combination of academic achievement and social behavior acceptable to authorities (Hasbrook and Harris 2000).

### ADOLESCENCE AND EARLY ADULTHOOD

Adolescence is a period in which people move more fully out of their families, developing their multifaceted identities and negotiating the increasing challenges of the social world of schools. During adolescence, close friends and the peer network, more generally, take on increasing importance for the individual (Giordano 2003).

Although awareness of sex identities is foregrounded in elementary school, open references to the system of racial, ethnic, and class stratification are less likely, at least in formal settings. By adolescence, children are well aware of these distinctions, and their management of their self-presentation involves the complex intersection of their gender, racial-ethnic, and social class positions. For example, in a high school with a white and Mexican American student body, girls' use of markers indicating ethnic and class identifications were integral to their versions of femininity (Bettie 2000).

Though children are introduced to ideas about sex in their earliest years, sexuality moves to the center of attention by adolescence. Learning a sexual or erotic role depends on extensive social inputs into what appears to be a biological fact of life. High school rather than the home is the critical location for exploring sexuality and gender. While heteronormativity may be the most fundamental lesson learned in the site, it is also a place for experimenting, including playing around with possibilities that might be viewed as transgressive (Pascoe 2007). In U.S. culture, learning to think of oneself as a sexual being, learning how to feel sexual (what "turns you on" sexually), and learning how to interact sexually have been very different developmental experiences for males and females (Giordano 2003). Being a sexual actor requires knowledge of the physical aspects of sexual behavior, but it also requires familiarity with the social scripts. Like theatrical scripts, social scripts provide the person with the acceptable lines to say to others and with the cues that tell the person when the time for those lines is at hand.

The most basic and pervasive distinction between boys' and girls' socialization into sexuality traditionally has been the different pattern for learning physical and social elements of the role. Girls tend to learn the social scripts of their sexual behaviors before they actually feel physically "sexual." Conversely, boys learn about the physical aspects of sexual behavior, explicit descriptions of it, and large vocabularies of applicable terms even before they know how to have a conversation with a girl. Girls learn how to interact in situations that are either overtly or covertly sexual quite early (relative to boys). For example, small girls learn to sit with their legs together before they have any idea of the implications of having one's legs spread apart for sexual activity. Girls learn how to flirt long before they have any notion of where flirting might lead and how that might feel.

Greater exposure to sexual materials in the last few decades has somewhat decreased the difference in girls' and boys' familiarity with the social and physical aspects of sexual interactions. Nonetheless, gendered differences in defining situations and feelings as sexual arousal persist, consistent with the persisting emphasis on romance in socialization of females and physiological cues in the socialization of males. There are variations in the patterns of sexual activity among adolescents of varied social class, religion, and racial-ethnic backgrounds, but the difference between girls' and boys' paths to sexuality is typical throughout the culture.

Adolescence and early adulthood are dynamic periods in which many people experiment with how they define themselves. Identity is always presented within some social context(s); the individual's self-presentation is simultaneously constrained to some degree by the meanings (in that context) that are ascribed to her or his racial-ethnic, class, and sex statuses. Individual agency must take these expectations into account, although one may work toward rejecting them. Even those who present themselves as part of a distinctive subculture, such as Goth, will present an identity that is gendered or actively opposed to gender category. The shape of this presentation is influenced or constrained by one's racial-ethnic and social class characteristics (Wilkins 2008).

### ADULTHOOD: GENDER AND SEXUALITY

Adult socialization encompasses learning about newly acquired statuses, such as parental and marital statuses and occupational statuses. Socialization in adulthood is also necessary because of social changes that reshape previously learned rules. In addition, the development of **sexual identity**, or one's self-conception as heterosexual, gay or lesbian, bisexual, or transgendered, extends into adulthood. Because sexual behavior during adolescence is widely constructed as experimental, there is some skepticism when adolescents identify themselves as other than heterosexual. By adulthood, these constructions are more commonly accepted as representing some permanent identity of the individual.

Despite hegemonic depictions of gay men as unmasculine and lesbians as unfeminine, one's sexual identity is actually distinct from one's gender identity. For example, a heterosexual man may do gender in an androgynous way, that is, he may combine some behaviors culturally defined as feminine with some defined as masculine; a lesbian may behave in a way totally consistent with traditional notions of femininity (except for the sex of her sexual partners). In U.S. culture, however, this still surprises many people. When a hegemonically masculine male celebrity, or feminine female celebrity, is identified as having a same-sex partner, he or she is illustrating the difference between these two dimensions, sexual identity and gender identity (Connell 1999). However, performance of gender is regularly interpreted within the framework of the person's sexual identity, just as the enactment of her or his sexual identity will be interpreted within the framework of the ways in which she or he does gender. Like the intersection of race-ethnicity, class, and gender, gender and sexuality are distinct dimensions whose combinations are significant (Schippers 2000).

There is a continuing and dynamic debate about the causes of homosexual preferences, which is interrelated with views about the acceptability of homosexual behavior. Although it has become a less popular view, some individuals continue to classify homosexuality as an illness or a perversion, or both. In 1998, Trent Lott, then majority leader of the U.S. Senate, compared homosexuality to kleptomania. Though there was widely publicized criticism of his comment, he was not removed from his leadership position by his colleagues. The reaction to his comments showed that this is a particularly controversial notion.

A more scientific, rather than moralistic, view argues that there is a genetic predisposition to homosexuality, even that one's sexual preference is "hard-wired," or determined by some neurological structures in the brain itself. Although there are serious scientific challenges to this view (see Zicklin 1997 for a critique of this research) it remains popular, in part because it makes nonheterosexuality predetermined, rather than an individual's choice (for which one might be punished) or the result of flawed upbringing (for which parents are responsible).

People may change their sexual views, behaviors, and even their identities throughout their lifetimes. Some scholars of sexuality maintain that sexual preference is not a fixed characteristic, but is a product of social experiences and can be influenced by changing circumstances. For example, prisoners may be committed to same-sex partners while incarcerated, but revert to heterosexual relationships on return to the outside world. Emotional attachment to an individual at a particular point in one's life may make that person a sexually attractive object, even if he or she is of the sex one has typically not seen as sexually interesting. Although it is well supported by research, this more fluid view of sexual preference is less popular than biological and essentialist models (Zicklin 1997; Blumstein and Schwartz 1990).

The negotiation of the meanings of one's sexual behavior and preferences is affected by the social context and the expectations that others have. Racial-ethnic, age, and social class are connected to the ways in which behaviors are interpreted by others. For example, lesbian Latina migrant workers must navigate the changing meanings of their sexuality in the different communities that they move through, related to both family relationships and variations in the larger community patterns of racism and homophobia (Acosta 2008).

Like other aspects of the self, people's sexuality is dynamic through the life cycle and with changes in the social construction of sexuality. **Transgendered** is a category that has only recently gained widespread acknowledgment. Currently it includes people who have completed the medical-surgical procedures to change from one sex to "the" other (although they do not function reproductively as their new sex category), people who have made some changes to their bodies to be like the other sex, people categorized as *intersexual* by their inborn mix of physical characteristics, and people who subjectively experience themselves as fitting into neither of the hegemonic sex categories.

Women's increased participation in sex-integrated environments outside the family increased their sexual activity outside the family (Blumstein and Schwartz 1990). This resulted from the greater opportunity to form emotional relationships that, for most U.S. women, precede the experience of sexual desire. Thus, women's lives have provided them with more chances to develop a relationship in which they feel sexual, and technological and legal changes have freed women from the fear of pregnancy that might otherwise have served to limit their behavior. Nonetheless, access to reproductive services is often limited (see, for example, Brubaker 2007).

### FAMILY AND OCCUPATIONAL ROLES

Even in a life that looks very stable, the individual must learn new things because of normal movement through the life course. For example, being an experienced worker has different expectations attached than being a newcomer, and being "thirty something" involves different rules than being "young." Among a sample of involved fathers, Palkovitz, Copes, and Woolfolk (2001) found that some men saw their new roles as bringing to the fore characteristics they had previously had, while others perceived their entry into fatherhood as a "jolt." Regardless of how they perceived their transition to parenting, most of the men felt that being a father was more influential than any other facet of their lives had been.

Although people know something about family statuses (such as grandmother or widower) they have not themselves occupied, a more complex learning of their meanings is expected when people move into those statuses. These details exist for gendered statuses and also for the gender-appropriate performance of apparently gender-neutral statuses. Thus, a woman learning the executive role finds that it may be unwise to have pictures of her children on her office desk, but a man in that role learns that he may actually benefit from such a human touch. All roles also require learning something about the expectations for other, related positions (e.g., executives have expectations about the behavior of secretaries and of chief executive officers, and secretaries and CEOs have expectations for those same executives). People exercise agency as they learn more about dominant expectations of roles they are newly entering, and may actively shape different versions of those roles, as Miller found (2007) among the new mothers in her sample.

In adulthood, the gendered variations in the patient role are learned as medical professionals teach their patients what is expected of them. Male physicians may consider it sensible to have a nurse present while examining a female patient, but female physicians may not consider this necessary while examining a male patient. Both male and female physicians are enacting for their patients their assumptions about the gendering of sexuality (Giuffre and Williams 2000). Although it was long acceptable for a male patient not to consider using the services of a female physician, until recently, it was not considered reasonable for a woman to rule out using the services of a male physician.

People's ideas about gendered roles often change when they are established in households of their own, with family responsibilities and economic conditions beyond their control. Gender ideologies change through the life course, and do so in complex ways, reflecting both variety in experiences and differences in other social characteristics, such as race-ethnicity (Vespa 2009). Sometimes their practices (that is, the way they lead their daily lives) are more flexible than their stated ideologies, which may be slower to change. In research on Chicana cannery workers and industrial workers, Zavella (1991) described how the importance of a wife's earnings may be recognized or denied by her husband. Likewise, because of the work-related demands on a wife, a husband's participation in household and childrearing tasks may be adjusted. Therefore, changes in behaviors may lead to changes in beliefs. Using a multiracial perspective, Zavella's research illustrates that ideological and occupational variations are significant within a single racial-ethnic group. Currently, fathers with greater-than-average participation in housework and child care tasks develop self-images as more nurturant and competent people as they spend more time in these activities (Coltrane 1996).

Evidence suggests that fathers of girls become more egalitarian in their attitudes. In contrast, fathers with sons only have not shown this shift (Warner and Steel 1999). The researchers suggest that a man with a daughter becomes increasingly aware of possible limits on her life related to sexism. He shifts his views to be in line with his desires for her opportunities. In contrast, the man with sons lacks that motivation to change his views. He may actually become concerned about the possibility of decreasing opportunities for his son(s), fearing that expanded rights for females will narrow males' chances.

Research about men in a federally funded program for "deadbeat dads" provides another view of the possibilities of socialization in adulthood (Johnson, Levine, and Doolittle 1999). Unlike most stereotypes of noncustodial fathers who fail to pay child support, this program aimed at men who were economically unable to make payments. With few occupational opportunities, and high rates of both unemployment and underemployment, these men were often unable to maintain their own household, rather than living luxuriously at the expense of their children as per the stereotype. The program aimed to help its participants find stable and relatively better paid work. The reality of the communities in which these men live is one of poor prospects, but some possibility.

However, because individuals' perceptions of their opportunities affect their motivation and commitment to taking initiative, the program worked both to improve the men's chances for favorable employment and to change the men's perceptions of their opportunities and their parental roles. By the end of the experiment, the views of many participants about their roles as fathers had changed.

### SOCIAL CHANGE AND RESOCIALIZATION

People learn to change how they do gender because of changes in their surroundings and the requirements of their own lives. Changes in surroundings include ways in which the social world changes (such as the increased employment of women in positions of authority) as well as the individual's mobility (for example, from a rural to an urban community or from a blue-collar to a white-collar household). Mothers who expected to stay home to raise their children went back to school or work when the rate of inflation in the 1970s made their earnings essential. Men whose reservist wives have been called up to military duty may find themselves responsible for their children's care (even if they have female relatives who take charge of or share in the actual caretaking). People living in a "twenty-four seven" economy must find ways to coordinate increasingly complex work and family schedules. Although generally in hegemonically gendered ways, adult children of the frail elderly and parents of disabled children negotiate the expectations that become harder to meet as government reduces or fails to create support systems for caregiving. As people age, sources of their sense of self are often changed in ways they cannot control. For example, men whose physical strength has been important vocationally must adapt as they move through middle age (Gilbert and Constantine 2005). As sexual potency decreases with age, men are challenged to revise the ways they think about potency and its relationship to masculinity (Calasanti and King 2005). The availability of pharmaceutical approaches to potency (for those able to afford it) changes notions of how to adapt to biological aging.

A significant area in which to observe changing gender through the life cycle is in the second wave of feminism and how it influenced the attitudes and behaviors of women and men whose socialization began before 1970. Boys had to take the initiative in asking for a date or a dance, a major challenge for many young people. Flight attendants were all female (called stewardesses), and they had to smile constantly as part of their jobs. Men learned to take orders from a woman; gay and lesbian people learned to introduce their same-sex partner, rather than hiding the relationship; mothers learned to consider it acceptable to serve prepared foods, rather than cooking "from scratch." Even though family arrangements were very different in the 1950s and 1960s than they are today, people who are in their early 50s now were raised in those homes. Adults' attitudes and behaviors changed in response to changing cultural content, and children and younger adults resocialized them to newer expectations for the ways in which behavior and role performances are gendered (or are less gendered).

People adapt to changing times and changing personal situations. Many people in today's society are doing gender in ways fundamentally different than those by which they were socialized, in other societies or at other times. People born fifty years ago were taught that men should not swear in front of women (if a man erred, one popular acknowledgment of the slip was "Pardon my French") before the women's movement. White, middle-class women who grew up believing they would depend on a husband economically redefined their own earnings as more than pin money when they lost their husbands, or when their husbands lost their jobs.

It may be more common for us to notice people when they say or do something old-fashioned than to realize the wide range of ways that their daily lives differ from what they were raised to expect. The most immediate source of information about the extent of these changes is available to any student who knows someone over age 50. Compose a list of questions you may have about how things used to be done, and have a conversation with someone raised before the women's movement started to have an impact!

## DOING GENDER

People start to perform gender, and enforce, it at early ages. The active involvement of children in making sense of their world, central to schema theory, is illustrated in an analysis of how 4- and 5-year-old children offer and challenge competing claims regarding gender and athleticism. When their sex-segregated soccer teams both attended a special ceremony, girls asserted Barbie as a symbol of girl athletes despite boys' insistence that girlishness and athleticism are essentially mutually exclusive (Messner 2000). Children in a racially mixed summer camp actively applied an informal, hierarchical system of interaction for which age, race, and gender were central factors (Moore 2001).

As schema theory suggests, with increased maturity individuals develop more nuanced versions of gender identity (especially for their own sex). For some period during adolescence, Williams (2002) found that girls let go of some of the rigidity associated with notions of gender, instead experimenting with multiple approaches to doing femininity reflective of practices in their communities.

All performances of gender are simultaneously performances affected by all the actor's identities and social structural location (Ridgeway 2009). For example, consider, hypothetically, how a motorist behaves when stopped by a traffic officer. Gender, race, and age may intersect in portrayals of innocence. Presumably sharing the goal of avoiding "trouble," individual strategies differ by one's position in the social world. Thus, men of color learn to relate to traffic officers differently than women of color do, and these women presumably adopt different strategies than white women. For white men, learning to relate to traffic officers is probably heavily influenced by social class position (a factor not completely irrelevant to members of other categories). The relative age of the officer and the motorist also will shape the motorist's demeanor.

Of course, all these variations are multiplied if we move from the traditional expectation that the officer is a white male. The motorist would change strategy if stopped by an African American woman, for example. Strategies believed to work with a white policeman (e.g., deferential behavior by members of subordinate social categories) may be rejected and others developed. Drivers who react to any officer by being cooperative and quiet, or by offering a bribe, regardless of the officer's race and sex, are illustrating their assumption that the officer's occupational status is crucial. This illustrates people's ability to change throughout life. Those who do not immediately "change with the times" are likely to learn quickly that they are out of step if they indicate to the officer that he or she violates their notion of what an officer's race and sex should be.

The construction and performance of a gendered identity are influenced by one's access to the means for accomplishing one or another version of femininity or masculinity. Not everyone has equal resources needed when performing the dominant, or hegemonic, variations of gender. For example, the most highly esteemed performance of motherhood includes a woman's staying home full-time during her child's infancy, which requires economic resources that not all women have. There are other, socially recognized, ways to be a good mother, although they are not as highly regarded. Women also differ in their chances of performing these alternatives; some women have another family member to do child care. This arrangement is generally viewed as less desirable than staying with the baby, but it is more desirable than using an unrelated babysitter or taking the baby to an organized daycare center. However, not all mothers have this option. Kin may be unavailable because of their location, or because of their other obligations. Fewer people grow up in large families, and thus new parents have fewer siblings and cousins to call on for help. Options are even more limited because male kin (except fathers) are very unlikely to help out in this way.

People have learned to do gender in varied ways depending on their group memberships, which are interrelated with historical differences in access to the means to perform the hegemonic version as well as cultural differences in valuing different forms of masculinities and femininities. For example, African American women historically have been socialized into a more flexible set of gender-appropriate norms than white U.S. women have been. In contrast to a strong popular belief that machismo is the dominant version of masculinity among Chicano men, research shows a flexibility also in Chicano masculinities, which are strongly shaped by the opportunities and obstacles in particular individuals' social situations (Zavella 1991).

Cultural differences lead a South Asian immigrant father in the United States to expect to have the final say in whom his daughter will marry. A poor father may not marry his child's mother precisely because he shares the hegemonic view that a husband should provide some degree of economic security. However, by having contact with the child and providing financial assistance when possible, he can be defined as a good father. In contrast, the choice of a middle-class man to not marry the mother of his child traditionally prevented him from being viewed as a good father, even if he contributed to his child's upbringing.

One study of a small group of economically successful Chinese American men illustrates a variety of masculinities (Chen 1999). Because of stereotypes of Chinese American men, such as their supposed lack of aggressiveness, these men could not fulfill the hegemonic ideal of masculinity. Rather than passively accepting some demasculinized identity, each man actively responded to this situation. Some tried to challenge their marginal position by *excelling* within the criteria of hegemonic masculinity itself. Other men tried to excel in other ways, in the hope that their excellence would *deflect* attention from their shortcomings within the dominant version of masculinity. Some of the men Chen interviewed, however, simply *denied* the ways in which their lives differed from the dominant version among white American men; they accepted the hegemonic definition of masculinity and ignored the ways in which they could not satisfy that definition. In a theoretical discussion of these findings, Chen emphasized that cultural domination requires the cooperation of subordinated individuals. To avoid dealing with repudiation, or rebellion against their domination, powerful groups may accept the adaptations of marginalized men as achievements of masculinity. Regardless of the version of masculinity that they develop, however, marginalized men must assert dominance over the women within their racial-ethnic or class groups to win this acceptance.

One man in Chen's study did respond to the dominant definition of masculinity by rejecting it, and therefore rejecting the judgment that his achievement of masculinity was merely marginal. This man is gay and so is multiply marginal. In a related account about bisexual people's experience of marginality among both heterosexual and homosexual groups, Rust (1996) found that some individuals, whose families were racially or ethnically mixed, or whose identity was otherwise experienced as marginal, were actually especially comfortable in the marginality of their sexual identity. Social change may be more likely to come from people who cannot successfully adapt to the dominant definitions of gender and so have less to lose when they stop trying to. Finally, sometimes people reject the effort to do gender, choosing instead to work toward *undoing* it (Risman 2009).

## SOCIAL INTERACTION AND THE EVERYDAY NEGOTIATION OF GENDER

Through our everyday social interaction—at work, at school, on the street, or in the supermarket—we are acting on the basic rules we have learned, or we are reacting to the rules and expectations that the people with whom we are interacting are implicitly putting forward. Because social interaction is one of the most powerful ways in which the gender system is maintained, or might be challenged, we need to consider the kinds of interactions in which people are most likely to find themselves. The micro-social level of small-group or face-to-face interaction is a significant factor in maintaining or changing the meanings of gender. It is the way that the changes "out there" get translated (or not) into changes that "really" happen. Just as interaction with significant others and peer groups is important in childhood and adolescence, interaction is an ongoing means of socialization in adulthood. The gender system has an enormous influence on the settings in which people find themselves, and in that way the macro and middle levels are important to all kinds of interactions. Because I am a middle-aged, upper-middle-class white woman, my interactions with sales people as I browse in expensive shops will be very different than those of younger people, especially people of color. When I shop alone for a computer, a large appliance, or a car, I get much less attention than when I shop with a man; he, on the other hand, gets the same attention whether or not I'm with him. The appeal of movies in which people present themselves as the other sex (classics such as *Tootsie*) is in part the shock the character experiences in interactions.

A hypothetical example illustrates how gendered expectations may be reproduced or changed in a group interaction. Imagine that a gathering of a neighborhood's residents takes place in response to a flyer distributed by several homeowners, who want to get a fairer share of municipal services. As ideas develop, someone has to take notes. Who will take the notes? One who has never taken notes at a meeting probably doesn't think of doing so. On the other hand, if one has often ended up taking notes at meetings, she may volunteer. She might be happy to take it on, as something at which she is experienced and therefore does well, providing a way for her to make a special contribution. But if no one offers to do this job, and the meeting seems momentarily stalled, another person may speak up: "I'm tired of people always thinking that some woman is going to take the notes. I'm not going to do it; why doesn't a man do it for a change?" Something will happen: another woman may well speak up and volunteer to do it, or a man may deny any sexism in the group and volunteer himself. Regardless of the outcome, the speaker has "rocked the boat," has challenged what is taken for granted. The next time the group needs a note taker, this episode will influence what happens. One outcome may be that a man will volunteer to take notes. Or the woman who complained may be treated coldly by others, who refer to her as a "feminazi" behind

**BOY OR GIRL?** People are often uneasy when they do not know the sex of a child they see in public. Comments to the adult(s) accompanying the child are likely to be different depending on the child's sex; strangers may also be concerned that they will offend the child's companion(s) by using the wrong pronoun to refer to . . . it?
Photograph taken by the author.

her back. The leaders who call the next meeting may announce at the beginning the name of the person who will take notes and avoid another spontaneous outburst that might endanger the success of the group.

In other words, when the rules we take for granted are followed without discussion, we assume that adulthood is simply about following the rules we previously learned; groups need recorders, and some woman will either freely or regretfully acknowledge that she will do it. But when people confront those rules, or follow other rules (let's say that the chair of the meeting started with: "Let's rotate the note taking; today we'll start with the person to my left"), we learn that rules can be renegotiated. Our previous socialization is not all-determining. Social interactions in small groups are particularly promising sites for undoing gender (Deutsch 2007). Nonetheless, people are not entirely free to interact and develop some consensus about gendering independent of larger social patterns. Both the confidence to speak up in the meeting and challenge a pattern that is perceived as unfair as well as the authority to impose a new system for task assignments are more likely among relatively powerful people.

The previous hypothetical example showed a mixed-sex group sharing its area of residence. In contrast to this mix, friendship and sociability groups are overwhelmingly composed of people who are similar to one another, as are informal groups in work settings (McPherson, Smith-Lovin, and Cook 2001; McGuire 2002). This pattern of **homophily**, or preference for likes ("birds of a feather"), leads individuals to see and hear their own expectations and beliefs about the world echoed by those with whom they choose to interact. Children's informal social groups starting from a very early age are generally same-sex (while this is interpreted by some as proving claims of essential preferences, it can instead be interpreted as children's quick understanding that sex identity is a ubiquitous dimension of difference that matters to their significant others).

Nonetheless, sex-integrated interactions are far more common than interactions with mixed groups along social class or racial-ethnic lines. We might predict, then, that individuals have many opportunities to have their own ideas about gender and the "opposite sex" challenged, if not changed. But sex-mixed interactions are often with people who have different amounts of power. In a group of friends, in which all are believed to have more-or-less equal standing, people are free to disagree. In contrast, when some in a group have power over others, the subordinates disagree at some risk. When a professor tells a student that she has performed very well "for a woman" or a principal tells a teacher he works very well with small children "for a man," the subordinates will probably not comment on the speaker's prejudices (Ridgeway and Smith-Lovin 1999).

In such groupings, as decades of social psychological study have shown, the less powerful members often do not correct what they see as errors in the views of the more powerful. Meanwhile, the powerful have beliefs that are reconfirmed by the way their subordinates behave *in their presence*. An office assistant may be quiet and agreeable with the office manager and talkative and critical behind his back. He will not see this side of her, and his belief in her unsuitability for promotion may be based on his perception that she is too quiet to be a good leader. The same executive is unlikely to see the parallel to his own behavior changes in the presence of his own superior. In contrast, subordinates in interactions are likely to be more attentive and precise in the study of their superiors because of the power they wield.

The chances of being the subordinate or the superior in an interaction are not, of course, sex-blind. Despite some changes in the society in the last few decades, usually the person with more authority in a sex-mixed workplace interaction is male, and the subordinate is female. So there is a patterned difference in the kinds of information we get from and about one another.

In particular, the existence of very different interpretations of the same behaviors may not be communicated when people do not have equal standing in the setting. For example, men typically take "girl watching" as performing normal masculinity (Quinn 2002). Women who are the objects of this activity or who witness it may perceive it as a form of sexual harassment, making them feel like a "piece of meat" rather than a coworker. Even in groups with members of equal status, reporting such feelings may feel shameful. If raised casually, these feelings may become the subject of jokes; if raised seriously, they endanger an apparently comfortable working relationship.

As long as relatively powerful positions are held by men, women may feel they must conform to unfair arrangements in their work groups. As Martin and Collinson (1999) pointed out, members of organizations actively construct and reconstruct gender in their organizations. When women are relatively powerless in those organizations, they are less able to affect the organization's formal and informal definitions of gender. Even in an "alternative" organization (that is, one with a self-definition as critical of mainstream social arrangements or goals), members reproduced traditionally gendered patterns of unequal respect and resources (Cohn and Enloe 2003; Kleinman 1996).

People who in some way do not conform to hegemonic definitions of gender have diverse experiences of negotiating acceptance. For example, when men enter offices as temporary clerical workers, they adopt strategies to establish that they are masculine despite the gender typing of the work; simultaneously, they do not challenge the general female-identification of the workplace (Henson and Rogers 2001). Openly gay athletes encounter cold reception from other athletes, but have some success at gaining acceptance with a combination of athletic performance and performing hegemonic masculinity in all spheres other than sexuality itself (Anderson 2002).

Finally, different patterns exist among similar organizations (Ridgeway 2009). Fraternities vary in their treatment of women; the military academies have different records of sexual harassment and sex crimes during the decades since they became coeducational. Different employers in the same industry are viewed as more or less hospitable to women. This organizational variability, on the middle level of social life, can reinforce or interfere with small-group, or micro-level, arrangements. With cooperation among individuals and small groups who want to change the organizations, the middle level may change. Otherwise, there will be relatively little influence from the micro level to the middle level. The impact of the macro level (such as society) is often mediated by the middle level of social structures in its influence on our daily lives. It is often the middle level that has the critical impact on small groups' ability to work out and live with arrangements that are gender neutral (see Risman 1998).

In one coed softball league studied for several months, teams varied in the gendered construction of players (Wachs 2003). Several strategies were used regularly to limit women's participation, although some players (both women and men) developed patterned forms of resistance to those strategies. Women were limited formally or informally in the positions they were assigned to play and by being switched out of a position temporarily when the qualities of an opposing team or player made her position more important. Sometimes a male teammate extended his position, usurping plays that were clearly the woman's responsibility, and thus eliminating her chance to show her full potential. Women were socialized, and continually reminded, to opt for a walk to first base; in other words, not to swing at a pitch that might fall outside the strike zone. In contrast, competitive players are usually expected to swing at a pitch that might produce a base hit. In other words, women were expected to behave meekly while at bat. These strategies to limit women's full participation in the sport were not always successful, as some players protested verbally or simply did not comply with expectations of lesser participation. Men on the team, however, may be complicitous in women's refusal or may have to go along with the *fait accompli*. Either way, the gendered performances of men as well as women have changed, illustrating that gender is always relational. League sports are a useful setting for observing the ongoing negotiation of gender, as each game presents the occasion for one's own gendered system to engage with that of another opponent.

## GENDER AND THE BODY

In recent years, sociologists of gender and women's studies scholars, more generally, have turned increasing attention to the body, as a site for making claims of identity, for negotiating one's social position, and for embracing, enforcing, or resisting the gender system.

Much of the attention has focused on the individual struggle for control over one's own body, especially as contested by both governmental agencies and the medical profession. The body itself may be regulated regarding hair styles, the treatment of facial hair, the use of tattooing, and piercing. The gender-appropriate use of clothing and accessories, such as head coverings, cosmetics, and jewelry, are also closely monitored and may be regulated for students and public and private employees. The body and its presentation are central to the sense of self, as organizations such as the military and prisons acknowledge by starting the processing of new members with the stripping away of individual variations (Goffman 1962).

In addition, attention to the ways in which people arrange and display aspects of their bodies helps us understand the continued importance of appearance and attractiveness as a source of social power. Women's appearance is widely recognized as crucial to success; a trip to a cosmetics counter, to a hair stylist, or through a fashion magazine will reveal familiar expressions about the critical role of appearance. These sentiments, aimed at sales of goods and services, are persuasive because they reflect dominant views. Simultaneously, they shape such views. There are regularly published research studies on the connection between appearance and success, with greater height, less weight, and youth associated with greater success. Generally the findings report that these factors are more significant for women's achievement than for men's.

Current beliefs about attractive and healthy body weight and musculature are products of contemporary culture rather than reflections of some neutral and universal truth (Gremillion 2001). People are bombarded with images, songs, stories, and products that tell what it means to be attractive. These cultural messages, often tied to profit making through sales of goods and services, are not received passively by their audiences. Some may be persuaded; for example, the recent return of very pointy shoes to women's fashions has led some women to elect harmful surgery to remove those parts of toes that interfere with fashion (Harris 2003). Others may conform to fashion while asserting that they do so ironically, seeing fashion as an enjoyable vehicle for individual re-creation even though it is obviously commercially driven.

Profit-oriented organizations sometimes recognize population segments that constitute market "niches," with alternative tastes, needs, and values. Products and services are then developed for those groups. The recognition of the profitability of a niche may lag far behind the market's existence. For example, fashion manufacturers only recently realized that teenage and adult women who are larger than fashionable may still seek fashionably designed clothing (Haskell 2002). Similarly, manufacturers of bras are slowly responding to the women who reject the discomfort of wiring, regardless of its promise of providing a youthfully uplifted bust (Seigel 2004).

Once adulthood is reached, expected changes in the body move the person farther from cultural ideals of attractiveness. Sagging, wrinkling, thickening, graying, and hair loss are all viewed negatively. Though they are more fateful for women, such body changes are also significant for men. A growing industry aimed at profiting from men's concerns with signs of aging includes hair coloring, hair replacement (through transplants or hairpieces), and plastic surgery. The uses of both cosmetic surgery and chemical processes have skyrocketed in recent decades, with ever-younger women and rapidly growing numbers of men choosing to change the shape of their bodies or their faces. The strong devaluation of age, extending downward to the overt cultural preference for barely pubescent girls, has

Although Betty Boop has been a recognizable character in the U.S. for more than seventy five years, the shape of her body has changed to reflect the changing definitions of attractiveness. This small statue has the classically shaped head and face, but a thinner body than the original, curvier character.
Photograph taken by the author.

meant that women choose surgery not only to remove classical signs of aging, such as wrinkles and sags, but also to eliminate all signs of maturity beyond adolescence.

Cultural ideals of men's and women's physiques have changed in ways that value an increasingly exaggerated athletic appearance (Pope et al. 1999). Although participation in athletics can be a positive experience for females and males, the struggle to create and maintain a body meeting contemporary standards of the star athlete may actually undermine a person's health. Rather than being empowered by athleticism, current fashions may involve dietary, exercise, and even pharmaceutical regimens that undermine the person's well-being (Dworkin and Messner 1999). An analysis of the changing proportions of action figures found that if a human man were 6 feet tall and had the proportions of the 1964 G.I. Joe, the man's biceps would be 12.2 inches in circumference. By 1998, the biceps of the G.I. Joe Extreme toy had become grossly enlarged. A 6-foot-tall man with G. I. Joe Extreme's proportions would have biceps 26.8 inches in circumference! In contrast, even home-run king Mark McGwire (6′5″ tall) actually had biceps of only 20.0 inches in circumference (*New York Times* May 30, 1999). As we noted in Chapter Two, athletic performance is not the only reason that males use steroids. In growing numbers, boys are using steroids to achieve the hegemonically defined version of male attractiveness.

Illness may effect changes in the body that threaten one's gender identity. For example, young men who had testicular cancer needed to rethink what they had taken for granted about their masculinity, and particularly about their sexuality (Gurevich et al. 2004). Women who had hysterectomies revealed a view of femininity in which the loss of one's ovaries was more undermining of femininity than removal of the uterus alone, even though the ovaries may have ceased all hormonal production (Elson 2003).

Ideas about appearance vary somewhat among racial-ethnic and social class groups (Lovejoy 2001). Latinas who are not very thin are often defined as feminine, but white women of the same shape tend to be defined as fat (Haubegger 1994). In the late nineteenth century thinness first became a component of beauty among middle-class women, particularly white women (Hesse-Biber 2007). As we saw in Chapter One, overeating may be a rational choice, rather than a compulsion (Thompson 1992).

The cultural construction of large size as a symbol of strength may encourage overeating among African American women. Obesity is then a positive aspect of the self, rather than questioned for the harm it may be doing and the societally caused emotional pain to which it may be a response (Beauboeuf-Lafontant 2003). The assumption that an overweight black woman has embraced her size as part of her strength functions as a stereotype, marginalizing black women in the literature on body image.

Alternatively, a radical feminist approach focuses on women's socialization to explain their failures as personal inadequacies, rather than due to discriminatory practices in everyday life. Women must spend more time, energy, and money to meet the standards of appearance for occupational or social success. A trial lawyer with a court date may use time to prepare the case (sleeping enough to function well) and preparing his or her personal appearance. To meet the last requirement women must spend far more time than men to meet the minimum gendered expectations for professional dress and grooming. Although a multiracial feminist might argue that there are important differences among women in the appearance expectations related to jobs, any explanation of body problems in the United States will be more robust if it recognizes the relatively greater emphasis on women's appearance compared with men's.

People can resist the pressures of the larger culture, but they may find their resistance itself becomes co-opted. For example, the hair style that was adopted by a woman as an antifashion statement itself becomes fashionable. Even though the formerly unfashionable woman now appears to be conformist, she is able to spend less time and energy on appearance nonetheless (Weitz 2001). The ripped jeans that initially indicated the wearer did not care about material fashion became, themselves, fashion; denim is industrially processed so it can be sold as looking worn out. Although some people spend money to look fashionably clothed, others can get more wear out of their old clothes; again, though resistance to fashion is co-opted, it still saves personal resources.

Cultural constructions of beauty are highly racialized (Rockquemore 2002). The preference for blue eyes was central to commercials for tinted contact lenses ("Are your eyes brown like bark?"). When cosmetic surgery is used to change one's appearance, to make one better looking, the desirable shapes and sizes are those associated with Northern and Western Europeans. Noses, chins, lips, cheeks, and the skin folds around the eyes are obvious sites for change. When Barbra Streisand became an entertainment star in the early 1960s, however, journalists wrote about her nonconformity—she did not have surgery to make her nose smaller, straighter, less Semitic, and more beautiful. African Americans were long judged to be more attractive if their skin was relatively light in color, and "good hair" referred to relatively straight hair. The Black Pride movement toward the end of the civil rights movement tackled this construction, and many people who had chemically treated their hair to straighten it stopped doing so. Among some African Americans, lighter skin color is still viewed as an element of attractiveness; however, it is unrelated to self-esteem among economically successful women and women whose other characteristics are considered attractive (Thompson and Keith 2001). How much this standard continues to be used by white Americans is not clear, but black women in movies and on television screens tend to be lighter toned than men characters and the black population as a whole. There is a growing international use of skin-lightening products, although the ways in which lightening is marketed and interpreted vary (Glenn 2008).

People may choose to ignore or resist norms of physical appearance. For example, women may choose not to treat gray hair with dye. They may choose to accept the ways that their face and body do not conform to expectations. But they will have to deal with the social reaction to their decisions. Women who do not hide their aging by coloring their hair will have to deal with the age discrimination that exists throughout society. Women with very small breasts who do not choose to augment them surgically or with padded underwear are less likely to have an active social life. Men who go bald and do not opt for implants, toupees, or shaved heads will find age discrimination, although it tends to be less fateful for men than for women. The decision to undergo cosmetic surgery or other intrusive processes to conform to cultural constructs of attractiveness may be seen as an exercise of an individual's agency, as she (or he) decides to actively improve the quality of everyday life (Gagne and McGaughey 2002). At the same time, this conformity reproduces hegemonic standards, carries some physical risks, and requires time and money that might be unavailable or more productively otherwise used. The ideological dominance of the use of surgery to change appearance is epitomized by the federally approved reintroduction of silicone breast implants, despite mixed findings of research on their potentially harmful effects (Kolata 2003).

In addition to the symbolic importance of the body as it is clothed, decorated, or shaped, informal social rules constrain how the individual may use or experience the body, often with gendered dimensions. People who do not conform must face reactions from others, often others with authority or power over them. People who do not conform also may be unhappy with themselves. For example, in an interview study of white, middle-class women about the experience of childbirth, some women were concerned that their pain might have led to misbehavior, such as shouting (disturbing strangers) or failing to fulfill the conversational expectations that they had for themselves (Martin 2003).

Formal rules also affect the body; involuntary sterilization was common for decades, particularly for very poor women, women of color, and women with disabilities. Decisions and developments, made one step at a time and often without public policy discussions, have led to the ever-earlier possibility of a fetus surviving outside its mother, and thus to a steady undermining of women's rights over their own bodies by assertions of fetal rights. By 2004, the dominance of fetal rights had led to the charge of homicide against a woman whose refusal to undergo Caesarian section was blamed for the stillbirth of one of her twins.

Many states require that notices be posted in establishments that serve alcohol, warning that pregnant women may be endangering their fetuses by consuming alcohol. Such notices treat heavy drinking and an occasional glass of wine as equivalent, and they informally encourage members of the public to act as enforcers of this regulation of women's behavior. But no establishments post notices about the impact of alcohol consumption on family violence, despite the large body of evidence establishing the role of alcohol abuse in that social problem. Furthermore, wife beating is especially likely to start when the wife is pregnant, thus endangering the fetus. It is the pregnant woman whose physical behaviors are being cautioned or monitored by the state, not the man who may be returning home in a dangerous condition.

Similarly, as we shall see in Chapter Six, women's present or future childbearing has more often led to restricting women's participation in hazardous workplaces than to reducing or eliminating the hazards. Men are subjected to the hazards, even though their future reproductive capacity may be endangered. These rules are based on mothering's hegemonic importance to femininity and wage earning's for masculinity.

## SUMMARY

Socialization is the process by which the content of culture is taken into the individual. Rules are learned and internalized pertaining to particular statuses that the person occupies and to people with whom the person interacts in particular contexts. More generally applicable rules of behavior are also learned—individuals learn to "do gender" or to present themselves to all and sundry as real men or women. Socialization is a very efficient form of social control, because rather than being externally monitored, each person is self-policing. We continually encounter assumptions about differences between the sexes in personality characteristics, intellectual abilities, and behavior patterns. The extent of these differences is increasingly called into question by careful research; simultaneously, the differences that are discovered are increasingly viewed as products of social treatment, rather than innate characteristics (Brody 1999).

People learn how to act "appropriately," but they usually learn a range of acceptable behaviors from which they actively choose: They learn what is appropriate, but also often realize that they are unable to conform because of other aspects of their lives. For example, men learn that masculinity includes economic self-sufficiency; however, if jobs pay too little to support a family, men look for other ways to be masculine. The concept of socialization is an important component for understanding what people do, but it cannot be used as the ultimate explanation for what people do or do not do. Social structure, to which we turn in the following chapters, combines with socialization to explain more about the gendering of people's lives.

People are constantly adapting to, if not initiating, changes in their own roles and those of others with whom they interact. When adaptation goes smoothly, the ability to change goes unnoticed. Indeed, the ideology of U.S. culture, with its emphasis on economic mobility, assumes that individuals can adjust to new social rules as they move in the social structure. As the following chapters describe, the gender system in the United States has changed in many ways in the last forty years. The ability to relearn gender, to do gender differently, or even to behave in ways that indicate one's sense of areas in which gender is irrelevant have been essential for these changes.

### DISCUSSION QUESTIONS

1. Imagine you are visiting some cousins who say they are raising their child without any limits related to norms about doing gender. Develop a checklist to use at their home, which would capture the extent to which they consistently follow their philosophy. Explain how each of these items is related to children's learning gender.

2. Also develop a checklist to use when observing the child's behavior (including speech). In other words, think about the dimensions you might observe to see if the child is doing gender. Your lists should be usable with a child (and parents) of either sex.

3. Think about one person over 40 whom you know well. What changes has this person experienced that would require learning new norms or new ways of doing gender? In what ways do you think this person does gender in a way that a younger person would not? In what ways does this person do gender in a way that would not have been expected in his or her childhood? What influences have led to these changes? Create a plan for gathering the information, or evidence, you would need to arrive at answers that reflect the complexity of this person's life and experiences. ◆

# CHAPTER 4

# The Family and Intimate Relationships

A family is a group whose members are linked by ties of blood, marriage, or adoption. Although extended family ties have important influences on individuals' lives, the greatest significance of the institution for the gendering of social life is in the household unit based on kinship. Kinship need not be legally based: People are considered socially married if they are in a cohabiting, economically interdependent, sexual relationship with the expectation of permanence. This broader meaning is becoming more widely accepted. For example, cohabiting couples, heterosexual and homosexual, are increasingly accorded some of the legal rights and responsibilities of marriage.

Despite the diversity of lifestyles and of ethnic, racial, and social class backgrounds that characterize U.S. society today, one experience that remains common to almost all people is that of growing up in a family-based household. The large majority goes on to spend significant portions of adulthood in family-based households, although an increasing proportion of the population lives alone or with "roommates" (people who share housing costs, but are not otherwise economically interdependent) for sizable periods of their lives. Throughout the chapter we will note alternative arrangements that have become more visible in recent years. Although many people are accepting of a wide range of individual lifestyles (such as premarital sex, divorce, and childlessness), marriage and childrearing remain important goals (Thornton and Young-DeMarco 2001).

After a discussion of the family *as a social institution*, we will review the changing patterns of family structure in the contemporary United States. Despite these changes and its numerous forms, the family remains central to social life in general and the gender system in particular. Its durability stems in part from the functions that it serves. Our survey of these functions includes emotional and sexual intimacy, economic provision for members of the family-based household, housework, reproduction, and child rearing. Finally, we turn to problems of violence against children, partners, and the elderly.

### A SOCIAL GROUP AND A SOCIAL INSTITUTION

Popular thought on the family tends to focus on its character as a small group and on the family-household as the arena for the interactions of diverse personalities. From this viewpoint, people explain each family's arrangements (such as the initial choice of partners and the development of household routines) by the individual personalities of the particular members and the idiosyncratic ways in which their patterns evolve or are negotiated over time. Gender has been often only implicit in this way of looking at families through taken-for-granted notions of how biology and socialization influence personality development and personal preferences. Increasingly, the approach to the family does acknowledge the importance of gender in the social construction of the small group.

Although sociologists don't reject this perspective, they emphasize that the family is also a social institution, sharing many common patterns of structure and process, regardless of the particular composition of each small group. As unique as the personalities of individual family members may be, their family arrangements are rarely unique because of the influences of various socially learned expectations, attitudes, and behaviors. As patterns of the institution have become increasingly dynamic (for example, with wives earning more than husbands in a sizeable minority of married couples), the small group perspective takes on new sociological importance. Individuals work together on the project of constructing households as social units in a society in which the recently taken for granted is no longer at all obvious. Strategies for these recreations of family roles are themselves socially influenced.

Circumstances outside individual families are less visible, but very powerful in shaping family life generally and gender relations in particular. For example, the economic resources people bring to the family will limit the household arrangements they can choose. Battered women often stay with their husbands because they have neither the money nor the credit record to establish another household for themselves and their dependent children. What seem to be simply personal choices are not merely coincidentally similar among large numbers of women, but reflect their common economic vulnerability. Nor is that common economic vulnerability a coincidence, but results from *macro-social* patterns of occupational segregation and the lower average pay that women receive compared with men. The legal institution (including family courts and police departments) also influences the choices battered women make. On the *middle level*, in most jurisdictions law enforcement agencies provide inadequate protections for battered women who try to flee abusive partners. When a battered women stays with her batterer, outsiders may interpret her inaction as a product of her psychology. However, although the economic factors and the shortcomings of the criminal justice system may be unknown to outsiders, they are significant in their impact.

The inflationary spiral that began in 1967 provides another illustration of how macro-social circumstances affect arrangements within the home (Edwards 2001). At that time, white, U.S.-born couples expected that mothers of young children would stay out of the labor force. Instead, the rapidly growing cost of living led wives to return to the workforce sooner after the birth of children than they had anticipated. Larger proportions of child-less wives continued working. Husbands and wives might have agreed that this was an unfortunate decision, but they could not insulate themselves from the economic trends in society. They had to choose between common cultural values: the nonemployed mother or wife, or a materially secure (or even acquisitive) style of life. Although individual couples experienced the wife's employment as a personal issue, there were many cultural, social, and economic similarities among couples' lives. Seeing the common elements in these situations helps us understand the social patterns that have implications for the changing character of gender in family life.

Some large-scale social changes are obvious in their influence on people's home lives. The social movement aiming to extend to gay and lesbian people the rights enjoyed by heterosexuals in the United States began more than forty years ago. It has led to the formation of more households of committed same-sex parterns. As the visibility of lesbians and gays grew, so too did the ways in which they are denied equal rights, such as the right to adopt a child and the right to make medical decisions for an incapacitated partner. Not all same-sex partnerships are openly sexual, instead presenting a roommate rather than a partner relationship to the outside world. For the first time, the 2000 U.S. Census provided each household with the opportunity to indicate that people in it live together as unmarried partners. The results certainly understate the prevalence of same-sex partnerships because concerns persist of serious homophobic reactions of employers, neighbors, and extended family members. It is important to realize that views of homosexuality differ across our society. For example, norms about homosexuality vary widely among regions and religions, and for different occupations. Though remaining "closeted" seems very old-fashioned in some social contexts, in others it may be a realistic choice to safeguard oneself and one's job. Nevertheless, people in almost 600,000 households identified themselves as living in a same-sex partnership (U.S. Department of Commerce 2003).

Another large-scale area of social change affecting the family is the increasing life span of people in the United States. The family is also the first source of support for extended kin who need help. The ability to help one another varies, and geographic distances from kin undermine some kinds of help, but caring for elders is still a family responsibility (Hatchett and Jackson 1999). Although men often participate in elder care, the main burden lies on the shoulders of women family members (Hooyman and Gonyea 1997).

A careful examination of the family is essential to understanding the ways in which life experiences are tied to one's gender. Family household tasks (most crucially including tasks related to economic subsistence, child rearing, caring for elderly family members, and household maintenance) are at the core of the gendering of roles both within and outside the home. They are central to ways in which people, regardless of their sexuality, work out a sense of themselves as feminine or masculine (Connell 1995).

Finally, the home is the site of several significant social problems tied to gender. One set of issues is related to sex differences in longevity. Men of all racial-ethnic categories have the unhappy likelihood of shorter life spans than their female age-mates. The average life expectancy in 2005 was 75.2 years for men, and 80.4 years for women. Racial inequality is manifested in the lower life expectancies for African Americans than whites, with similar within-race sex gaps: Among blacks, men have an average life expectancy of 69.5 years compared to women's 76.5 years. Among whites, men's average life expectancy is 75.7 years compared with women's 80.8 years (U.S. Census Bureau 2009). We consider the possible causes of these significant racial and sex differences in Chapter Six. But the effects of these differences are pertinent in discussion of family-related social problems: The isolation and economic marginality of single elderly women are more extreme because of the cultural norms of households based on nuclear family rather than extended family or nonfamilial relationships.

More than half of elderly women (75 years old or older) were widows in 2007. In contrast, almost three quarters of men in that age group lived with their wives. Among elderly women, 29 percent lived alone, compared with 11 percent of elderly men (U.S. Department of Commerce 2009). Even though some elderly women prefer to live alone, others do not do so by choice. Alternatives to living alone, such as shared housing, have not been considered acceptable by most people in this culture, although there is growing interest in such arrangements among older women (Gross 2004).

Feminist interest in gender stratification on the level of individual experience has been important in directing attention to physical and psychological abuse, a long-standing reality that has only recently been defined as a problem. As we shall see in the chapter on political and legal institutions, gender politics on the macro level have been important in defining family violence as a societal problem and in pursuing justice for victims. Just as stable family arrangements reflect external influences, problems in the home or in dating relationships are more completely understood when placed in a larger context. For example, analyzing violence against women by intimates requires placing it within a broader pattern of violence against women (Feltey 2001). Further, rates of family violence rise in periods of high unemployment, downward mobility, and homelessness—all related to conditions of the economy (Chasin 2004).

In this chapter, we focus on the family as a changing institution in which gender is enacted, taught, and revised. We emphasize the ways in which the culture and the socioeconomic structure of the United States influence family arrangements, and the ways in which families are an active site for redefining masculinity and femininity (Roschelle 1999).

### PATTERNS OF FAMILY STRUCTURE

The experience of growing up in a household based on family ties is nearly universal in this society; however, the particular composition of households and individuals' timing of taking on new family statuses have changed greatly in recent decades. Although family life in the United States is more varied than ever before, it remains highly valued. For example, lesbians and gay men use a wide range of strategies to maintain or create kinship ties when faced with antihomosexual beliefs and assumptions among some relatives (Oswald 2002).

Only a minority of family-based households are currently composed of a married couple and their offspring. Many others are composed of married or unmarried partners, either childless or with grown children. Single-parent families and multigeneration families have become increasingly common and visible. Numerous influences have contributed to these changes, some of which (like the development of the birth-control pill) are explicitly related to gender-oriented social arrangements and ideologies. Other influences on gender arrangements have been the unanticipated consequences of apparently unrelated trends (such as the loss of well-paid "men's" jobs when industrial corporations relocated to other countries).

Most Americans still marry. Of the 105.5 million households enumerated in 2000, 54.5 included married couples (U.S. Department of Commerce 2003). However, the age at which people marry has risen steadily in recent decades. Men and women married, on the average, in their early 20s in 1970. By 2007, women's average age was 26 years and men's, almost 28 (U.S. Department of Commerce 2009). The average age difference between husbands and wives has been quite consistently about two years for many decades (Costello, Miles, and Stone 1998). Increasing proportions of heterosexuals in their late 20s and early 30s have never been married, and population analysts predict that a somewhat larger proportion of Americans will never marry than in earlier generations. Although such predictions are notoriously risky, the act of deferring marriage will result, for some women especially, in the permanently lost opportunity of finding a marriage partner. As long as it is normative for husbands to be older than their wives, the postponement of marriage by a woman increases the pool of women with whom she will be competing if she seeks a husband. However, not all unmarried people have deferred marriage—many have rejected it as a personal goal. Women are now more often able to afford to remain single because of expanded occupational opportunities. Thus, they are able to reject marriage, for reasons such as their educational goals, their perceptions of available mates or their own parents' marriage, or their responsibilities to their kin (Ferguson 2000).

The decisions to marry at all, with whom, and when are all intensely personal. Suggesting that they are influenced by macro-social patterns contradicts our own experiences of thinking about marriages and other intimate relationships. How do we bring together these two realities: the personal nature of decisions and the observable similarities between our own decisions and those of others throughout the society? These are linked by the impact of our perceptions of our choices and our assessments of their desirability. For example, if being sexually active before marriage is considered sinful, or if there is no place to get reliable contraception easily, then sexually mature adults will be motivated to marry earlier than they might otherwise. Cultural and subcultural beliefs, and social structural factors (like access to child care or the availability of contraceptives), all influence people's marriage decisions. Because these circumstances are common, there will be common patterns of personal decision making. Thus, people continue to believe that a married couple should be economically independent. Not surprisingly, people with more positive attitudes towards marriage are more likely to marry than people less positively disposed toward marriage. When individuals with similar attitudes are compared, the more economically secure people are more likely to act on those attitudes (Sassler and Schoen 1999).

In recent decades, homosexual relationships have become increasingly visible and acceptable, with a growing number of households with gay or lesbian couples and, sometimes, their children. Nonetheless, regional and religious variations in dominant views of homosexual behavior and relationships continue. The "Defense of Marriage Act" was signed into U.S. law by President Bill Clinton in 1996, defining marriage as a relationship between one man and one woman, and releasing states from any obligation to respect a marriage contract granted to a same-sex couple in any other state.

Public and private conversations and debates about same-sex marriage gathered momentum in 2003, after the Massachusetts Supreme Court ruled that same-sex couples were legally entitled to marry. Defining what is essential to all marriage is an integral part of these discussions. Ironically, some of those arguing against same-sex marriage are offering definitions that imply heterosexual marriage is not appropriate for many couples. In particular, the argument that marriage is based on the potential for procreation suggests that women who are not able to have children have no reason to legally marry. Similarly, couples who are committed to a relationship without child bearing have no reason to legally marry. Regardless of the outcome on the legal rights of same-sex couples, the national conversation will lead some heterosexuals to think more about choices they may have previously taken for granted.

A growing number of states offer some form of legally recognized "domestic partnership" for same-sex couples. These do not offer identical legal status as marriage, and some people argue that simply denying the label "marriage" would make such unions less than equal. In the last few years, several states have legalized same-sex marriage, through state court decisions based on antidiscrimination interpretations or on legislative initiatives. Without federal-level recognition, however, partners who are married in those states do not have the rights of married couples in other states, nor are they eligible for treatment as married couples for federal purposes (e.g., the Social Security and income tax systems).

Both men and women aspire to stable long-term relationships. Among heterosexuals, the decision to marry (and its timing) differs for women and men. Many women perceive that career advancement is slowed by marriage and that the chances of one's future occupational success are improved by postponing marriage. Younger women have grown up in a society with high rates of household dissolution and view their financial self-sufficiency as essential to their ability to achieve autonomy as adults. Although they hope to marry someone who shares their commitment to an equitable division of household labor, they perceive the need to establish their economic autonomy beforehand (Gerson 2002).

Deferring marriage is not, in contrast, useful for men's career advancement, so men lack that motivation for remaining single. In addition, men do less housework after they enter a marriage than beforehand, but women do more (Gupta 1999). Nonetheless, men are also marrying at older ages. They perceive that husbands continue to make more of an economic commitment to marriage than do wives, but that women have moved away from their traditional commitment to unpaid household responsibilities (Gerson 2002). Coupled with increased concern about the stability of their employment prospects, these perceptions contribute to men's changing age of first marriage.

More than other social relationships, marriage has been informally limited to those sharing important social identities, particularly race, religion, ethnicity, social class, educational attainment, and age. **Homogamy**, or marriage to a similar person, has weakened slightly in recent decades (Amato et al. 2003). First-generation immigrants are most likely to marry people of the same national background, reflecting family

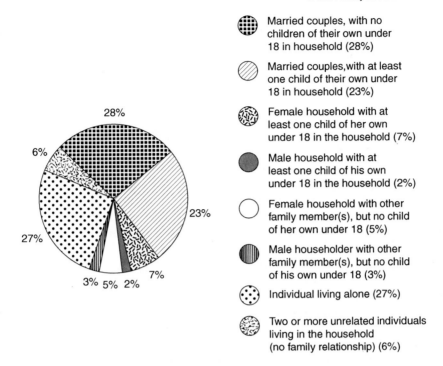

Married couples, with no children of their own under 18 in household (28%)

Married couples, with at least one child of their own under 18 in household (23%)

Female household with at least one child of her own under 18 in the household (7%)

Male household with at least one child of his own under 18 in the household (2%)

Female household with other family member(s), but no child of her own under 18 (5%)

Male householder with other family member(s), but no child of his own under 18 (3%)

Individual living alone (27%)

Two or more unrelated individuals living in the household (no family relationship) (6%)

**Figure 4.1  U.S. Household Composition, 2007**
Source: Statistical Abstract of U.S., 2009. Washington, D.C.: Govt. Printing Office, Table No. 62.

pressure, opportunities to meet, and shared cultural views. The children of immigrants, particularly those with more formal education, often marry outside their ethnic group (see, for example, Kulczycki and Lobo's discussion of Arab American marriage patterns, 2002). Ethnic groups vary in the gendering of intermarriage; for example, Asian American women are more likely than Asian American men to marry non–Asian Americans, but Arab American women are more homogamous than are Arab American men.

Family formation is not limited to those who marry (see Figure 4.1). Family-based households include single parents with their children, households composed of children and their nonparent relatives, and cohabiting couples (with or without children). Although cohabitation was rare in the United States until the late twentieth century, it then increased rapidly. By 1995, about half of all women in their late 30s had cohabited at least once. In 2006, the number of homes with unmarried heterosexual partners had grown to more than 5 million (U.S. Department of Commerce 2009), including childless couples and couples with one or more children of one or both adults. Like marriage partners, those who cohabit tend to share social background characteristics.

Until recently, cohabitation was socially constructed as a step before marriage. Now a large minority of cohabiting couples do not expect to marry. In part, this change results from the fading economic prospects of many working- and middle-class white men. The centrality of a husband's wage-earning role discourages marriage among U.S. women whose partners' future employment appears bleak (Manning and Smock 2002). Similarly, during the Great Depression of the 1930s, many couples did not marry. In addition to the costs of setting up a new household, very different norms about nonmarital sex precluded cohabitation for most.

Although teenage motherhood is still defined as a problem (i.e., "children having children"), the social stigma of illegitimacy has weakened in the dominant culture. Nonetheless, by 2002 the rate of teenage motherhood had reached a historic low (Martin et al. 2003). Having a realistic and attractive alternative to motherhood (educational or employment) is an important social structural factor that contributed to this decline. The rate began to increase, however, and in 2007 the birth rate among unmarried women reached an all-time high (Eckholm 2009).

A slight decline in divorce has occurred since 1980, when the steep rise throughout the 1970s reached its peak. Although most divorced people do remarry, remarriage after divorce has become less common, especially among women. In addition, remarriage does not occur as soon after the dissolution of the marriage as it did in the past, again particularly for women. Some of this drop in remarriage rates may be voluntary, as some women's occupations provide the economic security to live independently.

Despite the popularity of media portrayals of father-headed households, mothers continue to be the large majority of custodial parents after divorce. Because of the continuing earnings gap between the sexes, this factor contributes to a high incidence of poverty among single-parent households. Married couples have taken on parenthood later in their marriages and at a later age. Influenced by the increased years of formal education of both sexes, and the increased career orientation of young women, this shift has implications for family life. The later start of planned parenting decreases the total number of children a woman will bear, and the longer period of marriage before children is related to greater marital stability.

Changes in household composition and in family status through the life course have not been accompanied by equally large changes in the economic opportunities available to women. The much-heralded economic gains of the late 1990s were not widely shared among less educated and less skilled workers. In addition, many people formerly earning a middle-class wage in industries, such as steel and automotive workers, have been hurt by downsizing, the export of jobs, and corporate mergers. The export of jobs held by white-collar workers (such as programmers and customer service representatives) has expanded the downwardly mobile population.

Relatively low wages do not enable single mothers to afford quality child care, which remains scarce in the public sector. The number of mother-headed households living in poverty has risen dramatically. Moreover, the problem of homelessness, which skyrocketed in the 1980s, has had additional growth spurts. It initially disproportionately affected single adults, but has become a major problem for women-headed households in communities with shrinking numbers of affordable housing units.

The frequency of marriage among African Americans was similar to that of whites and Latinos until recent decades, although the marriages of African Americans tended to be more egalitarian in their gendered relations (Perkins 1997). African American women are currently much less likely to be married (U.S. Department of Commerce 2009). This pattern results from several factors. First, compared with white men, there is a greater prevalence of economic insecurity among African American men (Sassler and Schoen 1999). Further, African American men have disproportionately high mortality rates and incarceration rates, contributing to an imbalance between the numbers of marriageable African American males and females. The improved employment rates of the late 1990s and the concurrent decline in criminal convictions (Nasar and Mitchell 1999) were expected to influence this pattern in marriage rates. However, by 2004 the unemployment problem had again become critical (for example, see Scott 2004).

African American women have positively viewed, even if less desirable, alternatives to marriage. A tradition of women's strength and autonomy facilitates women's view of themselves as able to live independently of men and to rear their children successfully (Blum and Deussen 1996). Historically, the children of unmarried African American women have been more likely to have an ongoing connection to their father than have white children of unmarried women. Because of these different traditions and expectations, as well as the greater vulnerability of African American men's employment to economic downturns, African American women may be more cautious about entering marriage than are white women, even during periods of improved economic conditions.

### THE IMPORTANCE OF THE HOUSEHOLD AND FAMILY FOR SOCIETY

The family continues to fulfill essential needs for society, including reproduction, socialization, economic consumption, and care for dependent individuals. Labor power is reproduced by families, in which the physical and emotional needs of workers are most likely to be met. Fulfilling these functions is popularly viewed as a private matter. Instead, performing them can be seen as a form of civil engagement, with kin actively working to prepare, maintain, or return productive workers to their economic positions. When contemporary writers lament the decline in volunteer work and other public participation, they ignore the performance of household responsibilities and extended kin care, which especially when paired with hours devoted to paid employment leave little time for unpaid work outside the home (Herd and Meyer 2002).

Each of these functions is associated with the gendering of family roles. However, since the early 1970s, the assignment of related tasks has become less tightly linked to the sex of the family member. This reflects the influence of the women's movement and the inflationary spiral that diminished the spending power of husbands' earnings. The relative influence of these cultural and structural factors is a matter of disagreement (e.g., Mason, Czajka, and Arber 1976). The *structural approach* emphasizes the increased need for both parents in a two-parent household to earn money (due to factors such as inflation or the lowered earnings of men in traditionally well-paid jobs). The *cultural approach* emphasizes changing attitudes and beliefs about what it means to be a good wife and a good mother, particularly the greater acceptability of employment outside the home. There is no doubt that both culture and social structure influenced the loosening and even revising gendered arrangements within households. In addition, within relationships there may be a growing trend of *undoing* gender. Research indicates a slow but significant movement toward more equitable division of labor and responsibility in many homes (Sullivan 2006; Bianchi, Robinson, and Milkie 2006).

Many of these changes, such as the increased democracy of marital decision making, are associated with greater marital satisfaction among both husbands and wives (Amato et al. 2003; Springer 2007). As members of older generations are replaced with more recently socialized members of society, the traditional attitudes toward family roles are in decline, although they remain stronger among men than among women (Brewster and Padavic 2000).

## EMOTIONAL AND SEXUAL INTIMACY

In contemporary U.S. beliefs, couples are supposed to be emotionally and sexually compatible—indeed, they should not marry if they are not, and divorce is considered acceptable if their emotional relationship erodes. Providing a site for sexual and emotional intimacy serves an important societal function, serving as an emotional "shock absorber" for the difficulties encountered in the economic sphere. Emotional intimacy at home may be more crucial for men, because women have traditionally been more able to rely on friends and other relatives for emotional support (Cancian 1985).

For heterosexual couples, sexual behavior within, before, and outside of marriage—and how it is gendered–has been significantly influenced by changing contraceptive technologies (Goldin and Katz 2000). Since the mid-1960s, the availability of reliable contraception (coupled with at least partial availability of safe and legal abortion since 1973) has largely removed unwanted pregnancy as a deterrent to sexual activity. Furthermore, the availability of reproductive control with effective contraception and legal abortion has increased the ability of sexually active people to plan their futures rationally. Should a family invest savings in a down payment for an apartment that will require two incomes for its maintenance? Should a sexually active family member enroll in a training program that requires several years for completion? Couples can have sexual lives that are less charged by concerns of unwanted pregnancy, and people can make decisions about other aspects of their lives without having to be sexually abstinent. Sex before marriage is now widely accepted, which is one of the reasons that age at marriage is now later for the average U.S. adult.

Teenage sexual activity is somewhat less widespread currently than during recent decades, with a "culture of restraint" increasingly typifying high school student norms (N. Bernstein 2004; Villarosa 2003). Explicit vows of chastity, however, do not seem to have much long-term influence on teenagers' behavior. Though those who take them are somewhat older when they become sexually active, on the average, they often are then more active than their peers who never took them (Altman 2004b).

Over the last several decades, the link between sexual and emotional intimacies has become weaker among unmarried adolescents and young adults. Many do not date, instead participating socially in groups of peers. A sexual "hook up" (which involves varying degrees of sexual intimacy) has become a a common practice (Blow 2008).

In gay and lesbian relationships, unwanted pregnancy is obviously not an issue, but the AIDS epidemic and other sexually transmitted diseases introduce a dimension requiring negotiation between lovers. Questions of fidelity and trust for both heterosexual and homosexual partners become central when decisions about safe sex practices are made.

In addition, medical care for lesbians and gay men sometimes reflects societal prejudices and caricatures (Stevens 1996). For example, stereotypes about lesbian sexuality have led some practitioners to assume that AIDS is irrelevant to women in same-sex relationships. Thus, homophobia can interfere with receiving high-quality gynecological care for women who are open about their lesbian identities. In 1999, the American Civil Liberties Union sued a gynecologist and the health maintenance organization (HMO) to which he belonged for his treatment of a patient. When the patient explained that she didn't need a contraceptive strategy because she was a lesbian, the physician asked her to use another physician for her future health care needs. As a result of the settlement, the HMO agreed to have an educational program for its health care practitioners (American Civil Liberties Union 1999).

In the absence of normatively acceptable and technically effective reproductive control, economic circumstances often required the postponement of marriage. During the Depression of the 1930s, for example, the need to avoid pregnancy for economic reasons was widespread. When effective technologies are lacking and out-of-wedlock childbirth is considered deviant, premarital pregnancies press couples into early marriage, affecting both parents. In addition, although many unplanned pregnancies (within or outside marriage) result in loved children, some result in the birth of infants who are sooner or later abandoned or badly neglected.

The social construction of masculinity in the United States puts the highest priority on sexual potency. Further, male sexuality has traditionally, in this culture, been evaluated by the size of the penis, its ability to penetrate, and the capacity for frequent intercourse with climax. In other cultures, however, other aspects of male sexuality are not so overshadowed by penile function. The old expression "Slam, Bam, Thank You, Ma'am" refers to a particular male style of sexual behavior in which the man moves quickly to penetration and climax and takes the woman's involvement for granted. This style allows a man to prove how virile he is, because he is able to reach orgasm quickly. The woman is servicing the man in such an episode. During the 1960s and 1970s, sexual counselors and women activists paid increasing attention to changing popular ideas about male sexual performance, emphasizing foreplay and attention to ways of enhancing a partner's sexual pleasure. "Mutuality," or focusing on the sharing of pleasure with each other, became the catchword for such advisers.

Even though men of all ages occasionally experience impotence (or penile erectile dysfunction), it becomes more common in older men. Pharmaceutical companies have developed drugs, such as Viagra, to treat impotence. Public discussions about Viagra and about marital sexuality more broadly illustrate revolutionary attitude changes in just a few decades. For example, former senator and 1996 Republican presidential candidate Bob Dole appeared in testimonial commercials for Viagra, speaking in general terms about its benefits to his own marriage.

From the first, with criticisms of its high price, Viagra has been the focus of serious and comic attention. In 2004, a single dose cost $13.50, if purchased in a ten-pack size (falling below $10 only if purchased in large amounts, requiring a large expenditure); the generic competitor cost about a third as much, but the most reasonable cost also required purchasing a very large (and therefore an expensive) number of doses at once. This aid to sexual pleasure contradicts the old-fashioned view that "the best things in life are free." Other concerns about the impact of the drug on sexual intimacy were widely expressed after its release to the market. Behaviorally, there is the concern that the drug may act to undermine a slow, mutually pleasurable period of foreplay. On the level of social attitudes, it reinforces traditional beliefs in penetration, hardness, and orgasm as the lynchpins of masculinity. However, the drug has had a more complicated impact. Although it was designed for male use, its manufacturer did invest in experiments with women users. In 2004 the experimental program was ended, based on the finding that women and men tend to interpret symptoms of physiological arousal very differently, with desire in women usually depending on emotional as well as physiological conditions (Harris 2004).

### PROVIDING FOR THE HOUSEHOLD

Earning the money for consumption and reproduction of labor power has been primarily and centrally the man's responsibility since industrialization. Higher pay for men than for women has been traditionally justified by the belief that a man supports a family, but that a working woman does not have dependents. This "family wage" justification was widely accepted until the 1960s (Mason et al. 1976). Even among racial-ethnic and immigrant groups in which wives' wage earning has been essential, husbands' responsibility has been seen as permanent–even if times got better, husbands should earn, but wives need not. Indeed, until the passage of the Equal Credit Opportunity Act in 1974, wives' earnings could be ignored by banks and other potential lenders when judging a couple's ability to carry a mortgage or other loan. Single women's earnings could likewise be ignored by lenders who made the hegemonic assumption that at any time they might marry and leave the labor force.

With changing attitudes toward women's roles, and the growth of occupations employers saw as "women's jobs," U.S.-born white women's employment outside the home has increased dramatically across all age groups and family statuses. For example, mothers of young children have had an enormous increase in labor force participation since the early 1970s as Figure 4.2 illustrates. Increasingly, when both partners in a relationship work outside the home, they are both recognized as providing for the family. In a longer historical perspective, the period in which there was one provider (male) was quite short. That is, women and men were co-providers before industrialization and the application of the "separate spheres doctrine" to daily life. As noted in Chapter Two, the

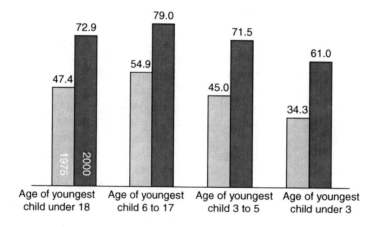

**Figure 4.2 Percentage of Mothers in the Labor Force 1975 and 2000**
Source: U.S. Department of Labor, Bureau of Labor Statistics 2001. Accessed June 8, 2009, at http://www.bls.gov/opub/working/chart16.pdf.

luxury of the wife staying out of the labor force was not universally shared, even during the height of the "separate spheres" belief. Then, as now, women of color were often co-providers for their families (Sudarkasa 1999), and rural women did farm work, even if unwaged (Rushing 2003).

Nonetheless, there are varied attitudes toward married women's employment. Some custody rulings reflect judges' continuing belief that a mother who hires a child care worker is a less adequate parent than is a father who relies on a child care substitute while he is at work. Ratcliff and Bogdan (1988) found that a majority of the unemployed women in their study encountered a lack of social support for their own interest in finding new employment. At the same time, they did encounter some support from members of their social networks for reemployment as a valued and legitimate goal.

For African American and immigrant wives and mothers, employment has traditionally been necessary and socially accepted as an important contribution, rather than for the "pin money" that white, U.S.-born couples might label women's earnings. Immigrant employment in settings dominated by immigrant group members, such as family-owned businesses, was unlikely to provide women with the increased standing at home that middle-class women associate with paid employment. A study of Korean immigrant women found that husbands helped out more with household tasks because of their wives' report of exhaustion, rather than because of notions of equality based on the wives' economic contributions (Lim 1997). However, wives may have felt that their complaints of exhaustion were more legitimate to express because of their economic contribution to the family.

When wives enter the labor force, or when working women marry, they face the challenge of managing employment (and related time demands, such as commuting), housework, and family care. In many households, this challenge is met through some combination of increased husbands' performance of household tasks and care giving, changed norms for the frequency or ways in which tasks were performed by women, and the loss of women's formerly discretionary time (sleeping or engaging in leisure activities).

Although both wives' actual employment outside the home and its acceptability have increased dramatically, pressures for husbands' employment have not declined. Unemployment of husbands is followed by their worsening health, suggesting that the failure to be a provider is a significant stressor (Stolzenberg 2001). Wives, to a lesser degree, also suffer health impacts from their husbands' unemployment. Both these patterns are found regardless of the financial status of the household. When men choose to retire but their wives do not, couples may face unanticipated stresses as their previous household arrangements no longer suit either spouse (Leland 2004).

In some households, the couple hires outsiders to provide labor for some or all of these responsibilities. Many homes, particularly in regions with large immigrant populations, are run to a greater or lesser extent with paid labor. Increased U.S.-born white women's labor force participation has been facilitated by the availability of international migrants. The particular sending countries vary regionally (e.g., Mexican women in California and the Southwest, Irish and Polish women in the Northeast), but the availability of cheap labor has enabled many families to maintain or improve their style of life through wives' employment and the inexpensive replacement of her unpaid household/family services by women who lack the U.S. credentials and networks to move into more desirable jobs.

The expansion of border crossing in the late twentieth century followed closely the growing prevalence of U.S. wives' long-term labor force commitment. Paradoxically, many household workers are not able to bring their own children when they migrate to the United States; their labor supports family maintenance for others, and their wages flow home to support their own families, from whom they remain separated for long periods of time (Salazar Parrenas 2000; Hondagneu-Sotelo 2001).

## HOUSEWORK

The patterns of who does how much of what tasks in the home are extremely varied throughout the U.S. population. Some responsibilities are largely unchanged, whereas some tasks have moved from one partner's responsibility to the other's or to a more gender-neutral status (e.g., men are more likely to wash dishes than their fathers were). Changes have come about quite gradually, and fall short of feminist goals of complete equity. Nonetheless these changes are significant (Sullivan 2006; Bianchi, Robinson, and Milkie 2006).

The notion remains in most couples that tasks have some "obvious" connection to one person or the other—although what those tasks are varies. The view that one partner should help the other out is different from a notion of shared responsibility for getting jobs done. In fact, in one study of young college graduates, researchers found that childless couples did have less traditionally gendered household arrangements. However, the gendered division of labor and responsibility conformed to more traditional patterns among those couples with children (Perkins and DeMies 1996). Cohabiting couples tend to voice more egalitarian ideas about the household division of labor, but behave in ways quite similar to married couples (Smock 2000). Men's gender ideologies are influenced by their economic situation, particularly the character of their economic interdependence with their partner (Cha and Thebaud 2009). Gender ideologies also tend to be more traditional among fathers than nonfathers (Vespa 2009).

As women's *hours* at paid work became closer to men's, the hours women put into housework and child care declined. The average overall decline, found repeatedly in various surveys, represents the combined effect of individual women actually changing their behavior as well as the stable behavior of younger groups of women, socialized since the beginning of the women's movement (Artis and Pavalko 2003). However, except for homes in which the wife works full-time *and* there is an infant, and homes in which the adults work two different shifts, there continues to be very little change in the amount of work done by men. Because women do less, there is a reduced couple total, and men's contribution becomes a larger percentage of the work done.

Men's employment continues to be taken for granted, and men continue to earn more, on the average, than the women with whom they live. One perspective on household dynamics suggests that earnings equity influences other ways in which household roles are gendered: The more that women contribute, relative to men, the more nearly equal the division of unpaid work at home. By 2006, wives' earnings were greater than their husbands' earnings in 26 percent of all dual-earner married-couple homes (U.S. Department of Labor 2009). In all households with a married couple, the wife's income was just over one third of the total family income (a median of 35.6 percent in 2006; U.S. Department of Labor 2008b).

As evidence mounted up that wives' employment itself did not bring an equivalent change in housework, researchers suggested that equity in housework might come if there were a change in the relative earnings contributed by each partner. In fact, couples in which partners earn about the same amount have the most nearly equal participation in household work. However, couples with wives' employment status greater than their husbands actually have more traditionally gendered divisions of household labor. For example, husbands who earned a small proportion of the couples' income were nonetheless described with "provider" language, rather than the "helping out" or "pin money" language that is generally applied to wives who earn such a proportion of a couple's income (Tichenor 1999).

Why isn't a gendered division of labor completely undone when women spend more time "bringing home the bacon," or even when they actually bring home most or all of the bacon? It appears that partners earning comparable amounts and doing comparable housework are not challenged about their femininity and masculinity, nor are they viewed as deviant. In contrast, those couples in which the wife is the primary breadwinner may revert to traditional household labor because they feel a need to assert their gender identity, or to avoid being stigmatized by others for their "role reversal" (Greenstein 2000). A more radical explanation that also merits study is the possibility that husbands pull back from household tasks to assert their dominance over their breadwinning wives.

Finally, although working women with relatively good wages may be in a strong negotiating position in dividing up household tasks, if the marriage were to end, they would probably lose economically. This reality must, for some, influence just how far they reach in attempting to achieve what they consider a fair division of labor in the household. In fact, in a study of dual-earner couples, Allen and Hawkins (1999) found that about 20 percent of mothers actually discouraged a more equitable division of labor with fathers. Like the women who earned more than their husbands, these women may be uncomfortable about the departure from traditional roles that their employment signifies, and choose to hold on to a version of femininity in which the mother is more involved than the father in daily tasks. Nonetheless, the majority of women in the Allen and Hawkins research did report a relatively collaborative household arrangement with their husbands.

There may be other ways, however, in which there is greater parity between the spouses. For example, Winkler (1998) suggested that women earning more than their husbands may have a greater say than other wives do in decisions about how to use household resources (e.g., savings, earnings).

In same-sex couples, the division of labor is more likely to be worked out in new ways, because partners cannot simply depend on a traditional division of labor to get the jobs done. Further, there may be more awareness of issues of justice and equity between the partners (Schwartz and Singer 2001). However, unpaid work in the United States (whether in the household or as volunteer work for community organizations) is ignored or underappreciated. Thus, the "use value" of unpaid housework and child (or other dependent) care is generally overlooked (Benston 1969). There is more widespread belief in equal sharing of tasks in same-sex partnerships (Patterson 2000). Some evidence suggests that the wage earner in a single-income same-sex relationship, like those in mixed-sex couples, takes for granted the house and child care labor of the unemployed partner (Sullivan 1969).

Most studies of household arrangements rely on individuals' self-reports. Research on the accuracy of such reports indicates that reports of one's own work are exaggerated, while assessments of other household members' contributions tend to understate actual work time (Press and Townsley 1998). Despite these methodological flaws, however, the patterned differences in partners' contributions to housework are well established.

Variations in household arrangements are associated with different racial-ethnic groups, but generalizations about these are difficult and can be misleading. First, important social class, regional, and national-origin variations exist within ethnic groups (for example, see Suárez 1999 on Cuban Americans, and Martinez 1999 on Mexican Americans). Further, as the period of time from the year (or generation) of immigration grows, assimilation continuously occurs. Household arrangements become less like those in the sending cultures and more like U.S. patterns. Thus, in Islamic families, younger men and men born in the United States are more likely than their immigrant elders to help out with traditionally female-assigned tasks (Carolan 1999). **Biculturalism**, the flexibility to move between the design for living of one's ethnic group and that of the dominant culture, allows people to choose the household arrangements that suit the requirements of their particular situations. As a result, even people with similar ethnic, class, and other demographic characteristics may lead quite different family lives.

The consequences of differences in performance of housework are varied. Clearly, one who does less housework has more time to use in other ways. But, there is also an impact on attitudes toward the relationship when housework is perceived as inequitably shared. Thus, in a national survey, women who perceived the division of labor in their relationships as unfair were more likely than other women to be depressed (Bird 1999). It was the perceived inequity, rather than the actual number of hours spent doing housework, that was crucial to the individual differences in depression. Dissatisfaction with the division of household labor influences women's decision to divorce (Frisco and Williams 2003).

In contrast, men's performance of housework generally promotes women's satisfaction with the relationship, although wives with traditional gender ideologies are satisfied with less sharing (Stevens, Kiger, and Rile 2001). Research has produced conflicting findings on the impact of greater housework on husbands' satisfaction (see Stevens et al. 2001; Amato et al. 2003). Although doing housework may not in itself be satisfying for men, its effect on wives may be; as several men comment in *Chore Wars* (a 1995 video), cleaning the toilet is useful for putting their partners in the mood for sex!

## REPRODUCTION

Having a child or children continues to be viewed as a central part of adulthood for many. Though most children are born to married couples, an increasing percentage of births occurs to cohabiting couples. Lesbian and gay couples are choosing parenthood in growing numbers, with gay couples and some lesbian couples adopting children from other countries.

As women's opportunities have expanded, attitudes toward becoming a mother have become more complicated. The social construction of femininity has long held that having children is central to being womanly. Essentialists see the choice to become a mother as a biological imperative for all women. But social researchers describe an extremely varied reality, rather than a biological one in which genes, brains, or hormones determine the decision to reproduce and to nurture children. Popular portrayals suggest that women are likely to value either motherhood or work (see, for example, the inaccurate but widespread characterization of professional and business women "opting out" of their careers; Kuperberg and Stone 2008). However, evidence shows that women are not in conflict about these roles; many mothers value both their motherhood and their employment. Among nonmothers, there is more likely to be a focus on the impact of mothering on discretionary and leisure time than on any employment impact (McQuillan et al. 2008).

Postpartum depression is a recognized problem among new mothers. A biological explanation focuses on rapidly changing hormone levels, but there is increasing understanding that the reaction may in part be due to women's mixed feelings about being a mother. The popular cultural beliefs that all women are meant to be mothers and that one immediately loves her newborn infant contribute to the difficulties of women who experience postpartum depression. A self-help movement of such mothers simultaneously asserts women's power to help themselves and accepts that something is wrong with a woman who does not immediately embrace motherhood (Taylor 1996).

## CHILD REARING

In addition to relying on a family group to reproduce new members, society relies on the family to take care of the young until they are able to survive independently. Gendered patterns of parenting are central to the everyday tasks we call "child care" as well as to the more highly regarded, long-term job of guiding the young to be emotionally and physically healthy as well as conforming members of society. The best ways to parent are frequent topics of popular media as well as visits to health care providers, and views about parenting from these "knowledge professionals" and their media popularizers are subject to ideological shaping. For example, the literature on breastfeeding in the last few decades has oversimplified the factors that families may need to consider in choosing their infant feeding practices. Although breastfeeding offers some (often exaggerated or unproven) health benefits, its costs are ignored—such as its effect on mothers' meeting other demands or choosing other activities and on the division of household and child care responsibilities negotiated before the birth (Law 2000).

As we discussed in Chapter Three, socialization into gendered roles (e.g., son, mother) and into gendered aspects of apparently sex-neutral statuses begins within the family-based household. The family is also the primary setting for learning how to "do gender," the gendered aspects of behavior patterns that transcend particular roles. The child learns rules that are not status-specific, but that apply, unless specifically overridden, as one behaves throughout the day or life. The family shares the responsibility for transmitting the culture to the new generation along with other social institutions, such as the church, the school, and the media. Nonetheless, it is still the first teacher of the ideologies justifying patterns of macro-social and micro-social gender stratification.

Researchers studying one-parent families have repeatedly found that children do not need to live with adults of both sexes to learn about the gender system (e.g., Hannerz 1969). Conversely, in two-parent households, children's social development is not harmed by a traditional division of labor in which fathers have relatively little to do with child care activities (Lamb, Pleck, and Levine, 1986). Neither do children raised by same-sex parents suffer from the lack of one parent of each sex (Patterson 1995).

Greater paternal involvement with children's daily lives has emerged in many homes where both biological parents are present. There has been some increase in the daily tasks of child care by married fathers. The extent of fathers' involvement with their children's rearing (both daily caretaking and broader involvement, such as contributing economically to their support) is highly variable. Researchers have found that a man's involvement is strongly shaped by a wide range of factors, from the interpersonal (such as the quality of his relationship with the child's mother) to the institutional and economic (such as his employment opportunities) (Gerson 1993).

Although evidence shows somewhat increased paternal involvement *on the average*, this is produced by the growing involvement of some, rather than all, fathers. Involvement is greater among fathers who live with their children (whether or not the parents are married) and those who have reached a point in their careers that allows them to pull away somewhat from work to increased family activity (Yeung et al. 2001). On the whole, fathers' increased involvement occurs on weekends; workplace demands shape family availability, rather than the other way around (Ranson 2001). In contrast to stereotypes of upper-middle-class men as less traditional than working-class men, the latter are actually more apt to participate in undoing gender in parenting (Shows and Gerstel 2009). This is especially likely for fathers when the earnings of the two parents are similar, and when workplace and household schedules are complementary rather than in conflict.

As we discussed in Chapter Three, more active involvement in child rearing has a major effect on fathers, as well as their partners and their children, and is generally viewed positively. The Million Man March and the Promise Keepers, two social movement organizations that flourished in the late 1990s, sought to increase men's performance of their fathering roles. However, people vary in their definition of those roles—some activists argue for a return to a patriarchal household, and others want a democratic partnership with the mothers of their children.

Because mothers generally provide the great majority of child care time, their responsibilities at home are more likely to shape their work involvement. Furthermore, as we shall see in Chapter Six, employers' assumptions of motherhood's responsibilities continue to affect women's workplace opportunities. Cultural messages about mothering add to some women's tensions because mothers are expected both to be intensely involved with their children and to aim for goals of individualistic achievement in their lives (Hays 1996). In contrast, immigrant women, women of color, and poor and working-class women are increasingly pressured by the changing occupational structure and the increasing prevalence of "nonstandard" work schedules that interfere with maintaining a stable and reliable pattern of household and child care arrangements (Presser 2003).

Increasing numbers of lesbian and gay couples are choosing parenthood and developing interpersonal strategies to establish acceptance for themselves as parents and for their children (Dunne 2000). Same-sex parents often simultaneously challenge heterosexual family patterns while adhering to some traditional aspects of gendered parenting (Dalton and Bielby 2000).

Mothers in same-sex partnerships have particular challenges to establishing their maternal identities. If one partner is the biological mother, she tends to have an easier time winning recognition as a mother, and for her child, within her extended family. The co-mother (the nonbiological mother) usually has more difficulties gaining acceptance for the child with her own kin (Hequembourg and Farrell 1999). The couple and their relatives may have concerns about the child's family ties, should the couple break up. As more legal jurisdictions recognize same-sex unions, extended family, adoptive parents, and coparents can be more certain of having a continued relationship with a child regardless of the long-term future of the couple.

Practices and policies outside the family also affect families that want to raise their children in more gender-equitable homes (Risman 1998). Choosing to stay home full time is often more isolating for men than for women, who relatively easily find other women in the same situation. Fathers at home may feel uncomfortable as the only male in a group of child-rearing parents (Marin 2000). Even public facilities may interfere with equitable parenting. For example, many public facilities have infant changing tables in women's rest rooms only. This obviously adds to the difficulty for men who might travel with or spend several hours away from home with their young children (and obviously for any single or homosexual fathers). Moreover, if a wife and husband go out together, there may be no practical way to share responsibility for this very real parental task—the architecture mandates that it be "women's work." One father gave up his job as an employment discrimination attorney to take care of his infant. As a result of his initiative, the Lord & Taylor department store chain reconfigured its restroom areas, providing changing tables in men's rooms, or a "family" restroom area for parents of either sex to use with their small children (*National Law Journal*, 1995).

Taking unpaid leave for child care is less realistic for the parent who earns more money—and so economic differences in men's and women's earnings interfere with many couples' choosing a nontraditional arrangement of father at home and mother at work. Couples with a serious commitment to an equal involvement in child rearing can choose to do so, but many who might want to do not consider it sensible to give up income to exercise this option. The decision to stay at home involves a complex set of factors: the income (and other benefits) that will be lost, the short- and long-term effect on employability for the parent who leaves the workplace for a few years, the quality and costs of available child care if no parent is at home, and the costs of working (such as transportation and clothing expenses).

Public policies toward formal day care facilities have varied since World War II, when the U.S. government encouraged them so that mothers could work, helping to redress the labor shortage. When that war ended, the facilities were closed down, even though many families still needed mothers' earnings. Consistent with the view that children should be cared for at home, the welfare system considered child care sufficient reason for mothers to stay home. Poor widows with children were eligible for (subsistence) Aid to Dependent Children from the initiation of that program in the 1930s.

By the 1970s, however, women in many two-parent households were in the labor force along with their husbands. Congress passed the Comprehensive Child Development Act in 1971; President Richard Nixon vetoed it on the grounds that it would "commit the vast moral authority of the National Government to the side of communal approaches to child rearing over against the family-centered approach" (*Congressional Record*, in WWSPIA 2004).

Later in the decade, a tax credit for child care expenses was added to the tax code, providing some public policy support to two-earner families. By 1997, paid child care was used by about half of all families with at least one child younger than age 13; most of these were households with at least one child younger than age 5 (Giannarelli and Barsimantov 2000).

In many households, employed fathers are more involved in their children's daily lives than they were in previous generations. This may be a choice made because of beliefs about the appropriate relations between men and women, or it may result when parents work on different shifts. There is still a significant difference between working mothers and fathers in the hours spent in child care, with more affluent men still having extended contact, largely on their days off.

Concerns about the influence of organized care on infants persist. However, research comparing infants who were in full-time (thirty or more hours weekly) care and those receiving only family care found fathers of those in organized care spent more time themselves interacting with their babies, offsetting time lost from infant–mother interaction. Children who had been in full-time care in their first 6 months showed no effects at 15 months, when compared with toddlers who had not spent time in organized care as infants (Booth et al. 2002).

Policymakers now consider it essential that mothers of noninfants be employed, rather than receive support from the government (as we discuss in Chapter Six). Care by a father or an extended family member is preferred by mothers of infants and young children, but the unavailability of the preferred alternatives is common (Riley and Glass 2002). Nonetheless, many families who can afford to have a parent at home do not consider paid care an acceptable substitute. Shift work is sometimes chosen so that children can be cared for at home even though both parents are employed. A national survey of working women recently found that spouses or partners working different shifts was most common among those with children under 18 years old (Greenhouse 2000). Some men who participate in such arrangements gradually take on housework tasks that are not male-identified, as well. Further, they may come to accept responsibility for their participation, rather than define it as "helping out" (Coltrane 1996).

In more than a quarter of households with gay couples and one or more children, one of the fathers is outside of the labor force (Bellafante 2004). Although a slightly higher proportion of heterosexual, married couples have a "stay-at-home" parent, these are mainly mothers.

### CARING FOR KIN

In addition to the care of healthy infants and children, family members contribute to the well-being of healthy adults. Kin also have primary responsibility for chronically ill or disabled children and adults, the frail elderly, and adult kin with acute illnesses. These responsibilities are related to gender in complex ways.

Although the medical profession is often viewed as the way that people receive health care, there are many equally or more established informal patterns for maintaining health. Household members benefit from having regular and nutritious meals, from attention to minor ailments and injuries (so they may not become major), and from reminders to take medications and facilitating the use of professional health care. Many lay people use unwritten, informally transmitted advice, popularized health care books and magazine articles, and Web sites, both popularized and professionally maintained. As obvious as the routine maintenance of good health practices is, the contribution of family members to lowering rates of illness and extending life is largely overlooked.

Historically, expertise regarding health and illness has been associated with older women. The greater life expectancy of married than unmarried men has been documented for many years. This largely reflects the "protection effects" men gain in marriage, such as the regular care provided by wives (Verbrugge and Wingard 1987; Wu et al. 2003). Wives are more likely than husbands to provide "health reminders"—to get more sleep, to exercise, or to take medications (Stolzenberg 2001). The importance of wives' involvement in managing men's health-related behavior is evidenced by the worsening of men's health associated with wives' putting in many hours at work. Women, in contrast, do not experience negative health effects when their husbands work more than forty hours per week, reflecting husbands' relatively minor involvement with management of women's health-related behavior.

The contribution of impoverished African American mothers to their adolescent sons' survival is an extreme case of the invisibility of family members' caretaking. Violence is a public health problem; neighborhoods lacking supportive public services challenge all parents to protect their children. Rather than appreciating their attempts at protection, the dominant culture demonizes black mothers (Richie 1999). Another area of invisibility is the caretaking that adult siblings often provide one another (Eriksen and Gerstel, in Garey et al. 2002). The Family and Medical Leave Act (F.M.L.A.) requires certain categories of employers to allow workers to take leave if they are needed to care for family members—but care for an adult sibling does not qualify a worker for leave. Likewise, single, childless uncles and aunts, who have traditionally benefited from the care given by younger kin, are not qualifying relationships.

The gendering of caregiving activities is not surprising given longstanding beliefs about women and men's capacities (Olson 2003). Just as more fathers have become involved in direct child care performance, men are involved in the provision of care to elderly and ill kin. The extent and nature of their assistance depend on their relationships with other family members. Thus, when wives or daughters are active caregivers, husbands (or fathers) tend to participate in caregiving to some extent, supplementing the care giving by their female family members. In contrast, men whose sisters provide care to their parents are less likely to participate; their sisters substitute for them. When there are only brothers, men do more parent care, indicating that they have the capacity to do so (Gerstel and Gallagher 2001). The kinds of care provided are often gendered; men are very unlikely to bathe the elderly or to clean someone after an episode of (or with chronic) incontinence. The person receiving care may prefer this arrangement, as well. Though receiving this care may be profoundly embarrassing under any circumstances, receiving it from a male may be even more so (Isaksen 2002). Even when the kind of care is not gendered, the men who are giving it often describe it in ways that conform to hegemonic masculinity (Russell 2007). For example, they may focus on those tasks that make use of male-typed characteristics, like physical strength needed for lifting a dependent adult. When accounting for their commitment to performing care, most men in Russell's sample focused on their reciprocating—they are providing care to people who had previously taken care of them. In contrast, they accounted for women's caregiving as an outgrowth of their (presumably) essential nurturance.

When children are labeled with a chronic problem, such as attention deficit disorder, the responsibility falls disproportionately on the mother—both for its initial development (what did she do wrong?) and for negotiating the possible approaches toward its treatment. Efforts to get the best treatment for children (e.g., from schools and from medical service providers) are regularly the mother's rather than the father's responsibility (Malacrida 2002). As public resources are increasingly scarce, this responsibility involves added demands on women's time.

Caregivers pay in many ways for their responsibilities, depending on how much time they devote to care giving, how extended a period is involved, and the degree to which the burden is shared. Those with relatively elite jobs often have less job-related stress when they need to provide care. Although the F.M.L.A. protects some categories of workers from job loss due to certain family care responsibilities, it does not require that employers make any payment during the time on leave. Low-income workers, also less likely to have any paid "personal" days, are therefore less able to take advantage of the act's protection. Sharing the burden of care can mean paying for help, which requires economic resources many people lack. Those who do pay for caregivers often benefit from the underpaid labor of women of color and immigrant workers (Olson 2003).

Caregivers may also suffer depression and other emotional and physical health costs, although these are less likely when there is social support (Cannuscio et al. 2004). Social support of the primary caregiver is itself gendered; for example, more help is offered to men who are caring for a spouse or parent than to women caregivers. Caregivers may also derive satisfaction from nurturing their kin or by providing an alternative to moving into institutionalized care (Olson 2003). Nonetheless, when men retired from the paid labor force provide care to wives suffering from mental disabilities, they often have difficulties related to the isolation of their new (care) workplace, and the invisibility of the work they perform. In addition, some have moved from work in which they could point to some product into the kind of work (like doing dishes) that simply restores or maintains taken-for-granted conditions (Campbell and Carroll 2007).

Increasing numbers of middle-aged people (primarily women) will be caring for elderly family members as demographic changes reduce the numbers of adult children available to help and increase the length of old age, and with the mounting cuts in public support services, begun during the Reagan administration. Involvement in caring for one's husband is associated with women's retiring earlier than their female peers, but men who care for their wives tend to postpone retirement longer than their male peers (Dentinger and Clarkberg 2002). These gendered patterns may reflect different economic costs of job leaving for men than for women: Those who earn more will lose more income on retirement, and retiring from jobs that provide benefits such as health insurance coverage is more costly than retiring from jobs without such benefits. The retirement difference is also consistent with the pattern of caretaking wives continuing their other household work, but caretaking husbands not regularly assuming their wives' chores (Allen and Webster 2001). The care work performed by elderly people has been little studied, reflecting the more general problem of the lack of attention to aging and the aged in contemporary U.S. culture. To the extent that attention has been paid to the elderly as caregivers, it tends to focus on their role tending to grandchildren (Calasanti 2006).

## TECHNOLOGY AND THE FAMILY

The kinds of work that are done in the home and the ways they are performed reflect contemporary technologies, which have been shaped in part by cultural values and beliefs about the nuclear family (Cowan 1983). Some technological innovations have been unsuccessful at least in part because central production of these services violated notions of the family as a private sphere. For example, early attempts at marketing full meals to be produced centrally and delivered to households may have failed because of their impersonality, which contrasted with the rhetorically loving touch of the wife and mother. By the time the microwave oven was marketed (decades after its initial development), the growing pattern of family members' differing schedules contributed to its success. For example, almost half of the employed women in a national survey worked different hours than their husband or partner (Greenhouse 2000).

However, the common assumption that successful innovations reflect the choice of the market is oversimplified. Often the market has only a limited range of choices, which reflect the imagination and judgment of people with capital to invest in "debugging" innovations, developing systems of production, and carrying out a marketing strategy. Further, many innovations do not function alone but must be supported by a technological system (e.g., how would a minivan function on unpaved roads?). When the community or society puts a supporting system in place, it is unlikely to contribute to other systems necessary to support alternative technological choices.

Perhaps the most expensive example of a technological system with huge implications for family roles is the combined development of the automobile, the construction of roadways to serve it, and the destruction (either actively or through slow disintegration) of systems of mass transportation. The results for parents are significant (Wajcman 1991). Parents have different tasks in areas with excellent public transportation systems than they do in areas where children can travel only by car. A standard keychain tag or decal to put on car bumpers or inside their windows says, "Mom's Taxi." This reflects the central role that transporting family members has for suburban mothers. When mothers are not available to transport their children, substitute labor must be found, or children's choices of after-school and vacation activities are greatly limited. Not only the affluent are dependent on the private automobile: Other uses for family resources must sometimes be shortchanged when families must keep cars running to provide essential transportation (Freund and Martin 1993).

Technologies of reproduction, such as in vitro fertilization, sex determination, and surrogate mothering, are also shaped by dominant cultural forces (Rothman 1987). Not all potential technological innovations are pursued with capital investments and human expertise. Instead, the choice of which challenges to take on is influenced by researchers' view of what is a problem and what kinds of solutions are acceptable, as well as designers' ideas about what innovations the public will adopt (Casper 1998). As we saw in the last chapter, the technological changes enabling earlier fetal survival have been accompanied by increased government regulation of individual women's bodies.

The greater possibilities offered by technologies of contraception and fertility are limited by the costs of devices and procedures. The dominant cultural preference that people bear children is connected to the much greater availability for those with private health insurance policies, that is, for medical services to insure reproduction than for services to avoid it. Prescription birth-control pills, legal for more than forty years, were almost never paid for (even in part) by insurance plans (King and Meyer 1997) until the development of Viagra. With its quick acceptance by insurers, the lack of coverage for oral contraceptives became a widely recognized inequity. By 2000, many policies had changed, but others continued to be inequitable (Lewin 2000).

The extremely costly medical care required to support very premature births (and often the chronic problems of people whose very premature births would previously not have been sustainable) has a significant effect on the other medical and surgical services that society can afford to provide its members. Finally, individuals with public health insurance (Medicaid) are in a very different situation. The social policy, and thus their insurance coverage, discourages reproduction, providing contraception but no subsidy for infertility treatments.

### VIOLENCE IN INTIMATE RELATIONSHIPS

Until the 1970s, violence between intimates went largely unnoticed. Ideological views that the state should not interfere in domestic matters and police reluctance to do so were challenged with feminist activism, and the state acquired a stronger political and criminal justice foundation for intervening when children or adults were victimized by an intimate. The home is still the most likely place where a woman will be murdered, and her husband or partner is the most likely murderer.

Abuse or neglect of children is a matter of grave social concern. Laws have been changed that had placed the career of a school nurse in jeopardy if she mistakenly reported suspicions of abuse. Now educational professionals and administrators are at risk of prosecution if they do not make such reports. There is controversy about what to do when a child has experienced abuse. Many child and family advocates argue that children will do better if their families receive serious therapy, rather than if the children are removed (often to inadequate foster placements or state-run residences). Other child advocates argue against extending children's vulnerability by leaving them in the home. Either approach is costly, and, despite the serious public concern, both approaches are underfunded.

The situation of adults alleged to have committed abuse is affected by their access to economic, legal, and therapeutic resources. Poor women and men are least able to argue successfully that they have been unfairly charged, and are least able to afford the kinds of treatment that might persuade government officials to allow them to keep their families together. Without the availability of public resources to improve the situation at home, children are removed. More affluent families are able to keep their children by paying for attorneys or therapists whose treatments should make the children's future safe.

It is often reported that mothers are equally, or more, likely than fathers to abuse children. These reports neglect to mention that the average child spends a great deal more time with a mother around than with a father (in two-parent as well as single-parent homes). When we compare the rate of abusive acts by parents *per hour that they spend with their children*, child abuse by fathers turns out to be a more serious problem than generally thought. This does not negate the existence of child abuse by mothers, but suggests that it is inaccurately viewed as *the* most likely abusive relationship (Featherstone 1996).

There is a push toward framing and discussing family violence in gender-neutral terms, which mask the differences in the patterns of violent behavior by and toward women and men (Kurz 2001). To understand the dynamic of each demands being aware of which sex we are discussing. For example, research on elder abuse is usually cast in gender-neutral terms, although the most frequent pattern, by far, is younger men's abuse of elderly women (Whittaker 1996). As we saw in the section on the role of knowledge professionals in culture, the way that a question or problem is phrased will influence the ways in which experts think about answering or solving it. Ignoring the gendered pattern interferes with developing more sophisticated explanations of the patterns of elder abuse and designing effective strategies to end elder violence.

Similarly, the term *spouse abuse* is often used instead of *wife abuse*, removing the problem from an explanatory framework that foregrounds the salience of the gender system (Berns 2001). On the other hand, using *wife* abuse contributes to the invisibility of dating violence as well as violence in same-sex relationships and other nonmarital relationships. Some researchers have maintained that rates of abuse by women toward husbands have been underreported and are actually comparable to the rates of violence by husbands against wives. These reports receive much popular attention (an interesting exception to popular fascination with sex differences). However, more careful analysis of the evidence used in the reports reveals that acts of women against men are likely to be something like a slap in the face by a smaller woman to a larger man or a jab in the shoulder. Violence by men against women is more likely to be physically threatening or actually harmful, such as being shoved against the wall. Homicide rates clearly indicate that more men, rather than women, have murdered spouses or present or past "girlfriends," despite the popularity of movie and television plots to the contrary (see Figure 4.3).

In addition, some surveys and journalistic accounts are misleading because they combine very different kinds of incidents. "Common couple violence" occurs around narrowly focused disputes, rather than being oriented toward establishing control over the partner. It usually does not escalate. In contrast, "intimate terrorism" is motivated by the desire for control, rather than by a particular issue; it is overwhelmingly male-on-female violence (Johnson and Ferraro 2000) and is sometimes, therefore, called "patriarchal terrorism" (Johnson 1995). Other types of intimate violence, rarely studied and apparently quite uncommon, are "violent resistance" (in which an abused partner, usually female, is violent toward the abuser) and "mutual violent control" (in which both partners are attempting to gain control in the relationship through the use of intimate terrorism). Violent resistance has decreased in the decades since the rise of the battered women's movement in the 1970s; women who would previously have seen no other way out have seen a growth of alternatives to killing a violent partner (Johnson 2008).

Although the study of intimate violence has largely focused on heterosexual cohabiting or married couples, it is also a problem in dating relationships and in gay and lesbian homes. The cultural framing of the problem interferes with friends' and kin's seeing the problem, and until recently this also stood in the way of social scientists and policymakers framing the problem. Other cultural obstacles add to the difficulty of making quantitative comparisons among groups. Ethnic differences in the degree of shame associated with family violence may contribute to different levels of denial by victims who seek assistance for injuries or by community members to whom victims go for support. Families with more economic resources are probably better able to avoid reports of violence between partners.

Social researchers have long established that all forms of family violence are more common during economic hard times; men's abuse of women is often related to the

**Homicides of intimates by gender of victim, 1976–2005**

**Proportion of all homicides involving intimates by gender of victim, 1976–2005**

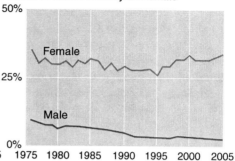

**Figure 4.3 Homicide and Intimacy.** According to the U.S. Department of Justice, women are much more likely to be murdered by present or former husbands or boyfriends than are men to be murdered by present or former wives or girlfriends. The intimacy victimization of men has declined steadily and significantly from 1976 to 2005, whereas women's murder by intimates was stable from 1976 until 1993. It then declined somewhat, but has changed little since 1997. Looking at homicide rates from a different angle, we see that female murder victims are far more likely than male murder victims to be killed by an intimate. For example, in 2005 about one third of female victims were killed by an intimate, and about 2.5 percent of male victims were.
Source: U.S. Department of Justice, Bureau of Justice Statistics. "Homicide Trends in the U.S.: Intimate Homicide." Accessed at www.ojp.usdoj.gov/bjs/homicide/intimates.htm.

woman having relatively greater resources than the man (see, for example, McCloskey 1996). Whether the resources are financial, prestige, or interpersonal (e.g., connection to a supportive family network), simply having greater resources makes a woman a threat to the dominance so important to some men. Some men whose violence has brought them into the criminal justice system see their behavior as highlighting their superiority to their partners in strength, power, and rationality—three features of hegemonic masculinity. Simultaneously, they complain of their powerlessness (relative to the criminal justice system and/or to the partners they construct as controlling) and of social changes undermining their traditional authority; in this context they refer to their violence as a means to construct masculinity (Anderson and Umberson 2001).

Although violence obviously has physical and emotional costs, it has economic costs, as well. Because violent men are likely to resent, and be set off by, some challenge to their power in the relationship, a woman's pursuit of economic independence, or simply of some improvement in her economic situation, is often related to increased violence against her. Women receiving welfare may find it difficult to take training courses or jobs because their partners either undermine their attendance or are actively violent to make participation impossible (Curcio 1999). With the changing welfare legislation (discussed in detail in Chapter Six), welfare support is limited to five years in an individual's lifetime, with no more than two years of support during one period of assistance. The law allows states to waive these limits for victims of domestic abuse.

However, most victims of domestic abuse are afraid to report it and thus are likely to lose this one, if inadequate, source of economic subsistence as they reach these personal limits. Previously abused women who move out of welfare sometimes turn in desperation to their abusers for financial or other forms of assistance, increasing their vulnerability to further abuse (Scott, London, and Meyers 2002).

Even though nonpoor women also suffer physical abuse from intimates, the rates of victimization are lower. This difference probably reflects a combination of factors: (1) among women seeking help, poor women may have fewer alternatives to official reporting than more affluent women have; (2) more economically secure men do have alternatives to physical power over their female intimates—they are likely to have the power to reward or punish with money and other economic resources; and (3) conflict and violence are more common in stressful situations, and poverty adds stress to people's lives.

Finally, violence in intimate relationships between people who do not live together has received growing attention. News reports are common about the murder of people who have ended a dating or more intimate relationship; the murderer is the rejected suitor or lover. These cases are overwhelmingly attacks by men on women. In the 1990s, laws were passed in several states against **stalking**, or the practice of following another person with whom one is (typically sexually) obsessed. The majority of people subjected to stalking do not report this crime to the police (Olson 2009). Stalkers sometimes are rejected lovers, although they may be relative strangers. Like other forms of intimidating behavior, stalking is much more commonly practiced by men, with women as victims. Both radical feminism and multiracial feminism bring insights to the study of violence in families and the ways in which family units are perceived by outsiders and treated by public agencies.

The radical feminist viewpoint would explain the push toward gender-neutral language and the exaggeration of maternal rates of child abuse as patriarchal attempts to mask the much greater rates of male than female violence toward intimates. The multiracial feminist approach would bring our attention to the differences in resources that people have available to deal with family problems, as well as the hidden role of economic pressures on the occurrence of family violence. In addition, an increasingly common critique of media coverage of intimate violence is essentially a multiracial feminist account: The media give more coverage to the sexual victimization of white women, and especially nonpoor white women, than they do to lower-status women.

### SUMMARY

The household has been a site of dramatic changes in beliefs and practices in recent decades. Same-sex couples in Canada were extended the right to marry in 2004. In a number of European societies, for example, opposite-sex couples as well as same-sex couples choose alternatives to legal marriage that offer most, if not all, of the rights of marriage (Lyall 2004).

Nonetheless, the household retains special significance in the gendering of social reality. It is the locus of much work, particularly work that gets little social recognition and that is differentially assigned and performed depending on social meanings attached to the biological categories of male and female. As we shall see in Chapter Six, gendered arrangements in the home have implications for the occupational experiences of women and men.

The household is the primary site for early childhood socialization and for emotional and sexual intimacy in adulthood. It is the primary unit of economic consumption and as such is the unit of deprivation when the adults are unable to gain sufficient income. This ability, as we shall see in Chapter Six, remains strongly related to membership in gender, racial-ethnic, and social class categories. Work arrangements also have implications for the reality of home life, because these two spheres are not separate for men or women. The economic discrimination against men of color and the deteriorating workplace conditions for white working-class men result for many in an inability to succeed as stable breadwinners. Although breadwinning is no longer an exclusively male responsibility, it remains an essential aspect of the roles of husband and father. Thus, when productive work with adequate earnings is precarious, family life is vulnerable. In the U.S. economy, the educational institution forms a crucial link between family life and occupational experience. In the next chapter we examine the gendering of education.

### DISCUSSION QUESTIONS

1. If each person were to have the opportunity to achieve satisfaction in both family and occupational activities over her or his lifetime, what would that require? What aspects of social structure would need to be changed?
2. Reflect on several current television shows and the ways that they present gender relations in intimate relationships. In what ways do they seem accurate, and in what ways inaccurate, compared with the description of contemporary patterns in this chapter?
3. With the economic crisis that began in late 2008, unemployment rates grew rapidly and even stable housing arrangements were made vulnerable by mortgage foreclosures. How are these and related developments likely to affect family and intimate relationships, and why? ◆

# CHAPTER 5

# Education

The social institution of education includes the many ways in which a society trains its members for future activities. In the study of gender, we have a particular interest in the educational institution for the ways in which it influences individuals' development of identity and ideologies of gender, for the ways in which individuals are encouraged to seek or discouraged from seeking training for particular kinds of work, and, finally, as an important work setting with significant differences in the opportunities available to people, depending on their social identity as male or female. As we shall see, every level of the educational institution exemplifies the important influence of the intersection of gender, class, and race-ethnicity in the opportunities and obstacles the individual is likely to encounter. Because employment paths in the United States depend heavily on the kinds of formal as well as informal experiences and credentials that people acquire, patterns of difference in the educational system are significant forces affecting people's life chances after leaving school. Along all these dimensions, change has been uneven, rapid in some areas and very slow in others. As we review the kinds of changes that have taken place, we will see the importance of political and legal forces, as well as their limitations.

Almost all children attend school, although for diverse reasons, increasing numbers choose to "home school" their children (U.S. Department of Education 2009). School attendance is required well into adolescence, and many people continue attending institutions of formal education into their twenties. Furthermore, it has become more common for people to return to schooling during adulthood, to earn the minimum credential for semi-skilled employment, to prepare to change occupations, or to move into more skilled positions within their previous employment. Although most people who are in school or college actually attend classes, a small but growing number make some use of "distance education" to earn credits without physically traveling to a campus. Of these, only about one quarter are in programs entirely without on-campus participation (NCES 2002). Women above "college age" are particularly likely to pursue distance courses and programs.

In this chapter, we will review both the formal and the informal curricula in primary and secondary schools and then turn to higher education. The enrollment of females in college and graduate school has increased steadily for decades, although gender differences remain in the fields that women and men choose. To some extent, student demographics mirror the composition of faculties in different areas of specialization. After a description of gender in educational employment, we end the chapter with an overview of athletics, both organized and informal, in schools and colleges.

## SCHOOLS: THE MIDDLE LEVEL OF SOCIAL LIFE

The formal authority of schools is significant, ranging from the right to regulate students' dress, grooming, and comportment to the ability to require or forbid the study of particular materials. Most notably for the study of gender, school authorities are able to channel students to courses viewed as appropriate within the gender system. That system, as we have seen, is complex, with different versions of masculinities and femininities associated with particular social class and racial-ethnic groups. Though there are limits to schools' formal authority, students (and their families) find that challenging school authority is difficult.

Schools are social systems with various formal and informal groups. Peer groups (through school-affiliated clubs and teams, friendship groups, and cliques) are especially powerful during adolescence, but recent research on younger children indicates that peers wield considerable influence before puberty as well. School authorities often remain uninvolved in the informal social interactions among students, permitting the use of badgering and bullying that enforces locally hegemonic systems of race, class, sexuality, and gender (Hand and Sanchez 2000).

Like families and large-scale organizations, schools and school systems vary considerably in how gender is enacted and limited. For example, some schools require sex segregation in the lunch room, but others do not (Ellis 1999). Whichever patterns and norms exist in a particular school, the families who send children to it find that the preferences and norms modeled and taught at home simultaneously can be reinforced or contradicted. The micro level of the home confronts the middle level of school organization and the competing small-group norms of friends, classmates, teachers, and administrators. For example, if a couple with a child in kindergarten decides that the father will volunteer to be class parent, the school official setting up the network of class mothers may not go along with that decision. Indeed, as long as the call for volunteers names the job "class mother," that couple is unlikely to have responded! As long as the larger organizations of which we are a part do not change their basic rules of gendering, micro-social redefinitions of the place of gender will not matter. However, if one or two or three fathers volunteer, the official title of the job may be changed for the future. Or, it may be changed that year and revert back to the gendered title in the future. In other words, the negotiation of change is ongoing. Eventually, after several consecutive years of calling the job "class parent," it would be hard to revert to the "class mother" language. And, as we saw in Chapter Two, the gender neutrality of the word will be irrelevant if men who volunteer are treated as inappropriate for volunteering.

Because of the considerable autonomy many teachers have in their classrooms, they can create experiences for students other than those that fit the hegemonic gender system. For example, a teacher might structure woodworking into every child's routine, rather than making it optional. If an activity is optional, children may be self-conscious about electing it; children who have not been exposed to an activity in a gender-traditional home may not be interested in choosing it. This teacher's approach makes it possible for girls to become comfortable with woodworking tools without declaring themselves gender renegades. Similarly, activities traditionally assigned to girls, such as sewing, may be introduced as an all-student activity in a matter-of-fact way. Even if students comment on it, as they attempt to enforce or show their knowledge of gender norms learned elsewhere, they will eventually have the required exposure and may become involved in a lesson that they enjoy. Although many teachers are probably content to convey conventional gender ideology in their classes, the relative freedom of teachers has been an important source of alternative possibilities to many who pursue activities not traditional for their sex.

### FORMAL AND INFORMAL CURRICULA

Education was one of the most significant and rapid areas of change produced by the second wave of feminism. Previously taken-for-granted segregation of students in physical and health education classes, formal limitations on curricular choice based on sex, and the implicit messages about gender in instructional materials were all targeted for change by activists, both professionals in the educational institution and feminists outside it.

Boys could not take cooking or sewing; and girls could not take shop. Guidance counselors routinely steered people to different courses depending on the sex, race-ethnicity, and social class statuses of the person, even when the courses were formally open to all. Vocational tests were scored with different keys for male and female test takers; the same set of answers was interpreted as indicating the potential for different occupations depending on the sex of the test taker.

With the passage of the Women's Educational Equity Act in 1974, the U.S. government adopted a policy overturning these previous practices. The Act made funds available for research and pilot programs, to develop new curricula and pedagogical approaches that would facilitate females' integration into previously male-defined specialties. During the 1970s many all-male and some all-female schools and colleges became coeducational. Few single-sex institutions remain, despite their positive impact on students (discussed later in this chapter).

Children are exposed to teachers' and administrators' worldviews quite apart from the curricular materials they encounter. Thus, teachers communicate the assumption, in many ways, that sex is a relevant basis for classifying people. For example, when holiday grab bags are planned, each child may be instructed to bring a gift that is appropriate for a child of the same sex. The world of play is officially segregated into things for girls and things for boys. More important, attitude studies continue to report that many teachers tend to define some behaviors (such as passivity) as problems if exhibited by boys, but not if exhibited by girls. Other behaviors (such as physical aggression) are more likely to be defined as problems if they are shown by girls than if shown by boys. In other words, boys are normal if they are independent, even to the point of aggressiveness. Girls are normal if they are dependent.

Teachers often encourage sex segregation through formal and informal practices. From the earliest days of school, many teachers and school officials structure routines in ways that imply that boys and girls are fundamentally different (see Thorne 1993). Despite official integration, play areas in day care centers, nursery schools, and kindergartens are usually informally sex segregated. And sex integration is not always the official rule. Teachers who would never ask white children to line up on one side of the room and children of color on the other side see lining up by boys and girls as entirely appropriate. In the 1990s, the principal of a suburban middle school punished *all* fourth grade boys because *many* fourth grade boys had misbehaved at a school event. He would never punish all members of a racial-ethnic group because of the misbehavior of *many* members of that group. Differences in treatment based on race tend to be more subtle and less overtly defended than differences based on sex.

In the early years of school, children themselves structure informal activities during recess. Teachers generally intervene only in the case of violent disagreements. Play is usually based on traditional views of gender. A few boys generally dominate the physical territory of the playground, including the fixed equipment (such as the monkey bars), portable equipment (for example, the soccer ball), as well as the available open space.

The domination of this arena by the most aggressive children leads to the enforcement of their worldview, including their notions of gender. Children (more often girls than boys) do venture into areas or groups identified with the other sex. Even when some boys are open to girls' approach, the dominant boys are likely to be intolerant of mixed-sex games. Precisely because these boys usually excel physically, they are likely to embrace a version of masculinity based on physical prowess. Thus, the real or potential ability of girls to be competitive at the boys' level threatens their masculinity. Most other boys usually go along with the enforcement of all-male play (McGuffey and Rich 1999).

Although the tendency to sex segregate varies with children's ages, peer groups are usually either all boys or all girls, rather than mixed-sex. However, research has shown that children interact in mixed-sex groups that adults set up, even if children did not typically create and choose such groups themselves (Thorne 1993). Similarly, when playground activities were limited (e.g., with a ban on fighting and a limit on the dominance of soccer), the hegemony of physical prowess was weakened and both boys and girls sometimes explored alternative versions of gender (Epstein et al. 2001).

Teachers often encourage gender distinctions in both subtle and obvious ways. Teachers' expectations that children prefer same-sex contact probably focuses their attention on children's expression of that preference and leads them to ignore or be less attuned to different messages from other children. When authorities accept or even initiate sex segregation, they limit the opportunities children have for choosing activities, playmates, or work groups. More basically, they endorse sex as a basis of differential treatment and expectations of girls and boys.

Like others in U.S. culture, many teachers assume that individual intelligence is set rather than immutable. Despite evidence to the contrary (Fischer et al. 1994), students are rarely expected to improve over their past performances. Thus, a poor experience with one teacher's classroom may depress the potential for improved performance with the next. Teachers' expectations and perceptions of students are also influenced by characteristics such as social class, race-ethnicity, sex, and family structure. Teachers vary in the expectations they have about the relation of these intersected identities and student potential, but decades of evidence have clearly shown that teachers do not treat all children the same way.

White teachers and administrators often more readily characterize African American boys as chronic "bad boys" than they do when looking at the same behavior in other categories of students (Ferguson 2000). Even when the students and teachers are from the same racial-ethnic group, some teachers' expectations about the intersection of class and gender are sufficient to lead to lowered academic expectations for certain students, while the teachers are quick to notice their misbehaviors.

Among white students, speaking up in class is sometimes seen as less acceptable for girls than for boys. Gender appears to be related differently to speaking up among African American students (Grant 1994). Young African American girls are typically more comfortable than are white girls in participating. For almost thirty years, research has documented teachers' (of both sexes) tendency to direct more attention to boys than to girls (see Figure 5.1). The sex difference in teachers' attention is less

---

1. *Is less expected of women than men?*
   *For example:* Are women asked easier questions and men asked more challenging ones?
2. *Are common stereotypes taken for granted?*
   *For example:* Are men made group leaders and women made recorders?
3. *Are women excluded?*
   *For example:* Are women speakers interupted, with the interruption unchallenged by the teacher?
4. *Does the same behavior get different reactions depending on the student's sex?*
   *For example:* Is there an interested look when a man speaks and an impatient one when a woman does?
5. *Do women get less attention and encouragement?*
   *For example:* Do men get more time to think of an answer than women?
6. *Is politeness used to define women as outsiders?*
   *For example:* Does a man insist on doing something for a woman, showing he assumes it would be hard for her and taking away her opportunity to have the experience herself?
7. *Are women singled out?*
   *For example:* Does the teacher ask a black woman student, "How do black women feel about this?"
8. *Are women defined by their sexuality?*
   *For example:* Are women praised for their appearance and not for their intellectual performance?
9. *Is there overtly hostile behavior toward women?*
   *For example:* Do men in the room hiss or ridicule students who raise women's issues?

**Figure 5.1  Thinking About Microinequalities in the Classroom\***
\* Microinequalities are small everyday inequities through which individuals are often treated differently because of their gender, race, age, or other "outsider" status. This term was created by Mary Rowe.
Source: Adapted from "Ways in Which Men and Women May Be Treated Differently." Bernice Sandler, in the Summer 1999 issue of *About Women on Campus* (Vol.8, Number 3).

pronounced for students of color than for white students: white boys lead in teacher attention (which is not always positive). Although these patterns are now less extreme, research confirms that they persist (Sadker and Sadker 1994).

Teachers may resist dominant norms, which places them in a contradictory position. They simultaneously represent the institution responsible for reproducing social arrangements and work to prepare students to be different or to make change. Many teachers of African American children push them to the highest standards of performance, motivated in part by a sense that outstanding performance is essential for survival in a racially discriminatory system. By explicity presenting (in age-appropriate ways) the reasons for their classroom norms, these teachers explain that mastering the dominant culture's academic requirements is important to better survive in a racist system, and should not be interpreted as somehow denying one's race (Tyson 2003).

Discipline in public education has changed in recent years, particularly after the Columbine massacre of 1999, when two heavily armed students murdered many other students and teachers. School systems have adopted "zero tolerance" policies aimed at removing potentially violent students from the school. As we will discuss in Chapter Seven, many behaviors formerly perceived as discipline problems for school authorities and parents to handle are now more likely to be treated as criminal acts. This approach focuses on preserving (or recovering) safety in school, but may permanently harm students whose misbehavior is so readily labeled. Even students who flaunt dress code violations have found themselves turned over to civil authorities (Rimer 2004). This approach usually substitutes for, rather than supplementing, important lessons about constructive, nonviolent approaches to conflict resolution. Slowly, however, increased attention is being paid to the long-term importance of treating rather than simply punishing bullying behavior (Klass 2009).

Reporting about school violence is another topic that illustrates the biases of news sources. Although children in poor urban areas are much more routinely harmed by violence in school (often by intruders), it is the violence in schools for affluent communities that is reported. The reporting generally fails to point out the clearly gendered pattern of multiple shootings or bombing plots: They are overwhelmingly committed (or planned) by white boys, and targets are usually girls.

In explaining variations in teenage boys' delinquent and criminal behaviors, Messerschmidt (1993) used an intersectional, multiracial feminist perspective. Looking at the present and future opportunities of teenage boys helps makes sense of their different choices of victims, sites for acting out, and modes of criminality. All boys trying to establish masculinity must cope with the emasculating character of the high school environment. Those who expect ultimately to achieve hegemonic masculinity will restrict their misbehavior to nonschool settings, safeguarding their academic and hence their occupational futures. Those who believe they will always be outsiders have less reason to behave in school. The Columbine-style violence extends Messerschmidt's analysis by highlighting the lives of boys who feel themselves to be outsiders despite their hegemonic racial and class memberships. Here, a radical feminist approach might point to media explanations of such behavior based on the construction of women (and girls) taking over access and privileges that men (and boys) previously took for granted.

Gender-traditional messages from peers complicate the worldview of children raised by parents with feminist beliefs. In a study of families headed by feminist couples, their children generally held on to the abstract values of their parents' ideology. However, they formed a variety of perspectives that accepted as real the practices and values encountered among their peers (Risman 1998). The peer group influence usually overwhelms the parental influence in shaping everyday behavior, although the family's egalitarian values remain dominant. Whether behavior is based on an internalization of the peers' patterns or more pragmatically based (i.e., "going along to get along"), as children's worlds expand, their parents are often surprised to see them adopt behaviors and attitudes different from those in the home. It is not unusual for children who play in sex-integrated groups in their neighborhood to shun their other-sex playmates at school. This, of course, perpetuates teachers' beliefs in children's preference for same-sex interaction.

Discussion of peer group influence often overlooks the various friendship groups within the larger peer group of the student's environment. In some schools (particularly in poor urban areas), friendship groups help African American students counter-balance some peer groups, especially those that define pursuit of academic goals as "acting white." In this construction of race pride, rejecting academic pursuits is a form of resistance against the oppressive white-dominated system, which discriminates against African Americans regardless of their ability. Yet, many African American students are successful in school, even when some peers consider this as "acting white." By distinguishing among their peers, successful students can reveal and share academic achievement goals with supportive friends, while emphasizing other aspects of their selves with those peers who consider resistance necessary to achieve a positive sense of self (Horvat and Lewis 2003). Friendship groups thus contribute to the construction of a worldview in which academic achievement and a positive sense of self are consistent. And, because a positive sense of self contributes to academic achievement, membership in such friendship groups helps students' school performance.

In their study of peer group influences on girls' participation in cheerleader preparation and competition for membership in the squad, Bettis and Adams (2003) also reflect on the importance of recognizing the complexity of the "peer group." For example, notions of appropriate facial expressions for adolescent girls vary among racial-ethnic groups. The constant smile that cheerleaders are required to display is a regular part of upper-middle-class white (hegemonic) femininity. However, for Native American girls in the school studied, a habitual smile was regarded negatively. Native American girls who considered trying out for the squad were affected by this variety of views of the constant smile, and some opted out of the competition because their ethnic peer group saw it as outside their ethnic norms.

The importance of supportive networks of peers sharing one's race and gender was illustrated in a study of Latinas who succeeded in college (Barajas and Pierce 2001). They saw the relationships they developed with other Latinas as contributing to their academic survival and their maintenance of a positive racial identity, despite the racially hostile experiences they often had on campus. Most Latinos in the study did not develop this kind of social support network with others of their racial-ethnic group.

## ACADEMIC ACHIEVEMENT

Children's gender, racial-ethnic, and social class positions are associated with their levels of academic achievement-how far they go in school, how well they perform in classes, and how they perform on increasingly important standardized tests. Social class often is related to how much formal education other family members have, which helps or hinders students as they encounter challenges in schooling. Middle-class parents are more able to train their children to compete and score well on achievement tests, to provide computer equipment and peripherals at home, and to afford tutors, SAT prep courses, or other forms of assistance to boost student performance. Social class is also related to how students do gender, with different interpretations of gender-appropriate behavior in school settings (Morris 2008).

Students in working-class and poor families are more pressed to have jobs before or after school, or both; girls are particularly likely to have family care responsibilities. These obligations take time away from school-related activities that improve higher education access, opportunities for financial aid, and expectations of success. Research that explores the academic performance of different categories of students often uses family income to measure social class position. **Wealth**, the possession of property and other financial assets, such as stocks and bonds, is a more accurate indicator of a family's financial ability to enhance student performance (Orr 2003). Wealth differences between whites and other racial-ethnic groups are generally more extreme than income differences. By using wealth measures, the difference in educational achievement associated with race is more clearly related to differences in families' economic circumstances.

Though it is currently extremely unusual in the United States, single-sex education serves as an instructive look at factors affecting girls' and women's educational experiences. Comparing the academic and social effects of attendance at same-sex and mixed-sex schools, Miller-Bernal (2000) analyzed the influence of one's immediate social environment on individual changes after early childhood. Research conducted in the United States and abroad, at both secondary and college levels, suggests that the sex composition of a school affects the outcome of the educational experience. Motivated by concern about boys' underperformance compared to girls, there is a growing interest and experimentation in establishing sex-segregated schools or classes within integrated schools (Medina 2009).

Although some criticize the single-sex school as an unrealistic environment, the absence of males benefits many female students, including in academic achievement and career orientation. Several hypotheses have been explored to explain this conclusion. For example, single-sex education may provide a social space in which people feel less pressure to "do gender," enabling them to devote more attention to the subject at hand. Although same-sex institutions are currently uncommon in the United States, they provide an important picture of the place of social arrangements on socialization and the potential for individual change after childhood (Tidball et al. 1999). Such schools help identify changes that could be made to mixed-sex environments to promote less sexist socialization experiences and outcomes. For example, women students profit from opportunities for leadership as well as standard practices that insure coverage of events featuring women participants and women's organizations in the student press.

## HIGHER EDUCATION

White men traditionally have had by far the highest rates of college attendance and graduation. For both men and women, social class position was even more important than one's academic performance in high school as an influence on attending college. With the college diploma increasingly defined as the minimum educational credential for entering middle-class occupations, rates of enrollment in two-year (community or junior) colleges and in bachelor's-level programs climbed throughout the second half of the twentieth century. In previous generations, the high school diploma was sufficient for many white-collar jobs. Economic trends (discussed in the next chapter), such as the sharp decrease in well-paid blue-collar work, have severely reduced the options for those leaving school after twelfth grade. In periods of high unemployment, people often choose to return to or continue their education to improve their chance for success in a very competitive labor market.

Social class of parents is related to attending college in both direct and indirect ways. Mediocre students can attend college if their families are able to support the costs and if they can do without contributions from the student to the household's income. When sending a family member to college is possible, but very difficult, making the necessary sacrifices may depend on the perception that a college degree will increase future earnings.

Social class is also associated with the type of college attended. Students with parents in higher income categories are more likely to be in four-year colleges, rather than in two-year colleges. Within four-year colleges, there are widely known distinctions of rank and prestige. Children from wealthy families are far more likely to attend elite colleges than are other students of similar levels of academic achievement. The ability to live in a school district with high rates of admission to elite schools is tied to economic position; obviously, the ability to send a child to a private ("feeder")high school with traditional, informal ties to particular institutions is financially based.

An important, although often overlooked, impact of colleges is the type of job network to which the college can provide access. Most jobs in the United States are found informally, for example, through kin, friends, colleagues, former roommates, teammates, or fraternity brothers. Because elite colleges have been sex-integrated for more than twenty years, some women have greater access to such networks than in the past. But, many college activities also tend to be segregated by sex, race-ethnicity, and social class. Thus, the elite degree, although an important asset, does not assure that all graduates from elite institutions will be members of elite informal networks, some of which remain closed to people of one sex or the other.

All population groups have had increased rates of college attendance, but the rates for students of color and white women have increased more than those of white men. In 2006-2007, 57 percent of people receiving bachelor's degrees were women (U. S. Department of Education 2009). Women have also been the majority of degree earners within each major racial-ethnic category (Hacker 2003). The gender gap is greatest among African Americans; black men's college enrollment and graduation rates are significantly lower than black women's (Arenson 2003). As described earlier, school experiences are often negative for African American boys, whose behavior is more quickly constructed as more fundamentally troublesome than the same behavior from members of other population groups. Though not all experience the same degree of labeling, the cumulative effect of discouraging school experiences may be aggravated when few job opportunities are perceived to exist for college-educated African American males (Beattie 2002). The presidency of Barack Obama is expected by many to have an impact on the aspirations and expectations of young African Americans (particularly males).

Although better educated workers may not be more useful for the actual performance of a job, credentials are a convenient way to limit the type of applicants who are considered.

The need for more specific credentials (for example, a degree from the employer's alma mater) may further limit access to some jobs and serve as an informal way to limit upward mobility. For example, a job may be advertised in a newspaper or trade publication, but often is also listed at only selected colleges' career service offices. Applications from such institutions may be far more likely to lead to interviews and job offers.

In many immigrant families, gender remains an important determinant of where a child will be sent or allowed to go to college. In ethnic groups that are protective of daughters, commuting to college may be the only option for women, yet men are permitted to go away to college. In addition, gendered expectations about the kinds of work the student will eventually do, and the relative importance of employment, affects a family's willingness to invest in the costs of education. If a daughter is expected to work sporadically, while mainly raising a family, there is less reason to finance her education than that of a son, who is expected to pursue a career as his top priority.

However, investing in a daughter's college was traditionally associated with investing in her marriage options. Attending an institution with more affluent students enhanced her opportunities to meet, date, and marry a relatively affluent man. Marriage options also influence college choice for families concerned about their children, especially daughters, marrying within their religious or ethnic group, or both.

Teacher training and home economics were the leading choices of major by women college students before the women's movement. Consistent with essentialist views of women's special capacities, these majors may justify women's higher education to people who question any need to invest time in women's education beyond high school. Traditional views of these fields conform to the gender hierarchy; women students are being prepared to serve in traditionally female professions, with generally little or no opportunity for upward mobility. They are preparing to use their nurturing and home-tending abilities, although for people outside the home. Even if they do not work outside the home, advanced training in these fields will enable them to enhance their performance as wives and mothers. As we saw in Chapter Two, Mormon women recently attending a public university explained their pursuit of higher education with these justifications. When students evaluate the usefulness of getting a college education, men are likely to focus exclusively on their job prospects, but women are likely to assess the effect on their family role performance as well (Mickelson 2003). Women's college attendance choice is less affected by their apparent occupational payoff than is men's, except for men from relatively high social class families (Beattie 2002).

Simultaneously, the study of traditionally female-identified fields legitimates women's movement into college and thus gives them access to a wide range of other ideas and experiences. Thus, the potentially libratory impact of higher education is, to some extent, available along with training in the most traditional of women's vocations. The initial development of these fields on the college level was instrumental in elevating the entire occupations for which they trained women. Teachers with college degrees had more social standing than less educated teachers. Among black women in the early twentieth-century South, domestic servants who had been formally trained in home economics could experience some improvement in the kinds of work they might find (Rushing 2002).

College campuses expose students to a widened range of ideas and experiences. Preparing people for the most prized jobs in society, colleges and universities potentially affect individual beliefs through curricular experiences as well as other organized and informal activities on campus. Contrasting views of higher education construct it as a site for reproducing the society's stratification system or, alternatively, a site for broadening views and creating or developing challenges to hegemonic ideological justifications for inequality. The persistence of both views reflects the simultaneous validity of both constructions. For example, Kane and Kyyro (2001) report that greater amounts of formal education are generally associated with rejection of segregation and rejection of victim blaming, but not with increased recognition of the existence of discrimination or increased approval of remedies such as affirmative action.

Curricular and pedagogical change have been spearheaded for more than forty years by feminist scholars on faculty and among graduate students. For example, at the 1970 national conference of the American Historical Association, feminists criticized the typical treatment accorded women by historical researchers, charging the discipline with either ignoring women completely or negatively stereotyping them (Evans 2003). The first women's studies courses were offered at the end of the 1960s, and organized programs proliferated throughout the 1970s. Interdisciplinary women's studies programs are often more supportive of feminist scholarship than the discipline-based home departments in which many feminist professors are employed.

Because feminist scholars commonly see activism as part of their feminism, women's studies faculty are likely to work for change, or for the protection against the undoing of equity achievements, on their campuses. Their relatively high visibility made them a central target of the national attack on *political correctness* ("PC"), which exploded in 1990. The mass media widely repeated accusations that campuses were oppressive of conservatives in their communities, for example, people critical of affirmative action, women's studies, or policies to promote nonracist, nonsexist, and nonhomophobic language and behavior. These reports grew despite the small percentage of campuses for which there was any evidence of such incidents. In contrast, the larger numbers of documented problems of racism, sexism, and homophobia were underreported in the media (Evans 2003). This socially constructed "fact" of national domination of campuses by an intolerant left continues to persist.

As you read this account, you may assume it is false or inaccurate, so thoroughly has the claim that PC is a widespread phenomenon been integrated into what we take for granted as real. Returning to the challenge raised in the discussion of "knowledge professionals" in Chapter Two, what procedures can we follow to find out if the charges of "political correctness" are accurate or inflated? Students often dismiss claims in assigned readings or lectures as wrong, but assume that challenging the teacher would be risky, and would not be worth the effort. What counts as evidence has become even more complicated as people turn to the Internet for instant answers, often without paying attention to the sources of materials they find, especially if these are consistent with their beliefs about what is true.

## FIELDS OF STUDY

We still find many students making traditional major and career choices, even though more children than ever are brought up in families espousing nontraditional gender ideologies and schools increasingly integrate their courses. Although academic areas of concentration are not as sex-segregated as they used to be, women and men often

**Table 5.1  Bachelor's Degrees Awarded in the United States 2006–2007, in Selected Fields.**
Women and men often specialize in different areas in college. Information grouped in broad categories masks differences within particular fields. For example, whereas the social sciences and history have roughly equal sex representation, economics and sociology do not.

| Selected Fields of Study | Percentage of Degrees awarded to | |
| --- | --- | --- |
| | Men | Women |
| Architecture and related programs | 56% | 44% |
| Biological sciences and biomedical sciences | 40% | 60% |
| Computer and information sciences | 81% | 19% |
| Education | 21% | 79% |
| Engineering | 82% | 18% |
| English language and literature | 32% | 68% |
| Foreign languages, literatures, and linguistics | 30% | 70% |
| Mathematics and statistics | 56% | 44% |
| Psychology | 23% | 77% |
| Social sciences and history | 50% | 50% |
|     Economics | 70% | 30% |
|     Sociology | 30% | 70% |

Source: U.S. Department of Education, National Center for Educational Statistics. 2009. *Digest of Educational Statistics 2008*. Washington, DC: Government Printing Office, Table 275, "Bachelor's master's, and doctor's degrees conferred by degree-granting institutions, by sex of student and discipline division. 2006–2007." ✦

specialize in different areas in college. These differences are not always obvious, because information is often grouped in broad categories, masking sex and racial-ethnic imbalance among particular fields. For example, while the category "social sciences and history" has roughly equal sex representation, the categories of economics and sociology do not (see Table 5.1). Despite the fact that U.S. women are pursuing higher education in ever-greater numbers and now earn more than half even of doctoral degrees, women continue to be underrepresented in mathematics, physical sciences, and engineering.

Although there is a large defection among both men and women who start college with a plan to major in these traditionally male-dominated fields, men are more likely to persist in such majors than are women of similar ability levels (Parelius 1991; Lee 2002; England and Li 2006). Asian Americans are the only racial-ethnic group without a large gender gap in these fields. The loss of human resources has led to extensive government investigation of this gap. There has also been some government support for the development of programs to overcome both the gender gap and the persistent underrepresentation of African Americans, Latinos/as, and Native Americans. Rather than ever-popular explanations based on sex differences in cognitive strengths, current studies emphasize the effect of cultural differences among programs, with a friendlier climate more typical in social sciences and the humanities than in mathematics, physical sciences, and engineering (Lee 2002). Within the sciences, institutions and departments vary in their record of educating women; organizational approaches to improving the retention of women students, rather than a focus on the characteristics of individual students, are central to success (Fox, Sonnert, and Nikiforova 2009).

Choice of major is also influenced by social class. Students from working-class and poor families are more likely than other students to choose programs with clear vocational application. Upper-middle-class students are freer to choose "liberal arts" majors, with the financially realistic expectation that they can later pursue a vocationally oriented master's degree.

Although women now receive the majority of all doctorates earned by U.S. citizens (Smallwood 2003), they remain underrepresented in some fields. Graduate student women are even less likely than undergraduates to study engineering, computer science, mathematics, and physics. This underrepresentation is popularly explained by referring to some biologically based differences in females' aptitudes, despite a growing research literature to the contrary (Hyde and Mertz 2009). At the undergraduate level, women are made to feel like outsiders in the "chilly climate" of many science and technology classrooms and programs, in which informal group work with peers is enormously helpful for survival.

Research clearly identifies aspects of organizational culture and social structure within these areas of higher education that perpetuate this pattern (Fox 2001). For example, among the highest-ranked departments in the United States, women faculty are underrepresented in entry-level appointments, promotions, and tenure in these fields. In other words, while they earn disproportionately few doctorates, an even lower percentage of positions are filled by women than doctoral degrees are earned by women (Lewin 2004). This difference may be hidden by the "revolving door" by which a department regularly replaces some people from underrepresented groups with new hires from those groups; a percentage of members of those groups appears to indicate integration, but omits the reality that time in the department is limited and fraught with the knowledge that others who have gone before have not been retained. Several leading institutions (e.g., M.I.T.) have sponsored inquiries into the sex (in)equity within the faculty, identifying material problems, such as less space for women's experimental work, and smaller budgets for their essential instruments and materials. The lower rates of retention of women faculty have indirect effects as well; doctoral students are less willing to work on a research team if they perceive its leader as a less-than-permanent member of the program.

### SEXUAL HARASSMENT IN EDUCATION

As a result of activism during the women's movement, women started to work against sexual harassment rather than taking it for granted as a difficult fact of life; through the consciousness-raising groups in which many participated (see Chapter Seven), women shared stories of experiences that previously they had been too embarrassed to discuss with anyone. It continues to be a charged issue in public discussions, in part because of the differing ways people perceive or evaluate similar behaviors, and in part because harassment is often invisible to (and thus charges of it are not credited by) nonvictims. Some men are concerned that they might have false charges placed against them. People who have experienced harassment are afraid of being blamed for their victimization, being told that somehow they must have invited the offending behavior. By avoiding open discussion of harassment, the development of a consensus about its meaning has been slow, and research on its prevalence has used mixed definitions and measurements.

The legal definition of **sexual harassment** includes three levels: gender harassment, unwanted sexual attention, and sexual coercion. As research has begun to accumulate, it is clear that many kinds of harassment are common in school life.

Most attention to harassing behavior before college has looked at peer-on-peer harassing. Though both girls and boys experience harassment, that experienced by girls is more frequent and more severe; further, girls are less likely than boys to be harassers; girls also consider harassing actions more harmful, on average, than boys do (Hand and Sanchez 2000).

In higher education, there has been more attention to the ways in which faculty may harass their students (at the undergraduate and graduate levels). Some verbal harassment may function to discourage students from remaining in a class. However, if harassment comes from one's major professor, leaving is costly. "Putting up with" harassment may make doing one's best work difficult. The most serious form of harassment is *quid pro quo*—the victim is expected to give something (a date, or sexual intimacy) to get something (a grade, a letter of recommendation, or a job).

The wide range of seriousness among the levels, from being subjected to sexist jokes in a class to being sexually coerced, helps explain the lack of consensus when people share perceptions of the frequency of harassment. One study of harassment in higher education found that a large minority of both men and women students, with similar proportions within sex for various racial-ethnic groups, reported an experience falling within the definition of gender harassment (for example, hearing sexist remarks from the professor in class), although not all students used that label for their experience (Kalof et al. 2001).

Educational institutions have established formal policies for handling harassment charges. Because of the great power disparity between students and faculty, however, many students choose not to pursue formal charges. As in any case of accused misconduct, it is necessary to protect the rights of the accused, but procedures established to do so may be interpreted as making it impossible for the accusation to be fairly heard.

## AFFIRMATIVE ACTION IN EDUCATIONAL INSTITUTIONS

Affirmative action has been the focus of perhaps the most passionate arguments related to women's rights. It requires that employers and educational institutions pursue action to affirmatively improve the representation of women and racial-ethnic minority groups among their workers and students. Although evidence clearly shows that reverse discrimination (against whites and men) has rarely occurred, the perception that it is common is widespread among whites, particularly among white men (see Reskin 1998 for a thorough review of the research). White women have been the largest group benefiting from affirmative action policy, despite the popular conception among whites that affirmative action is largely about race, rather than sex.

The most recent criticisms of affirmative action have emphasized the plight of poor and working-class white men and women in U.S. society. They propose to replace race and sex with an income measure to better identify those people who should have preferences extended to them in employment and educational decisions. While addressing social class inequality makes sense, these proposals generally argue for removing race and sex, arguing that when individuals come from economically comfortable families they do not experience racism and sexism in ways that will harm their access to equal opportunity. Unfortunately, sufficient evidence exists to show that biased treatment has limiting effects on minorities and white women of all social class positions.

### EMPLOYMENT IN SCHOOLS, COLLEGES, AND UNIVERSITIES

Educational employment has been a mix of remarkable change and stability since the beginning of the women's movement in the late 1960s. Including administrators and teachers at all levels, more than 6 million people had professional jobs in education in 2003 (U.S. Department of Labor 2004). One major shift has been the change in career paths of women who would, before the women's movement, have chosen to become educators. With the opening up of other professional and managerial jobs, the selection of education has become less common among the academically strongest women students (Postrel 2004).

The distribution of women and men in educational jobs has changed dramatically in the last forty years. Female administrators are far more common than they were before the legal and procedural challenges of the second wave of the women's movement. In the mid-1970s, for example, less than 5 percent of school systems had female superintendents. Principals and assistant principals were also very likely to be male. In the 1999–2000 school year, in contrast, 44 percent of principals in public elementary, middle, and secondary schools were women. Of private school principals (who are generally lower paid than public school principals), 55 percent were women (N.E.A Research 2003). Of all full-time educational administrators—including college administrators, school district managers, and assistant principals as well as principals—almost two thirds were men in 2008 (U.S. Department of Labor 2009); further, the average woman administrator's income was only 75 percent that of the average man's (2003). Leadership in teachers' unions (affiliates of the National Education Association and of the American Federation of Teachers) was, likewise, disproportionately male until recently.

The percentage of female teachers and administrators is highest in the youngest grades. Some of the historical differences in educational employment were actually legally mandated. For example, until 1968 New York City did not permit men to be licensed as kindergarten or first-grade teachers. The unspoken reasons for the ban were probably the belief that normal men could not be sufficiently nurturant to meet small children's needs and would not want to teach small children, so the normality of those who would want to was questionable. In fact, even in 2007, men were less than 2 percent of preschool and kindergarten teachers.

Men who choose to teach young children continue to face informal challenges to their masculinity and their professional ability. Their occupational choice, in itself, implies that they do not adhere to a hegemonic masculinity, yet they are expected to serve as role models for the boys they teach. Those who are also parents must avoid the nurturing behaviors they perform at home, lest they be suspected to be pedophiles. There is no version of masculinity that satisfies all the demands they face. To defuse concerns about their masculinity (in particular their heterosexuality, because homosexuality is frequently presumed to incorporate pedophilia), men who teach early grades spend time and take great care to present themselves as appropriate. To meet the children's needs for warmth and nurturance, these men develop alternative techniques, such as enthusiastic greetings, the generous giving of kudos for student accomplishments, and the verbal comforting of students in need. The men's role performance is under more intense scrutiny than women teachers'. Thus, men are simultaneously pressed to prove that they are just like their women peers (e.g., not sexually motivated) and to craft different ways of teaching and interacting with adults to avoid behaving in ways associated with deviance in males (Sargent 2001).

Male teachers also have to devote energy to negotiating their relationships with administrators and other teachers. They may be pressed to take on disproportionate amounts of extra work activities that are traditionally male-defined (such as working with electronic equipment). Female peers may distrust their commitment to teaching, assuming that men plan to move out of the classroom quickly. This lowers the level of interaction with their peers, limiting an important source of professional information and contributing to feelings of social isolation. Although some men in female-dominated professions are eager to move into supervisory positions, and may find themselves on a "glass escalator" upwards (Williams 1992), those who do not want to move up are often stigmatized for their commitment to a woman-defined field (Sargent 2001).

In the elementary and middle school grades, men are slowly increasing their proportion of the teaching staff (19 percent in 2007); women earned, on average, 90 percent of what men were paid. Nevertheless, faculties are still disproportionately female, and schools are among the few places with women regularly in charge. The grouchy old maid stereotype may be a thing of the past, but popular discussions of boyhood continue to reflect that women teachers unfairly single out boys more than girls for bad behavior. In the classroom, a woman teacher shows that women can have authority, but children also notice teachers' interactions with each other and with administrators. The gender system within which educators function simultaneously affects professionals' lives and serves as a model for children of gender in the workplace. Teachers and administrators also reproduce and communicate gender through their own enactments with one another.

High school teachers have a similar wage disparity (women earn 91 percent of men's average income). By high school, teachers are more apt to be perceived publicly as subject area specialists rather than people who are simply good with children. In the United States in 2007, 56 percent of secondary school teachers were women. Further, starting in high school there is a pronounced gendered division of subject matter, with women teachers underrepresented in mathematics, technology, and the sciences (parallel to student choice of majors, as described in Fields of Study earlier in this chapter). This pattern becomes more extreme as the level of institution rises to colleges and graduate-degree-granting departments.

The more prestigious the college or university, and the academic department, the lower the proportion of women faculty. The proportion of females in a department at any one moment also can understate the inequities in employment, because of the "revolving door" described previously, in the section on Fields of Study. Meanwhile, the department seems to have achieved some degree of integration, because there is always some female presence on its faculty.

Women were 46 percent of all postsecondary teachers in 2007, but they were disproportionately employed in part-time and temporary work. Of all those employed full-time, the women's average income was only 78 percent of the men's average income (U.S. Department of Labor 2008). In the next chapter, we will explore the range of explanations that scholars offer for the continuing failure to fully integrate occupations and professions and specially areas within them.

As the use of electronic technologies has increased in educational settings, the same gendering found in the technology workplace is performed in front of students. As Jenson and Rose found when they studied computers in Canadian schools, there is often a perpetuation of traditionally gendered tasks even among technology specialists (2003). For example, a sex-integrated technology teaching team made a presentation at a technology conference. The more technical presentations (about hardware and software) were made by men, and women made the less technical ones (such as a theoretical discussion of computers and pedagogy). Men in sex-integrated technology groups often interact in traditional patterns (for example, interrupting women speakers). When the men do not use the social skills that might facilitate the group's productivity, those who have such skills (often women) find their social skills are acknowledged, and they perceive themselves acquiescing for the sake of the group's effectiveness. Often, as in this case, women do acquiesce to their assignment.

### GENDER AND ATHLETICS

Athletics in school has long been an important site of individual development. Sports become more organized and formalized as children get older. Teams are formed in classes and as school-sponsored, extracurricular activities. Girls' and women's participation in sports has radically expanded from its level before the beginning of the women's movement.

An important change in athletic opportunities for female students came with the 1972 passage of the Higher Education Act. Title IX is the section of that act that orders equal access to sports in public schools and colleges. This section has been one of the most energetically disputed pieces of legislation concerning girls' lives. Both cultural and social structural traditions were threatened by Title IX. For example, it threatened traditional beliefs in the relative weakness and passivity of females by assuming they would and could take advantage of equal opportunities in sports.

Although most of those beliefs have become outdated, the social structural obstacles are still significant, because of the measure's impact on schools' and colleges' budgets. Though some additional monies might be given to girls' and women's teams, athletic budgets are not doubled. Therefore, to achieve equity some spending on men's teams must be reduced.

Athletic programs and their achievements may affect a school's financial support from alumni and legislators. Leaders of schools are reluctant to cut budgets of teams that bring in money (in some cases from contracts with sports broadcasters). This combines with most administrators' continued belief that women's sports do not have many fans. In fact, most institutions' men's teams lose money (Zimbalist 2000). And, the enormous positive reaction to the U.S. women's soccer team in the 1999 World Cup contest made sports enthusiasts rethink the potential audience for women's sports.

Inequities continue in terms of which sports are open to each sex, and the quality of coaching, equipment, uniforms, and physical facilities assigned to boys' and to girls' teams. As women's teams came to be viewed more seriously, coaching women's teams became a more attractive, better paid job. Like the aftermath of the racial integration of public schools, when many African American teachers were refused employment in formerly white schools, many women coaches found themselves closed out of coaching jobs for newly reputable women's teams.

The ways in which athletics and opportunities for participation in them are gendered have serious implications for the development of both females and males. The involvement of preadolescent and adolescent girls in organized sports contributes to the development of a strong, positive self-image. Girls who participate in sports tend to do well academically. Thus, the goal of equitable athletic opportunities for girls has broader consequences than does sports achievement alone. Women of color who participate in sports at majority-white colleges and universities find that their teams (typically more integrated than their other activities) provide a space where they are able to assert their racial identity (Stratta 2003). Although cheerleading squads also offer a physically demanding team experience, calling it a sport is controversial. If it were accorded the status of "sport," there would be greater respect given to the participants in it (Grindstaff and West 2006).

Athletic boys and men of color are able to achieve hegemonic masculinity through participation in school and college sports. In their study of Latinos and Latinas in college, Barajas and Pierce (2001) found that athletically outstanding boys found their sports participation helped connect them to other aspects, including the academics, of their secondary school experiences. For example, some were mentored by supportive coaches, who encouraged them in their academic pursuits as well.

In colleges and universities with highly competitive athletic programs, varsity participation may be a way to get to college for poor and working-class men, but is associated with lower academic achievement than the potential indicated by those students' earlier academic performance. In schools with less professionalized varsity sports, participation in athletics does not generally have this negative impact. Unfortunately, as women's sports have become more professionalized in higher education (related to Title IX), the negative effect on recruited men has become more common among women who are recruited to a college on the basis of their athletic abilities (Bowen and Levin 2003).

Women and gay men continue to be outsiders in many collegiate sports settings. At one university where women worked as trainers with men's varsity teams, they were never performing as professionals who happened to be women. Their sex was central to their identities, and they had to use their energy and attention to manage their gender identities in ways acceptable to the team members (Walk 2000). Although Title IX may give women's teams the formal right to share facilities with men's teams, informal struggles for access and for respect can be ongoing. An unanticipated benefit is the strengthened group feeling of the women's team members and an increased awareness of the need to struggle for sex equity. Even if the team's claim for equal resources becomes accepted, however, the heightened feminist sensibility may be lost in following years, in which new teammates do not realize that their resources were not automatically granted (Pelak 2002).

Gay men (as discussed in Chapter Three) must deal with homophobia among male athletes, and many gay and lesbian athletes outside of school settings have chosen to form or join same-sex teams and leagues so they can enjoy athleticism without having to face down the hegemonic hostility toward them (Pronger 2000).

Social class and racial-ethnic positions have a major impact on the transition from participating in athletics in the school years to thinking about pursuing athletics as a career. The decisions made by successful amateur athletes both reflect and influence young men's shaping of their masculine self-definitions (Messner 1989). Athletic prowess is a significant source of masculine identity throughout the culture, but some men abandon it as their primary source of masculinity sooner than others. Differences in pursuing or abandoning athletic achievement reflect the tremendous variation in opportunities for establishing masculinity, rather than any difference in cultural values or beliefs about masculinity. Good athletes whose social class backgrounds provide other reliable opportunities for economic success were more likely than players from lower-status backgrounds to let go of their athletic sources of self-esteem while they were still performing well.

## SUMMARY

Children spend a large portion of their lives in schooling, where they actively do as well as learn gender. The peer group, friendships, teachers, and formal and informal schoolwide rules shape these experiences. Children's experiences differ to some extent because of their varied combinations of racial-ethnic, class, and sex identities. As adults, their lives will be affected by the kinds of experiences they had and the credentials that they earned.

Extensive change in the educational system followed from the women's movement. Academic and athletic programs opened to girls and women, and employment patterns for women and men in education also changed. Curricular and pedagogical innovations were introduced to overcome traditional patterns of gendered education in the formal and informal curricula. Some aspects (such as the employment of men as early childhood educators, the homophobia of organized athletics, and the study by women of engineering and the physical sciences) have been much slower to change. Formal governmental policies, particularly addressed to equal employment and educational opportunity and to affirmative action, have been crucial factors in the changes that have taken place.

We turn next to gender in the economy and at work, having had an introduction through a brief view of work in the educational institution. As we shall see, the rapidly changing economy of the last several decades has made the educational credentials of workers, both female and male, more important than ever in affecting whether they secure desirable or even adequate employment.

## DISCUSSION QUESTION

1. Imagine that you have just started to teach the first grade. What kinds of arrangements (rules, physical layout of your classroom, projects, parental involvement, group structures) would you create to help each student get the most out of the class? Explain how each of your plans is connected to what we know about individual development, in general, and educational settings, in particular.
2. Reflect on how the behavior and interactions in each course you are now taking are related (if at all) to the sex and race-ethnicity of the teacher and of the students. Do you think your own behavior is related to these aspects of your self? What might you get out of the course if you behaved differently in it?
3. You have been selected to lead a national task force to reduce the gendering of students' choice of majors, as illustrated in Table 5.1. Develop a plan with both cultural and social structural features, and explain how and why you think it will work. ◆

# CHAPTER 6

# The Economy and Work

An individual's links to the economy have crucial influences on many aspects of the quality of that person's life: Political power, material well-being, access to educational opportunities, and even length of life are closely tied to one's position in the stratification system. So, too, is the ability to set one's offspring on the road to economic well-being. A household based on kinship involves economic interdependence: Individuals who themselves earn no money are usually connected to the economy through others in their home. Children's economic position is initially the same as the adults with whom they live, and because of the importance of class position, parents typically do all they can to assist their children's future economic status. For those with "something to lose," decisions are made with an eye to maintaining all current advantages. For those low in the economic hierarchy, decisions are made in the hopes of improving the children's opportunities. Obviously, decisions are made among choices that are perceived as possible, or realistic.

Because work has been central to definitions of masculinity, changing opportunities for economic participation have significant implications for men's identities. Before industrialization, many men were self-employed or worked in family enterprises (farms or workshops), in which most women worked as well. Industrialization meant that most men became subordinate to an unrelated "boss" at work. In addition, few men now have jobs with demands for physical strength, which used to be a common way to establish one's masculinity. Indeed, in the late nineteenth and early twentieth centuries, technological and organizational changes throughout society led to a crisis in the cultural definitions of masculinity and required a revisioning of the justifications of patriarchy.

Over the last several decades, in each stage of the life course, men and women have come to share similar labor force participation rates, as Figure 6.1 illustrates. They have also shared the experience of living with radically changing employment possibilities. During the late 1960s and early 1970s, wives' and mothers' employment outside the home became increasingly acceptable even in the absence of economic hardship. By the end of the twentieth century, young women found it hard to believe that being employed could threaten any definition of femininity. To understand how gender is related to the economy, and how that has changed, we need first to review the enormous changes that have occurred in the last several decades.

### THE NEW POLITICAL ECONOMY

The dynamic nature of the economy came to national attention in the 1980s with an awareness of the loss of U.S. dominance globally, the changing structure of the job market, and the increasingly "high-tech" character of work. The changes in the economy have been as significant as changes in cultural beliefs in the process of shaping the relation of gender to individuals' economic participation and to gendered arrangements within families and households. In the early 1970s, OPEC (the Organization of Petroleum Exporting Countries) took an aggressive stance toward the amounts and prices of oil that it would make available to importing countries, including the United States. Oil shortages and skyrocketing fuel costs contributed to the development of economic **stagflation**, or low growth but high inflation rates. In the following years, U.S. corporations increasingly became transnational, rather than legally and physically located only in this country. Manufacturing jobs, particularly those in unionized industries, were exported to low-wage regions of the United States and the world. Corporations also sought locations with fewer government regulations (e.g., of polluting industrial processes and of occupational hazards to workers) to increase their profits and thus the dividends they could pay to those people participating in the stock market. Well-paid jobs held by men disappeared, and inflation raised the price tag for maintaining a household's existing standard of living. As a result, women's employment outside the home became crucial to a growing number of families.

Starting with the "Reagan revolution" of the 1980s, corporate mergers and takeovers occurred at the highest rate of the twentieth century. Either closing down competitors or combining their equivalent departments (such as sales or engineering) led to a significant loss of jobs. Thus, employers gained considerable leverage in the demands they could make on employees, and many corporations laid off large portions of their workforce. Those who remained were expected to work longer and harder, and they usually did so in hopes of keeping their jobs. Despite increased economic productivity, wages did not increase. **Downsizing** is the process of cutting the size of a corporation's workforce, but not its profits. In addition to relaxed federal policies regarding mergers, a number of corporate changes shaped the cutbacks in human resources. For example, positions were eliminated through the automation of both factory and office jobs (spurred by the newly developed computer microchip). Continuing a decades-long pattern, businesses transferred tasks from paid employees to consumers (e.g., entering one's account number on the telephone before or instead of speaking to a customer service employee). As mergers and takeovers reduced

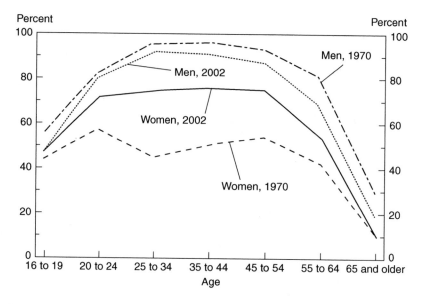

**Figure 6.1 Labor Force Participation Patterns Over the Life Course Have Become More Similar for Men and Women**
Source: U.S. Department of Labor, Bureau of Labor Statistics. 2003. Figure 5, "Women's Labor Force Participation Patterns Are Now More Like Those of Men." In "Women at Work: A Visual Essay." *Monthly Labor Review* 126 (October): 45–50, 48.

competition, the quality and quantity of customer services also could be reduced. These reductions led to further job loss. Finally, a reduction of federal involvement in corporate practices (such as occupational safety regulations and consumer protections) reduced the kinds and numbers of jobs required to ensure compliance with such regulations.

The labor market has also changed as immigration to the United States has surged, bringing people from Asia, Latin America, and Eastern Europe. New workers come from a wide range of educational and social class backgrounds, affecting the labor markets in places where they relocate. They often perform jobs for which there is a shortage of U.S. workers, but sometimes crowd a labor market and allow employers to hire at lower wages because of worker surpluses. Immigrant women tend to hold jobs at very high rates compared with other groups of women. The multiracial composition of the new immigration adds complexity to the intersection of race, class, and gender. It also contributes to the rate at which the U.S. population is becoming more racially and ethnically diverse, with projections that only a minority of the population will be white within the next few decades. Certainly, political decisions will begin to reflect the changing composition of the electorate, having some effect on the inequalities currently associated with racial-ethnic identities.

In the 1990s, the economy underwent a major expansion, with a fast growth in jobs. Skilled workers were in demand in many occupations. Starting in 2001, and escalating after the attacks of September 11, unemployment returned to high levels that had not been seen since early in the 1990s. Even during the expansion, however, the fastest growing jobs were those at the low end of the hierarchy. Wages in this sector did rise during the expansion, but not as rapidly as pay for jobs at the top of the employment scale. And, although most people who are "dislocated" (by corporate moves abroad, mergers, or downsizing) do find work within a year, on the average their new jobs pay less and are otherwise less desirable than the jobs they have lost. Older workers are particularly likely to lose work and to have trouble finding new jobs, partly because of age discrimination. The economic boom of the mid-to late 1990s left out a large minority of individuals, who dropped even further below the average than they were already (e.g., Kilborn and Clemetson 2002). Similarly, these low-end jobs rarely provide health care coverage. The lack of health care coverage continues to motivate people to use welfare (Edin and Lein 1997). In 2009, the controversial issue of how to organize health care financing moved to center stage in the U.S. Congress. The outcome of this political struggle (unknown at this writing) will have many implications, including whether the newly shaped approach removes the incentive of remaining on welfare to have some health care protection.

The Aid to Families with Dependent Children program (AFDC, or what most people referred to as welfare) was ended in 1997 after sixty years. Marking a fundamental shift in the governmental policy approach toward families living in poverty, AFDC was replaced by a far more frugal system. In the Temporary Assistance to Needy Families program (TANF), the federal government sets strict limits on both a single episode of need (two-year maximum) and for an individual's lifetime (five-year maximum). The new system forces parents to accept any work they can find. For those who receive public assistance and can find no job, there is usually a workfare requirement. If a recipient has a child over a year old, the agency is supposed to provide child care. This puts pressure on an already inadequate child care system. In 1999, New York State failed to use a substantial portion of its federally funded child care allocation, because there were too few openings compared with the demand (Sengupta 1999).

With a workfare requirement, people must do assigned jobs to receive a stipend typically below the federal minimum wage. While receiving welfare, people are doing jobs that might otherwise be available to the overall labor market (e.g., cleaning city parks, enabling the city to decrease the number of park workers paid a higher wage). When they approach the time limit, or even earlier, individuals are forced by the new and punitive procedures into taking very poorly paid work. This depresses the prevailing wages in their area, thus having a negative impact on semiskilled or unskilled workers who have not received welfare.

In other words, the public systems for connecting unemployed individuals to the economy negatively affect the employment situation of people who have been in the labor force all along. In addition, although immigrants generally have not displaced workers from desirable jobs, their availability has expanded the labor supply, which helps to keep wages low even in a booming economy. Finally, the boom boomeranged for those who became homeless, as the competition for housing among the affluent removed many previously affordable units from the price range of the working poor.

The increasingly rapid decline in the U.S. and the world economy in the fall of 2008 affected many dimensions of work and family life. Housing foreclosures affect the shelter of renters, whose landlords lose their property, as well as homeowners themselves. The unemployment rate rose quickly, and many people who kept their jobs experienced losses in income and benefits. Early in 2009, the U.S. government undertook enormous economic interventions, including a "stimulus package" putting funds in the hands of governmental and nongovernmental entities.

The impact of these initiatives depends in large part on the decisions and actions of state and local governments, non-U.S. governments, large and small private employers, and individuals. For example, if some federal funds are available to states for use on bridge repairs, the states will plan how they will use the funds. Which bridges will be repaired? If bridges are targeted that are far from populations of color, the beneficiaries of these jobs will disproportionately be white workers. Which companies will win the contracts to do the work? Are they companies with a strong program of zero tolerance for sexual harassment on the job, or are they companies with no women workers? Will work be done around the clock? If so, will workers have rotating shifts, which make arranging child care particularly difficult?

Other kinds of changes that affect gendered arrangements in the family are also likely, and also hard to predict. For example, there may be increased availability of paid child care offered by women who have lost better paid employment. If the cost of child care and the ease of finding it change, this will affect the employment choices of parents, particularly women. The impact of these changes and the uncertainty about future economic security on household arrangements is unfolding in unpredictable ways. The greater our understanding of the fundamental interrelationships among different dimensions of social life, the better able we will be to understand the implications of varied policy and personal decisions.

## IDEOLOGY AND THE ECONOMY

It is hard to convince people that economic opportunities are gendered and that social treatment depending on one's sex is interrelated with categorization by race, ethnicity, and social class. The difficulty lies in the strong belief that people control their own destinies, a central tenet of U.S. ideology. In this view, people *should* have different rewards if they have made different efforts. In particular, it is popularly believed that the more formal education one has completed, and the more work experience one has accumulated, the better off a person will be economically. Although education does, on the average, raise a person's earnings, disparities exist between men and women at all educational levels. Moreover, for both sexes, at each educational level the average earnings of whites are higher than those of blacks and Hispanics (Institute for Women's Policy Research 2008).

Despite evidence to the contrary, it is similarly believed that anyone who is willing to work can be self-supporting. During the Reagan presidency, in fact, this belief was often expressed by the leader of the country. For example, Reagan asserted that homelessness was nonexistent—a fantasy as patently unreal to those with homes as to those without in most American cities. Eventually, he did acknowledge that he was mistaken. Similarly, when problems of poverty and unemployment were raised, Reagan cited the number of pages of "help wanted" ads in the Washington papers. He ignored the fact that many of these positions either required credentials beyond the reach of most of the unemployed or would pay too little to bring a family above the poverty line. Such outright denial of people's limited control over reality can be understood among the successful, because these people are generally unwilling to attribute their success to luck or privilege. At extraordinary moments, when a local economy is hard hit by the closing of a major employer, or by a natural or social disaster (such as a hurricane or the destruction of the World Trade Center), people do recognize the limits of individual agency. Nonetheless, a good deal of evidence has clearly demonstrated that, in ordinary times, persistent economic inequality is associated with gender, race, ethnic group membership, and social class origins. As we see in the following sections, members of some social categories find it significantly easier than others to pull themselves up by their bootstraps.

### ECONOMIC OPPORTUNITIES AND GENDER

Clearly, people's economic lives are not completely determined by their sex, race-ethnicity, and childhood social class position. It is more accurate to think of the system as one in which individuals' probability of affecting their economic situation will vary depending on these characteristics. For example, a white, middle-class man has better odds of being well rewarded for his work than an equally hard-working member of one or more of the lower-status categories. These odds fluctuate with the condition of the economy (i.e., the benefits of some booms do reach many people). But, more fundamentally, these factors have varying relationships to particular aspects of economic well-being (see Browne and Misra 2003 on the varied impact of intersecting statuses associated with different aspects of one's employment). For example, one's *earnings* are influenced strongly by the combination of race and sex, but one's likelihood of being *unemployed* is much more influenced by race than by sex.

Most fundamentally, one's sex, social class, and race-ethnicity are related to whether or not one is considered to be in the labor force at all. To be a participant in the labor force means that a person is either employed or actively seeking work (unemployed). To qualify for unemployment insurance, for example, one must be formally labeled as actively seeking work. The status of others' participation is more difficult to classify. That is, new graduates or dropouts who are not receiving unemployment benefits and are not employed are not included in official unemployment statistics. Sophisticated federal research procedures give a *relatively* accurate labor force participation rate for the population, and for many specific subgroups. But they are seriously flawed for those who choose not to report their employment, such as those who are paid "under the table" (to avoid taxation or because of the employer's preference), those employed illegally, undocumented immigrants, people receiving benefits limited to the nonemployed, and individuals employed in illegal activities. However, these sources of inaccuracy are consistent over time (although their prevalence may not be), making the long-term comparisons of labor force participation fairly reliable. This allows us to get a picture of how the economy is doing and how various groups are faring, compared with one another and also compared with themselves at different points in time.

The participation of women in the workforce has increased steadily for more than fifty years. Only one third of all women between 25 and 64 years old were in the labor force in 1948 (early in the baby boom, when many women who had worked during World War II had returned home and were bearing and raising children full time). By

2008, 75.8 percent of women 25 to 54 years old and 59.1 percent of women 55 to 64 years old were in the labor force (U.S. Department of Labor 2009a). White married women born in the United States have traditionally had the lowest participation rate of all women. Although a majority of married women of color and immigrant women were also traditionally at home and not counted as "in the labor force," women from these groups were less free than white women to stay out of the labor market. Some immigrant groups were more likely than others to have women do home-based work, thus respecting a cultural belief that women should not be actively involved outside their home (Davidson and Gordon 1979). For example, some groups have been especially likely to start family-based businesses, in which all family members are put to work (see Rosen 1987). Women's employment sometimes served the goal of their family's upward mobility, often motivating migration to the United States (Amott and Matthaei 1991). The need for women of color and immigrant women to work for money to insure their families' subsistence reflected the lower wages paid to men of color and immigrant men compared with white men of equivalent skill levels. White, U.S. born women without employable husbands have also participated in the labor market traditionally. Finally, many women who were not counted as workers were in fact doing financially productive, unreported work. For instance, they prepared food for sale, raised chickens, sold eggs, did sewing and other textile work, and took in laundry.

The connection between women's family statuses and paid employment has changed profoundly in the last several decades. As illustrated in Figure 4.2, mothers are now far more likely to participate in the labor force. More generally, women's labor force participation is higher for those with more education, due at least in part to the growing significance of women's educational level for their earnings (England, Garcia-Beaulieu, and Ross 2004). Because white women's educational level is higher than that of African American and Latina women, it is not surprising that the racial-ethnic differences among married women have decreased. For example, in the twenty-year period from 1976 to 1996, white wives' labor force participation rates increased from 44.1 percent to 60.6 percent (U.S. Department of Commerce 1976; Jacobs 1997). Both African American and Hispanic wives had a smaller increase: 56.7 percent to 67.3 percent for African American wives and 41.6 percent to 52.5 percent for Hispanic wives. Indeed, the white pattern of labor force participation became more like the African American pattern (the 12.6 percent gap between the two groups' rates of 1976 shrank by half to 6.2 percent) and less like the Hispanic pattern (the 2.5 percent gap of 1976 grew to an 8.1 percent gap in 1996).

Both men and women of color are, and have historically been, less likely to be fully employed than white men and women who are in the labor force (Reid 2002). That is, they have been more likely to be out of work, to work fewer hours than they want to work, or to hold jobs for which they are actually overqualified. In contrast, until the 1970s white women were more likely than other people to simply stay out of the labor force if jobs were scarce; thus, their relatively low unemployment rates overstated the opportunities available. This has changed in the last forty years: Many unemployed white women, rather than opting out of paid employment in a bad market, define themselves as looking for work and are thus counted among the unemployed. This makes it more valid to include white women's unemployment rates in recent group comparisons.

White women share with women of color a pattern of significantly lower average earnings than men of the same racial or ethnic category, as indicated in Table 6.1. Historically, the higher pay for men's work was justified as a "family wage." That is, the earnings of the family's one wage earner were expected to provide also for his wife and children. Labor unions fought for and won acceptance of the concept of the family wage. Conversely, labor unions actively accepted low rates of pay for women. This contributed to the pattern of smaller earnings differences among groups of women than those *between* men and women.

Clearly, this model was never perfectly suited to reality because some working men had no economic dependents, and some working women did. Furthermore, not all working men were paid a family wage. Wage discrimination was routinely practiced against men of color and immigrant men (in contrast, women's earnings were more similar). Their wives were traditionally more likely to participate in the labor force than married, native-born white women. As the economic changes of the 1970s and 1980s unfolded, many of the men who formerly had earned a family wage found their pay devalued by inflation, pulling women into the labor force who had previously not needed to be employed.

Interrelationships among earnings and employment rates require detailed attention. For example, while African American men and white women's average full-time, year-round earnings are similar, African American men's higher unemployment means that they often do not work full time, year round. More complexities exist than even these comparisons show. Racial-ethnic categories include people from subgroups with distinctive economic experiences; for example, Cuban Americans' earnings are significantly higher and Puerto Ricans' are lower than most other Latinos' and Latinas' (Benitez 1998). Differences also appear depending on the particular age groups being examined.

When evidence is presented showing gender and racial-ethnic variations in economic position, the ideological response is to assert that these differences result from differences in people's educational levels. Although some people acknowledge inequalities in educational opportunities (related to one's family's economic position as well as to residential segregation by race), it is still popularly believed that those who overcome class-, race-, or gender-related obstacles, or all of these, to achieve educationally will have an equal economic outcome. Thus, employers are not seen as discriminating, but simply reacting to the differences in credentials among people, regardless of their category.

The evidence contradicts this view (Smith 2002; Reskin and Padavic 1994). Although differences in economic position among categories defined by gender and ethnicity are multidimensional and complex, gender continues to be a significant factor in people's economic experience. For example, the earnings gap among college graduates aged 25 to 34 is smaller than that of the 35-to 44-year-old group (women's median earnings were 83 percent of men's in the younger group, and 74 percent of men's in the older group) (Hecker 1998). This is consistent with previous findings that lower rates of promotion and pay raises for women gradually enlarge the gap between women's and men's earnings.

Rather than being produced by the differential treatment of individuals in similar jobs, many of the differences in earnings result from the continuing pattern of de facto occupational or job segregation by sex (Reskin and Padavic 1994). The **glass ceiling** is

**Table 6.1 Earnings and Unemployment Rates**

| | 2008 Weekly Income[*] | As a Percentage of | | | Unemployment Rate, 2008[**] |
| --- | --- | --- | --- | --- | --- |
| | | White Men's | White Women's | Men of Same Race/Ethnicity | |
| **Men** | | | | | |
| White | $825 | — | — | — | 4.9% |
| Black or African American | 620 | 75% | — | — | 10.2% |
| Asian | 966 | 117% | — | — | 3.9% |
| Hispanic or Latino | 559 | 68% | — | — | 6.8% |
| **Women** | | | | | |
| White | 654 | 79% | — | — | 4.4% |
| Black or African American | 554 | 67% | 85% | 89% | 8.1% |
| Asian | 753 | 91% | 115% | 78% | 3.5% |
| Hispanic or Latina | 501 | 61% | 77% | 90% | 6.9% |

*Note:* Persons whose ethnicity is identified as Hispanic or Latino may be of any race and, therefore, are classified by ethnicity as well as by race.

[*] Median weekly earnings of full-time civilian wage and salary workers for 2008 from U.S. Department of Labor, Bureau of Labor Statistics (2009a). Current Population Survey. *Household Data Annual Averages.* Table 37, "Median weekly earnings of full-time wage and salary workers by selected characteristics." Accessed June 9, 2009, at www.bls.gov/cpsaat37.pdf. Percentages calculated by the author.

[**] Unemployment rates for 2008 for all members of the civilian noninstitutional population 20 years and over who were employed or actively seeking employment from U.S. Department of Labor, Bureau of Labor Statistics (2009a). Current Population Survey. *Household Data Annual Averages.* Table 5, "Employment status of the civilian noninstitutional population by sex, age, and race." Accessed at http://www.bls.gov/cps/cpsaat5.pdf, and Table 6, "Employment status of the Hispanic or Latino population by sex, age, and detailed ethnic group." Accessed at http://www.bls.gov/cps/cpsaat6.pdf. ✦

the barrier limiting women's promotion beyond particular levels in many organizations (Alessio and Andrzewski 2000). However, because people are often uninformed about others' job experiences (e.g., income levels), and because people usually generalize from their own experience, there is a gap between the reality and the perception of employment inequity in the United States today. At the beginning of the women's movement, the average woman earned 59 percent of a man's earnings (one popular button said only "59¢"). By 1990, women's average earnings had climbed to about 70 percent of men's, but the pace of change then slowed considerably. As Table 6.1 indicates, the wage gap has by no means disappeared.

In a study of two-physician marriages, Hinze (2000) shows how the earnings gap is the product of a complex interaction of multiple factors (at the macro, middle, and micro levels) that contribute to gender inequities in earnings among people in the same occupation. Women tend to be concentrated in a small number of lower-paid specialties (such as pediatrics, rather than surgery). This pattern results from a combination of discrimination and decisions made by the physicians reflecting gendered performance of family responsibilities. Women are also more likely than men to reduce hours devoted to their careers, and their incomes are more closely tied to the number of hours they work than are men's. Men are more likely to focus on increasing their incomes to better fulfill their family responsibilities.

## SEGREGATION AT WORK

Before the women's movement began in the late 1960s, most jobs were "men's jobs," with relatively few women working in them (e.g., laborer, carpenter, or dentist). Most women used to work in occupations that were 80 percent or more women (e.g., secretary, nurse, or elementary school teacher). In response to the women's movement, occupational segregation began to decrease. Despite changes in the kinds of jobs considered appropriate for each sex, many occupations remain dominated by one sex or the other.

Women's occupational distribution changed most rapidly in the 1970s, following legally mandated policy reforms. Pressed to comply with affirmative action requirements, corporations took advantage of experience among their existing female labor force and transferred women into previously men's jobs. For example, publishers of college textbooks integrated their previously male sales forces by moving women from secretarial to sales positions. Some of the statistical indications of increased occupational integration may have overstated the move toward integration (Cohen 2004), because they included homemakers (an almost entirely female category) entering the paid labor force.

The sex integration of occupations slowed down in the 1980s, and it slowed further by the early 1990s. This is consistent with the evidence of a plateau in the gendered wage gap. The largest numbers of women who were freed up to change occupations had already done so. This reflects that the rapid decrease in many overtly discriminatory personnel practices was not followed by a similarly rapid decrease in more convert or subtle practices (Benokraitis and Feagin 1994).

Women are now less likely to be in extremely segregated jobs, but their jobs are predominantly female, nonetheless. That is, for the most part, women have jobs in which only the *majority* of people are women, rather than jobs in which *nearly all* people are women. Though men's entrance into predominantly female jobs was initially slower than women's exit from extremely female jobs, it did increase somewhat (Wootton 1997). In the bigger picture, men and women are more likely to have coworkers of the other sex than they did thirty years ago.

Just how much integration has occurred? The **index of dissimilarity** is one way to indicate the extent of occupational segregation. Starting with the percentage of each sex in each occupational category, the index is calculated to show what percentage of people from one category (e.g., women) would have to change occupations to reach equality as indicated by the percentages of both women and of men employed in each occupation. For example, if the index of dissimilarity for the United States were zero, it would mean that the proportion of males of every occupation was the same as the proportion of the whole labor force that is male (in 1995, this proportion was 53.9 percent). An index value of 100 would mean that the labor force was completely segregated by sex. The dissimilarity index, thus, refers to the extent to which women's and men's occupational patterns are different—the higher the number, the more segregated the occupational structure.

Using this indicator, slightly more than half of all employed women (53.5 percent) would have had to change occupations to make men's and women's 1995 occupational patterns identical. This rate was slightly lower than in 1985, when the index was

58.1 percent. In other words, out of 1,000 working women, instead of 581 changing into male-dominated occupations to reach complete integration (1985), only 535 would have had to do so in 1995. The improvement is more than a drop in the bucket but not by much! In analyzing changes in a sample of occupations during the thirty-year period from 1973 to 2002, Queneau (2006) found a continuing decline in the rate at which occupational desegregation is occurring, with 1993–2002 having an even slower rate of change than the preceding decade.

The index of dissimilarity is also used to describe the extent of segregation between smaller categories of population, thus enabling us to learn more about the intersection of gender with other major dimensions of economic stratification. It reveals that the segregation of the sexes is at about the same level within each of the three major racial-ethnic groupings (1995 index of 52.9 for African Americans, 54.1 for whites, and 56.0 for Hispanics; Wootten 1997, 18).

There are serious limits to the index of dissimilarity. Even where an occupation has comparable numbers of women and men, individual firms often restrict the hiring of members of particular groups into that occupational position (**job segregation**). For example, although both sexes are food servers, waiters (males) usually work in more expensive eateries than do waitresses. As a result, they are paid a higher hourly wage, get larger tips because meals are more expensive, and have help on their job (such as workers who clear tables). In contrast, waitresses' workplaces often require servers to do other tasks as well, such as cleaning bathrooms at the close of business.

Federally collected statistics often summarize information in ways that hide significant differences in the situation of men and women in the same occupation. For example, the servers' jobs just described would be lost in a report that puts all food service workers together. Similarly, a report of the total numbers of men and women physicians would mask the disproportionate employment of men in the more prestigious and better-paid medical specialties and work settings (Lorber 2001a). Perhaps one day, federal statistics will show that an equal representation of men and women from each racial-ethnic category are selling new cars. But, car salespeople are paid on commission: We will still need to know who is selling luxury cars and who is selling the budget models. Will it be like real estate, where white women have moved in to dominate residential sales, but people of color remain outside? Or, will it be like automobile sales today, where a few men of color do have jobs but women of all categories are largely absent? Are the industry and the occupations integrated, but not the workplace and the jobs? More detailed information is usually available from the same federal agencies; however, media reports tend to focus on what are often oversimplified summaries, overlooking how the summaries understate patterned economic differences between the sexes and among racial-ethnic groups. Thus, Table 6.2 masks the full extent of employment inequality among its four comparison groups.

When we compare the occupations that are predominantly male with those that are predominantly female, we also see differences in intrinsic rewards. Traditionally, jobs that are predominantly female have less autonomy, less decision-making power, and fewer opportunities for training and promotion. Similarly, predominantly male jobs have better extrinsic rewards—in addition to pay, jobs vary in their security and in fringe benefits, such as health coverage and pension plans. These are each related to the

**Table 6.2 Occupational Distribution of Employed Men and Women in Four Major Racial-Ethnic Categories, 2007**

| | African American Men | African American Women | Asian American Men | Asian American Women | Hispanic or Latino** Men | Hispanic or Latina** Women | White Men | White Women |
|---|---|---|---|---|---|---|---|---|
| **Occupational categories** | | | | | | | | |
| Management, professional, and related | 22.3% | 31.2% | 49.3 | 46.8 | 14.3 | 23.1 | 33.2 | 39.5 |
| Service occupations | 19.2 | 26.8 | 13.5 | 18.9 | 19.7 | 30.7 | 12.4 | 19.3 |
| Sales and office | 18.7 | 32.7 | 18.4 | 26.0 | 13.2 | 33.1 | 16.7 | 34.4 |
| Natural resources, construction and maintenance | 14.0 | 0.8 | 7.4 | .9 | 31.0 | 1.8 | 20.4 | 1.0 |
| Production, transportation, and material moving | 25.7 | 8.5 | 11.3 | 7.4 | 21.7 | 11.3 | 17.3 | 5.7 |
| Totals | 99.9%* | 100% | 99.9%* | 100% | 99.9%* | 100% | 100% | 99.9%* |

Notes: * Percentages do not add to 100 due to rounding off.
** Persons whose ethnicity is identified as Hispanic or Latino may be of any race and, therefore, are classified by ethnicity as well as by race.
Source: U.S. Department of Labor, Bureau of Labor Statistics. 2008. "Labor Force Characteristics by Race and Ethnicity, 2007." Table 4, "Employed persons by occupation, sex, race, and Hispanic or Latino ethnicity." Accessed June 9, 2009, at http://www.bls.gov/cps/cpsrace2007.pdf. ✦

racial-ethnic composition of people in the occupation, as well. White men's work historically has been better paid, with more opportunities for advancement. Men of color have had, on the average, lower rates of pay, much less autonomy, fewer fringe benefits and protections, and higher rates of unemployment.

When unions won better conditions, including fringe benefits and better protection in the event of job loss or retirement, the gains were generally restricted to white men. That is, unions often excluded men of color and all women from membership. Employers providing improved working conditions in an effort to forestall labor organizing also restricted these conditions by race and sex. Until the 1970s, men of color and all women were largely excluded from unionized jobs as a result of agreements between management and white men unionists (Reskin and Padavic 1994). In some occupations, individual male union members may continue to sabotage women coworkers, with little or no interference from union leaders. However, when union memberships are integrated, there is often less of a gender pay gap than is found on average in nonunionized jobs (Elvira and Saporta 2001).

Men's and women's jobs have also differed in their negative qualities. There has been a long-standing tendency to assign high-risk occupations to men. *New York Times* investigative reporters found that men suffered over 90 percent of the workplace fatalities in the United States resulting from employers' willful violations of safety laws (Barstow, Gerstein, and Stein 2003). The patriarchal ideology defines men as stronger and more capable than women and paternalistically assigns men the protection of women and children. Allowing women access to these jobs, or recognizing the hazardous quality of some women-dominated jobs (such as nursing and some women-dominated or sex-integrated agricultural work with exposure to high levels of pesticides), threatens the traditional justifications of male's higher status. In addition, jobs with hazardous aspects, whether traditionally assigned to men or to women, are disproportionately performed by members of lower-status groups (Mullings 1997). Higher-status groups are typically able to avoid such work. During the Vietnam War, for example, African American men were greatly overrepresented among combat troops, especially in higher-risk infantry units. Police work, despite its glamorous depiction in the media, is a high-risk, blue-collar service job. Traditionally performed by white men, recruits have been drawn disproportionately from the working class and from lower-status ethnic groups. Regardless of its acknowledged importance and difficulty, it is not an occupation that attracts economically and educationally advantaged people. Women do both paid and unpaid hazardous work, but its hazards are rarely acknowledged (e.g., the repetitive motion injuries of data entry operators and chicken-processing workers).

Recognizing the dangers of the work some women do will undermine one ideological justification of patriarchy. The paramount importance of wage-earning to masculine identities and the more punitive governmental approach to unemployed able-bodied men have facilitated corporate and public policies to exclude women from high-risk jobs, rather than to lower the risks of dangerous jobs (e.g., see Klein 1987 on lead exposure). Most owners and managers do not want to lower productivity by developing and implementing techniques to reduce hazards (see Clarke 1988). However, when the hazardous effects of an organization's activities cannot be limited to low-status groups, more powerful members of the community or the society may mobilize to demand changes. Otherwise, those people who don't have to do it often defend the persistence of hazardous work by saying that no one is forced to accept it. The lack of actual alternative opportunities is often ignored in such discussions.

Labor unions, which traditionally limited their organizing drives to occupations dominated by men, regularly would put a higher priority on raising pay for their members, rather than on workplace safety and health issues. This made sense, at least in the short term, when married women were expected to stay at home and entire families depended on a solitary male's earnings. The assumption that unions represented men with wives to take care of the home also explains their acceptance of undesirable working conditions, such as the rotating shift and mandatory overtime. Such common contractual features have made holding these jobs harder for mothers seeking better pay because ever-changing work schedules interfere with child care arrangements.

Jobs in which the work is done entirely in the worker's home (home-based work) have become more common in the last thirty years. These jobs differ from employment in which workers bring work home from their workplace. Women are more likely than men to do home-based work. Except for white men in urban areas, home-based workers of both sexes earn less, on the average, than "on-site" workers. Compared with other employed women, those who do home-based work are more likely to be married, to have more children, to have younger children, to live in rural areas, and to be self-employed (Edwards and Field-Hendrey 1996). It appears, then, that these women are particularly in need of the flexibility that working at home provides. The home-based women accept lower wages and are unable to unionize to improve their situation through the power of collective bargaining. Some home-based workers may be covered by benefits (such as health insurance) through another family member's employment.

There has been an increase, as well, in the phenomenon of individuals working full time as "independent contractors" even though they are working long term and only for one company. The job she or he does might otherwise be done by employees, who, unlike contractors, are legally free to unionize. Whether independent contractors work at home or on-site, they cause labor unions the same concern: The bargaining power of on-site employees is undermined if employers can turn to the services of independent contractors.

In the late 1990s, Perdue Farms (the poultry company) was sued by a large group of African American men, whom Perdue changed from employees to "independent contractors" in 1991. The workers argued that they were de facto employees and should have the rights of employees (Greenhouse 1999). In the settlement of this and several other suits against Perdue for labor law violations, the corporation was ordered to pay millions of dollars in back pay to workers. The "contractors" regained their employee status (United Food and Commercial Workers 2004).

Jobs and occupations vary in the degree to which they are available full time or part time, whether they are seasonal or year-round, and whether they provide higher pay as employees get more experience, more on-the-job training, or additional formal education. Research by sociologists and economists has established that people of color and white women continue to have less favorable work situations, along each of these dimensions, than do white men. The *extent* and particular *kinds* of inequities vary among people depending on where they are located in the intersections of race, class, and gender as well as region, age, and educational attainment (McCall 2005).

## EXPLAINING THE SEGREGATION OF OCCUPATIONS AND JOBS

Describing the differences in "men's" and "women's" work is the easier part of the job. Analyzing the causes of these inequalities is more complex, however, and more susceptible to the influence of differences in ideology. Nonetheless, an accurate analysis is essential to a successful strategy for reducing inequality. Given the strong U.S. value of equality, a push for change is likely when the justifications for segregation are understood and shown to be invalid.

The prevalence of cultural beliefs about what men and women can do, or can best do, is a significant factor in job segregation, affecting the behavior of job seekers and employers. Even if an applicant is willing to do a "nontraditional job," the employer may not be willing to hire her or him. Segregation is influenced by cultural beliefs about what a masculine man and a feminine woman should *want* to do. Thus, as we discussed in the last chapter, men who teach young children must manage their presentation in ways that assure people they will not be inappropriate with the students.

These traditional cultural beliefs in support of segregation have many flaws. Women's exclusion from managerial work was often justified with claims of their lower educational achievement, which was simply inaccurate. Women's automatic exclusion from physically demanding jobs (such as fire fighting) is equally questionable when we find that typically there are no reviews of veteran workers to ensure the maintenance of the physical abilities required when they were first hired. It is uncommon for men to test the barriers to their entry into "women's" jobs, because these are usually less prestigious and lower paid. In this culture, few people are willing to sacrifice pay and prestige, and endure recurrent challenges to their gender identity, because of the intrinsic appeal of a job. Many men who do enter traditionally women-identified jobs, such as nursing or elementary school teaching, do so in pursuit of administrative or other higher status positions in those fields, and do not stay long at the entry level (Williams 1992).

A second factor in creating and maintaining segregated jobs is the different experience (educational and otherwise) that individuals bring to the workforce, which itself is gendered (see Chapter Five). So, the likelihood that boys take more math than girls in high school means girls are less likely to meet the minimum entrance requirement for certain training programs. Experiences girls have had in caring for younger children in the family, or as babysitters, will enhance the sense that they are capable of working with young children, but young men may feel they would be incompetent.

Third, segregation may result from past local practices that became habitual. Indeed, some corporations with locations in different regions in the United States report that certain jobs viewed by employees in one region as "women's work" are viewed as "men's work" by employees in another region (Kramer 1991). In contrast to such varied beliefs about which sex should do a particular job, what is stable in different places and at different historical moments is the notion that some jobs are appropriate for men and others for women.

The practical aspects of a job also have gendered implications, contributing in a fourth way to segregation. For instance, people with primary child care responsibilities (usually women) will probably not apply for a job with mandatory rotating shifts. A man who is expected to be the main breadwinner at home will not apply for a particularly low-paid job, such as nursery school teacher. Not surprisingly, the good fit between family and work roles of the past makes a poor fit for desegregation if those family roles have not changed. However, a man with a wife earning a high income may decide to work as a nursery school teacher, after all. In 2006, about a quarter of dual-earner couples reported that the wife earned more than the husband (U.S. Department of Labor 2008).

The continued segregation of men's blue-collar occupations is due, in part, to the declining number of such jobs. Women entering the labor force are unlikely to choose occupations with poor future prospects. More generally, seeking "nontraditional" work (jobs typically held by someone of the other sex) depends on the attractiveness of that work, in comparison with other available jobs. What constitutes attractive work and what is perceived as available will vary depending on local opportunities, patterns of race discrimination, and the financial needs of the woman. In contrast to a middle-class woman who wants to be a neurosurgeon, a working-class woman who wants to be a welder gets less support from family and friends (Kramer 1991).

Pay disparities between blue-collar, semiskilled jobs mainly held by women and those mainly held by men are often small at the entry level. But, after years of employment, the differences in raises and promotion possibilities will be greater. However, this may not be obvious to the new worker, who may not be planning to stay at the job for years anyway. Further, expectations of sexual harassment may discourage women from trying to integrate male-dominated blue-collar jobs. Working-class women who want to improve their economic position instead often have the option of moving into higher-status women's jobs, such as skilled office work. Many blue-collar women view these jobs as at least preferable to blue-collar "women's work." The lack of opportunities for advancement, the low rate of pay increases, and the growing lack of autonomy in female-dominated, white-collar jobs are not well known or are not perceived as significant job characteristics because they are seen as "less dirty" than blue-collar work and, therefore, are considered more feminine. Defining blue-collar jobs as undesirable and understanding the shortcomings of office and sales work are tendencies that aspiring working-class women share with other people in society.

Men's very slow rate of movement into predominantly women's jobs makes sense when we remember that these jobs typically have lower pay scales. There is still a 15 percent wage gap between men in female-dominated jobs and men in male-dominated jobs (Boraas and Rodgers 2003). In U.S. culture, the money one earns is generally considered more important than the satisfactions that come with performing a job, or the ways in which one's position facilitates other roles and outcomes. Although many men are interested in spending more time with their young children, few feel they can afford to accept jobs with lower pay or fewer hours (Gerson 1993). Even if "women's jobs" pay well, the socialization of boys and men into avoiding predominantly female activities seems to keep many men out. In 2008, for example, men were only 8 percent of registered nurses in the United States (U.S. Department of Labor 2009a).

The practice of discrimination in hiring and promotion is last on this list, but not least, and not simple. When treating men and women differently was legal and socially acceptable, it was easy to determine the role of employers in creating and perpetuating a gendered job structure. Since the passage of equal employment legislation in the 1960s, and after subsequent court cases established the seriousness with which the laws must be taken, many employers have changed their practices. But those practices that directly or indirectly make it more difficult for a person to get a job because of sex are hard to document, precisely because they are illegal.

Rather than based on biased beliefs about people who are being excluded, some employers' and managers' decisions are based on homophily, their preference for people like themselves. In other words, in hiring and promotion, some people are motivated by the characteristics they want, rather than particular beliefs about the people who they see as different (Reskin 2002, cited in Browne and Misra 2003). Such decisions have an equally discriminatory effect, but to reduce discrimination, it is useful to understand that those who make such decisions do not see themselves as discriminators.

Promotion into supervisory positions involves increasing gender inequity as one moves up the organizational hierarchy. Those women who do move above the glass ceiling encounter a larger income gap than do women at lower supervisory levels. Women also typically have control over fewer monetary resources and have supervisory authority over smaller numbers of employees than do their male peers. Though there are increasing numbers of women and minority men who supervise other employees, they are concentrated at lower levels of the hierarchy and generally supervise workers in the same category (minority managers supervise minority workers; women supervise women). This minimizes worker complaints that there are no opportunities for advancement, but keeps minority and female managers in marginalized positions (Smith 2002).

Economists do not agree on how much of the existing segregation is due to employers' discriminatory practices, but they do universally agree that such practices explain some part of the dissimilarity in jobs held by women and men. Even today, we can read about the legal settlements requiring major employers who have ignored the law to pay penalties for their discriminatory practices. For example, Texaco, which was sued for race and sex discrimination, settled after a high-level white male executive secretly taped a leadership meeting in which overtly racist and sexist comments were made. Mitsubishi settled after charges were pressed for the widespread sexual harassment of women employees in its illinois factory. In late 1999, Boeing agreed to pay more than $4.5 million in back pay and salary adjustments and to institute a range of procedures to insure against pay discrimination against minority and women salaried workers and executives.

A study of employers revealed two significant practices through which discrimination against black men can be made invisible. First, when a new workplace site needs to be chosen, the racial segregation of many metropolitan areas in the United States enables employers to avoid applicants of color by locating at a distance from the residential areas in which they are concentrated. Second, by building subjectively assessed characteristics (such as "people skills") into a job's requirements, personnel decisions seem equitable although they are based on racial stereotyping (Moss and Tilly 2001).

## CHANGING THE GENDERING OF WORK

The decline in occupational and job segregation results from feminist action and pragmatic changes in corporate, group, and individual practices. By *feminist action* we refer to legislative initiatives and legal suits resulting in antidiscriminatory judicial rulings. Individuals and groups who have worked for such changes may not call themselves feminists; rather, they may view their actions as simply aimed to achieve the cultural value of equality. Before the 1970s wave of feminism, women and men were considered fundamentally different in ways that made it inappropriate to seek equality of treatment in the economy. Just as we would now not deem it appropriate to treat children the same way that we treat adults, men and women's differences were defined as justifying (even, perhaps, requiring) different treatment in the economy. As long as that point of view was part of the hegemonic ideology of gender, people who worked for equal rights were likely to see themselves as political activists. Now that it has become "obvious" (at least in the hegemonic ideology) that one's sex should not be taken into account in judging one's job or earning potential, people working for equal rights may avoid any political identity.

Indeed, once the broad initiatives of the 1970s occurred, many people pursued nontraditional arrangements even though they did not have particularly feminist goals or worldviews. Thus, employers trying to hire increasing numbers of workers for expanding occupations were willing to take advantage of the existence of women's growing labor force participation. Women who wanted to earn more money were ready to move into attractive nontraditional jobs, such as accounting. Couples that needed two incomes, but did not want or could not afford to have a stranger care for their children, tried working different shifts. Financial needs, rather than a feminist ideology, have led to more involved fathering in many families (Gerson 1993; Weis 2006). In other words, "purely practical" reasons were sufficient motivation to challenge gendered constraints once the legal system had made sex an inappropriate basis for economic treatment.

Changes in laws, through legislative or judicial action, rarely make for widespread changes in behavior. With this in mind, the federal government led by President Nixon developed the requirement for affirmative action. Employers dealing with the federal government would have to file plans showing how they were going to undo previous patterns of employment discrimination. Despite all the rhetoric against these programs, evidence has clearly established that affirmative action programs were an important force in the desegregation of jobs. Despite common allegations, such programs only rarely led to cases of "reverse discrimination." Concerns that unqualified individuals would be hired ignored the fact that attention to race and sex were called for only *within the pool of qualified candidates*. White women, who outnumber men of color, benefited at least as much as did men and women of color (Reskin 1998). Whether or not labeled an affirmative action strategy, formalizing personnel practices is a significant factor contributing to the increased employment of women as managers (Reskin and McBrier 2000).

The evidence supports the effectiveness of affirmative action policies in creating more integrated organizations (Reskin 1999). It shows a neutral or sometimes positive impact of affirmative action policies on organizational effectiveness or profitability. It documents the perception among many people of color and white women that affirmative action is still necessary, because sexist and racist beliefs continue to survive (see, for example, Hulett et al. 2008). If affirmative action were dismantled, they believe this would reverse the progress that has been made. In Chapter Seven we will examine the patterned misperceptions of affirmative action policies and results.

Cultural representations of a range of nontraditional workplaces on television and in the movies may also have had an impact on individuals' perception of the possibilities available to them. As discussed in Chapter Two, despite their distortions, media depictions often influence people's ideas. Thus, the made-for-TV movies, situation comedies, and dramas with female characters performing nontraditional jobs may encourage women to broaden their job searches. For example, shows in the 1980s featured women police officers and attorneys in larger proportions than the real world. Numerous made-for-TV movies showed women taking on nontraditional blue-collar work, struggling with hostile coworkers, and triumphing in the end. *Grace Under Fire* was a comedy about a single mother choosing nontraditional blue-collar work because of its better pay; it often included material about the challenges of her workplace. Current dramas routinely feature women doing emergency rescue work and forensics investigations, probably in larger than actual numbers.

Many factors have drawn middle-class women into nontraditional work. Generally, traditional work has offered them low pay and prestige relative to their educational achievements. Entry into nontraditional middle-class work (such as accounting, which was almost all male before the women's movement began) involved no stigma and promised significant improvements in rewards and working conditions over bookkeeping jobs (i.e., predominantly female).

Despite factors discouraging women from moving into nontraditional blue-collar work, many blue-collar jobs have become less segregated (e.g., bus drivers, police, and corrections officers). Women have known about the hazards of certain occupations, and ignored dominant misperceptions of them, feeling that the positive aspects outweighed the negative. In addition, women who place a high value on economic independence are more attentive to the immediate or long-range monetary advantages of nontraditional work. Finally, cultural representations of nontraditional work (even if inaccurate) may ease women's concerns about the hostility they will encounter from coworkers, encouraging them to expect that some coworkers will support them even if hostility might occur.

When pressures from the individual level grow sufficiently strong, employers often change working conditions. During the economic boom of the late 1990s, for example, some workers with sought-after skills were able to negotiate creative arrangements, which both men and women increasingly desire, that allow combining work and family roles in new ways. As a result, some employers began to permit telecommuting (i.e., working at home while using e-mail, fax, and other technologies) for one or two days per week.

## GENDER ON THE JOB

Doing gender is an integral part of doing one's job. As we discussed in Chapter Three, it is through the actual interactions of people that macro- and middle-level meanings of gender are reproduced, challenged, or negotiated. The technology team members who assigned hardware and software issues to male presenters and pedagogical issues to female presenters illustrate the reproduction of gender. Restaurants whose female servers are required to wear revealing clothing rarely have such expectations for male workers. These differences in tasks or presentational requirements are generally taken for granted by workers as well as the other people who witness their role performances.

Individuals' expectations of the relationship between gender and work roles may prevail over indicators of formal equality. In a study of the financial services industry, McGuire (2002) found that, even for men and women with similar formal positions, coworkers provided more help to male than to female members of their informal networks.

In a study of three Korean-owned nail salons in New York City, Kang (2003) encountered different norms of job performance along with different performances of gender, each associated with the race and class composition of the salon's clientele, and the differing reliance on tipping among the salons. Workers varied in their emphasis on pampering clients or creating technically and artistically outstanding nails. Workers who pampered clients simultaneously used techniques to resist being constructed as subservient.

Workers in sex-atypical occupations are more obviously negotiating gender. For example, women corrections officers need to establish their ability to perform a role that is generally associated with hegemonic masculinity. They may do so by accentuating their difference and making use of strategies that fit inmate and coworker expectations of femininity, such as "people skills" (Britton 2003). A former day care worker interviewed by Britton emphasized the similarity between supervising inmates and supervising small children. Chicana attorneys, in organizational settings that continue to privilege white men, also develop strategies to gain the visibility required for professional advancement (García-Lopez 2008). In the last chapter, we described the situation of men who teach young children and develop teaching techniques that will reassure adults that they have no pedaphilic inclinations.

Lesbian and gay workers have a more complex negotiation of job performance. Sexual identity and gender identity are analytically distinct, but others do not necessarily accept this distinction. Police work, like corrections, is based on a traditional, hegemonic, and generally homophobic masculinity. Homosexual officers are thus seen as an implicit challenge to male officers' worldview. Performing their jobs well and working to minimize coworker hostility require more energy and care than the already high demands of police work by "unmarked" (i.e., heterosexual male) officers (Miller, Forest, and Jurik 2003).

Finally, gender on the job too often involves incidents of sexual harassment. Recognition of and attention to sexual harassment as a social problem developed with the women's movement. A significant judicial ruling in the late 1970s made employers liable for the harassing behaviors of their employees. When corporate leadership took that liability seriously, managers who had previously avoided tackling chronic or acute situations of harassment found avoidance became costly for themselves. Interest accelerated even further as a result of the Clarence Thomas confirmation hearings of 1991 (see Chapter One). Social and political policies in the United States have moved forward against sexual harassment, with the problem framed as a deterrence to achieving gender equality. In Europe, where sexual harassment is more apt to be framed as a one of a set of problems of the abuse of power (rather than a gender equity issue), policies are weaker (Zippel 2006). Research about sexual harassment is now in a period of rapid growth (Welsh 1999). Research on the three levels of harassment has increased identification of the organizational arrangements that are most successful for avoiding, eliminating, or at least reducing the frequency and the seriousness of harassing acts (Mueller, De Coster, and Estes 2001). It has also established that harassing behavior is racialized as well as gendered, with the styles of harassing related to the identities of both the harasser and his or her victim (Thierry Texeira 2002).

As we have seen, the organization itself affects the ways in which gender is built into expectations. For example, in Chapter Three we saw that teams in a coed softball league differed in how gender factored into construction of players. Corporate anti-harassment policies have successfully changed the organizational climate for women. Just as people may "do gender" in different ways, or undo gender by effectively rejecting its pertinence to their behavior, organizations may be more or less strongly gendered social systems. While some restaurants employ only male servers, and others employ only female servers, a third category has a sex-integrated wait staff. Once a job is integrated, this question arises: Are people who are in the same job given the same tasks (e.g., cleaning restrooms), the same opportunities (e.g., the assignment of more or less promising workstations), and the same obligations (e.g., regarding the presentation of their bodies and behaviors)?

### ALTERNATIVES TO EMPLOYMENT

What happens when people do not earn enough to subsist? This can happen to single individuals as well as to people living with kin. It happens when people cannot find full-time employment at a living wage, when they are too old or infirm to work, or when they must stay home to care for dependent children or adults. Finally, with the need for two paychecks to keep many households out of poverty, the breakup of a marriage or other intimate domestic partnership can lead people (especially women) to turn to the government for some form of economic assistance.

A maze of programs offers various forms of public support to people, depending on how the people are categorized. People in family-based households have different kinds and levels of assistance available than do single adults. This reflects a desire to protect children from the most extreme poverty, rather than any particular respect for the situation of the adults in their homes. Many people assume that anyone who makes a real effort will be able to find work and that working full-time raises people above the poverty level. For example, a major feature of the Family Support Act of 1988 is the pursuit of child support payments from absent fathers. This strategy is irrelevant when too few jobs paying a living wage are available. In 2001, almost 7 million workers had incomes below the government-established poverty threshold for their family size (Mosisa 2003). Using the more realistically computed "living wage," Appelbaum, Bernhardt, and Murnane (2003) estimate that more than a quarter of households with children and at least one worker are living with less income than what is required for a bare-bones budget.

Although the 1970s saw a striking down of sex-specific regulations regarding public assistance, the differential treatment of categories continues to have different effects on men and women. Ideas of how women should be treated have changed radically as middle-class mothers' increased labor force participation undermined the belief in using public funds to support "stay-at-home moms." Although economically secure parents can afford adequate paid child care, or can choose to give up a parent's earnings while raising small children, the poor no longer have that choice. The ideas have changed about what mothers should do, but the use of income-transfer programs to enforce those ideas has not.

Under TANF, the welfare system enacted in 1996 when Aid to Families with Dependent Children was ended, recipients *must* participate in workfare unless they are caring for a child under one year old. Going to school typically does not exempt a recipient from this workfare requirement, so pursuing an education to improve one's job opportunities is difficult. In some states and welfare offices, case managers may have the discretion to define attending college as a work-related activity. However, case managers' decisions are influenced by their perceptions of the client's potential, which may be affected in turn by the case managers' biases (Pearson 2007). Nationally established time limits for receiving assistance can be shortened by states without federal approval, but such approval is required if a state chooses to extend those limits. Significantly, the time limits on receiving public assistance are being enforced, but the supports promised by the law (e.g., child care, medical insurance, and food stamps) to facilitate the transition are often lacking (Schorr 1998).

By 2004, the number of people receiving public assistance was even more sharply reduced than initially projected in 1996, despite the serious economic downturn nationally (Pear 2004). The closed cases include individuals who did find adequate employment. Some of that group would have been glad to work earlier, but needed the medical insurance that did come with welfare but did not come with the jobs they could find. Because the new law lets them keep these benefits for a time, they are now able to do what they wanted to do previously—work for their income (see Schorr 1998). However, staying off welfare will be difficult: the medical insurance lasts for one year only and the new jobs usually do not include insurance. Likewise, child care benefits are limited; unless former recipients can find the money to pay for child care, those with young children may have trouble holding a job after these benefits run out. Finally, the kinds of jobs many recipients are able to find are often the least stable, and former recipients were among the most vulnerable when unemployment rates rose to higher levels after the 1990s boom ended.

An intermediate category of former A.F.D.C. recipients consists of people who have had periods of both employment and unemployment during the brief time since leaving the welfare rolls. This pattern is far from economically secure and results in a very low income (they are not typically eligible for unemployment compensation from the kinds of work they have done), with minimum wage during periods of employment and no income otherwise. Former recipients frequently lack the skills that employers seek (Corcoran et al. 2000). Even with appropriate skills, women of color are less likely than white women to be hired into jobs with a potential for promotion to living wage levels. Stable employment is difficult in the growing number of jobs requiring "non-standard" hours; they sometimes make the use of public transportation impossible, and child care arrangements may fall apart as schedules change each week (Seccombe 1999).

In contrast to those who have left welfare for employment, a large minority of former recipients have simply "disappeared," giving up on an increasingly harsh and bureaucratically demanding system even before reaching their two-year time limit. A 1999 study, for example, of former New Jersey recipients estimated that 27 percent were receiving no wages to replace their welfare stipends (Kocieniewski 1999). By 2003, even the Bush administration's Assistant Secretary for Families and Children admitted that between 10 and 15 percent of former recipients were "significantly worse off financially" (Kaufman 2003). Finally, there are people in need who are not former recipients and who do not apply for welfare because of the discouraging prospects, as well as the active measures by welfare agencies to divert people before they file formal applications (Corcoran et al. 2000).

There is widespread, growing concern about the current and future well-being of children living with even less adequate supports than those provided by welfare (Schorr 1998). If policies are adjusted to respond to this fundamental flaw in welfare "reform," the changes are likely to be addressed to households with children. More typically headed by women, these households may get some improvement in their economic situation. The question of how to protect people who formerly were kept, by the "safety net," from an economic free fall will be on the public agenda for the foreseeable future. Men are likely to get short shrift if they are not attached to children. However, the symbolic support offered to women with children may not help much as they face the considerable challenges of raising the next generation with insufficient resources. One extreme outcome predicted from the new laws is an increase in the number of people who are homeless. The threat of homelessness has also contributed to the victimization of single mothers, who may have no alternative to putting up with sexual harassment by landlords (Tester 2008).

The emerging national policy for reducing welfare and insuring the well-being of poor women and children is remarkably similar to the historical practice of the "family wage." Rather than moving toward the eradication of sex and race inequities in the labor market, the expectation is that women should marry, creating two-income households that would enable family members to survive without government assistance. Funds are now earmarked to increase federal payments to states that have higher rates of marriage among their recipients, creating an incentive for state agencies to reward women who marry and punish those who do not.

By highlighting the importance of fathers' and husbands' performance of their hegemonic provider role, policymakers imply that it is only a matter of individual commitment (Curran and Abrams 2000). This ignores the depressed opportunity structure many poor and working-class men face. In addition to the lack of jobs in or near poor residential areas, there are depressed wages for existing jobs. Parallel to the occupational wage gap between predominantly male and predominantly female jobs described earlier, there is a wage gap between jobs employing high proportions of people of color and jobs predominantly employing white workers with the same level of qualifications (Kmec 2003). Macro-level changes in opportunity will be required before good fathering depends only on men's will (Lichter, Graefe, and Brown 2003).

Finally, new welfare policies may have serious unwanted consequences for poor families. The "family cap" allows states to freeze benefit levels on the basis of family size when the application for assistance is made. A woman who has another child receives no additional income to help defray added costs. This policy has led to a higher rate of abortion use among recipients (Jagannathan and Camasso, 2003). The marriage incentive may harm women and children, when abusive relationships are resumed or tolerated to comply with policy pressures.

### HOMELESSNESS AND GENDER

The growth of homelessness is largely a result of large-scale economic developments. Individual and social problems help determine which particular people will be without housing; but even with similar problems, before the 1980s people were not so vulnerable to homelessness as they are now (for an excellent overview, see Blau 1992). Families and individuals living below the poverty line twenty-five years ago simply did not experience homelessness at the current rate. Likewise, people with drug or alcohol addictions or with serious mental illness were not at today's risk of homelessness. The growth in homelessness is due to the declining number of privately owned, low-cost housing units, the astronomical increase in real estate values and rents, government abandonment of the construction of public housing, the growing proportion of the population working in low-wage jobs, and the declining buying power of the minimum wage. Another factor adding to the size of the problem is the change, starting in the early 1970s, of treating the mentally ill with medications rather than long-term hospitalization (which usually did not include therapy, but did provide shelter). Each of these factors is, itself, the result of a complex set of social and economic shifts.

The *relative* influence of each of the foregoing factors, as well as the size of the homeless population itself, is hotly debated. It is in many homeless people's interest to not be identified as such (e.g., mothers may lose custody of their children, or employers may fire workers), and so official counts are unreliable. Social support for homeless people is generally locally based and differs widely from one city and region to another. According to estimates from the National Law Center on Homelessness and Poverty, before the economic crisis of 2008 and 2009, approximately 3.5 million people in the United States experienced homelessness in a single year (National Coalition for the Homeless 2009). Even if the most cautious of these estimates is accurate, homelessness and fear of homelessness are significant aspects of contemporary U.S. life. Finally, those people who have never been homeless are likely to have distorted views of the problem and the composition of the homeless population. There may be more awareness of homeless men because we are more afraid of them and they are more visible. Homeless women may make great efforts to be invisible to protect themselves and their children from street crime or intrusion by welfare agencies who might separate members of the family.

Homelessness is gendered in important ways. First, vulnerability to it results from one's economic situation; and, as we have seen, the economic situations of people are gendered—women earn less than men, are more likely to be working part time rather than full time, and may be more constrained by child care needs than are men. When men leave, women's wages may not pay the rent or the mortgage payment, not to mention other household expenses. Many women become homeless because they have left a violent home and have no place to go or have had only temporary shelter with relatives or friends.

In addition, the available services for homeless people reflect how the society defines men and women, their family obligations, their capacities, and their needs.

Many homeless shelters were originally designed with single individuals, rather than family units including children, in mind. Homeless women are more likely than homeless men to be caring for their children. The particular difficulties of homelessness also vary for individual men and women. Women are more vulnerable to sexual assault, may have to manage menstruation-related hygiene, and often have a greater sense of physical modesty in U.S. culture.

Among white men, homelessness is more likely than for other population groups to be associated with psychological difficulties; white men without such problems are more able to earn a living wage than are women, as a group, or men of color. In the latter two groups, psychological and substance abuse problems appear to characterize a smaller proportion of homeless people. Their homelessness is often simply due to the kinds of work available to them.

These patterns are more complex than generally thought: The path to homelessness may not include psychological problems, but homelessness may itself produce such problems. If one has been homeless for a while, it would be hard not to become psychologically disturbed and not to seek relief through drugs or alcohol. Liebow (1993) described the lives of women in several shelters in the Washington, DC, area in the 1980s. Getting through each day was a challenge: where to spend the day, where to eat, how to safeguard one's possessions, how to arrange medical- or employment-related appointments without revealing one's lack of residence. Religious faith was an important support for many of the homeless women he got to know.

Although shelter space in most communities is more available for single individuals than for adults with children, it is usually of worse quality. In part, this reflects the greater prevalence of single individuals in the early years of the homelessness era. But it also reflects sexist beliefs about men and their independence. As long as a man has only himself to support, there is culturally no acceptable explanation of his homelessness—he must be to blame. So, the *quality* of shelter space for men is likely to be worse than for women, and especially for mothers with children. We more readily accept women's dependence and we may be reluctant to punish children for the perceived failures of a parent. However, higher standards for family shelters mean they cost more, and fewer have been made available. Public sentiments may be with families and women, but their lesser visibility reduces public pressure for providing the shelter they need.

Although men may more easily find shelter, it may be more dangerous than arrangements made for women (whether individuals or with families). Further, men's housing in public shelter appears to be enough of a solution, in policymakers' eyes. By contrast, there is more pressure to regard shelters as a temporary solution for women in families and more interest in developing permanent housing alternatives for them. This varies, too, with regional differences in views of the poor and views of the role of government in helping individuals in crisis (Blau 1992).

### EXPLAINING GENDERED ECONOMICS

A theoretical perspective is useful if it helps explain, or make sense of, a wide variety of our observations. The feminist perspectives introduced in Chapter One contribute different insights to understanding the gendering of economic life in the contemporary United States. Multiracial feminism is the most powerful explanatory perspective in studying work and the economy, but other perspectives help as we consider particular questions. Multiracial feminism takes power as the central explanation for stratification patterns; it emphasizes the differences among both women and men related to social class and racial-ethnic identities. Thus, although women share the experience of job and occupational segregation across racial and ethnic groups, racial and ethnic groups differ in unemployment rates and even labor force participation rates for married women. The multiracial feminist argues against simply adding the economic inequities associated with race to those associated with class, as well as to those associated with gender, looking instead at the ways that each intersection of statuses, at particular moments and places, is associated with various economic outcomes.

Multiracial feminism also helps explain the circumstances of young people in the top, and increasingly affluent, tier of the stratification system. Young women from the upper middle class and the upper class have left school with credentials to match their male peers and have been more successful than less-educated women, who have sought traditionally male blue-collar jobs. When these affluent young women marry and when older women of affluent marriages return to school and earn comparable credentials, their households achieve significantly higher standards of living. Even though such women often experience sex discrimination on the job, they are financially secure enough to survive divorce economically. Indeed, women's employment outside the home has been "blamed" for women's greater willingness to end unsuccessful marriages.

This position is consistent with the framing of gender as consisting of multiplicities of femininities and masculinities. The form that is hegemonic, or dominant, at some historical moment will be related to the structure of the economy. Thus, Connell (1995) describes economically hopeless Australian men who have stopped believing they must be the primary breadwinner to be masculine. This move makes sense; their lack of opportunities would make the hegemonic, breadwinning masculinity an impossibility. Instead, some have adopted an alternative masculinity—which Connell calls "live fast and die young." Athletic achievers in the United States are likely to give up dreams of professional sports if they have access to achieving hegemonic masculinity by providing a very comfortable home and other material assets through more conventional work. Lower-class athletes and athletes of color are more apt to pursue professional sports careers, despite the long odds and high physical costs, because the odds are apparently even worse for their economic success through "normal" avenues.

Achievement through climbing the corporate ladder conforms to our society's dominant definition of adult manliness. Where the chance to achieve economically through a white-collar route seems remote, alternative routes to manliness are pursued. As white men from blue-collar families found their traditional job opportunities had disappeared, some have been able to find other, but less well-paid work. As a result, in their households there is less inequity in the earnings of husbands and wives and there is also more involvement in childcare activities previously woman-defined. Rather than seeing this as a failure, men in this situation often focus on the ways in which they are conforming to the role of a good father. For example, they may emphasize the superiority of a family member rather than a stranger providing child care while a mother is at work (Weis 2006).

Radical feminism presumes a commonality among women of all classes and racial-ethnic groups that does help to explain the high rate of poverty among elderly women and its connection to the ways their earlier life experiences were gendered. But the radical feminist view does not ring true to most women in disadvantaged classes and racial-ethnic groups. In particular, the men with whom many racial-ethnic, or economically disadvantaged women share membership in low-status categories are not prime figures in women's oppression. An exclusive focus on gender stratification significantly oversimplifies economic realities.

Socialist feminists often examine social life for ways in which patriarchal beliefs divide groups that might otherwise unite and unseat the powerful through coalition. This helps to explain the cooperation of white men labor unionists with management to keep men of color and women out of the better jobs. The gendering of wages (even where identical work was done by both sexes) enabled men to retain power in their family relationships by virtue of their greater economic resources (Hartmann 1976).

Poststructural feminism's emphasis on social construction contributes to studies of the changing workplace, encouraging the researcher to move away from prior assumptions as social and technological changes reshape jobs and industries. It highlights the dynamic quality of social arrangements and recognizes the significance of power in shaping new arrangements.

### SUMMARY

It is easy to see the importance of economic arrangements for the quality of life. However, the extent of economic stratification by gender is usually underestimated. It is also justified by patriarchal ideology. Aspects of U.S. capitalist ideology, such as the belief in the ability to "pull yourself up by your bootstraps" regardless of external limits on opportunities, lead to the invisibility of discrimination on the basis of sex, race, ethnicity, and age against women and members of other groups.

Nonetheless, as labor force participation has become normative for white women, many have become aware of the existence of gender stratification (joining women of color in that awareness). Although some aspects of economic circumstance are not gendered—for example, men's and women's unemployment rates are comparable within racial-ethnic categories—other aspects, including occupations, rate of pay, and kinds of public welfare, are clearly gendered (Steinberg 2001).

The chapter started with a review of the "new economy." One of the most significant factors of that economy is the increasing earnings gap between the individuals at the top of the earnings hierarchy and those in the middle and below. This phenomenon is true for women and for men (Bernstein and Mischel 1997). Indeed, most of the shrinking difference in wage inequality between men and women has resulted from the stagnation or even decrease in earnings of low-wage male workers, rather than from women "catching up" to men's earnings levels. This is consistent with the socialist feminist focus on capitalism and the importance of the economic interests, rather than the ideological beliefs of employers in the shaping of occupational and wage structures.

Multiracial feminists demand more careful and complete attention to numerous dimensions of economic experience, arguing against simpler and more intellectually "elegant" models that emphasize only one or two dimensions and pay little or no attention to the variations that characterize their intersections. Future feminist research in the sociology of work and the economy will certainly make use of the multiracial approach as it successfully "makes sense" of a growing body of evidence (Browne and Misra 2003).

### DISCUSSION QUESTIONS

1. Review the many dimensions along which jobs and careers can differ, and the ways in which they tend to do so, depending on one's sex, racial-ethnic group, and social class.

2. Develop a checklist of economic conditions and public policy approaches that will have gendered impacts, to keep in mind as you follow the news reports over the next few months and years.

3. If men and women are to have equality in the quality of their lives, what changes are called for in the welfare system and in other governmental programs for the economically vulnerable? ✦

# CHAPTER 7

# The Political and Legal System

The political system provides people with a stable social structure and a point from which they can act as agents to change the structure. It includes government, oriented toward the maintenance of internal order and external defense, and all other activities aimed at changing or maintaining power arrangements in the society. In its regulation of organizations and individuals and its allocation of resources and responsibilities, government influences and sometimes dictates personal decisions and actions. However, diversity of beliefs and lifestyles among the population is not always supported by public policy. In fact, agencies of government may undo or preclude agreements negotiated by family and economic units. For example, because most state governments refuse to recognize same-sex couples as domestic partners, they cannot depend, as a unit, on health or other fringe benefits that are available to their married fellow employees. Nonetheless, in many instances, the government and nongovernmental groups respect the rights of families and work organizations to choose their own ways of functioning even through public policies may be undermined. Thus, employers in regions where the federal judiciary is hostile to equal employment opportunity have implemented the Family and Medical Leave Act more slowly than employers in other regions of the United States (Guthrie and Roth 1999).

The dominant social meanings of gender will always be those that are backed by the force of government policies and agencies. We begin with an overview of the ways government shapes the gendering of social life and the ways government backing is affected by nongovernmental ideas and actions related to gender. The focus will be on economic, cultural, and change-oriented group influences on government. In particular, we will examine the development and impact of the women's movement, men's activism, and the movement for gay and lesbian rights.

Social control is exercised through civil and criminal law in the regulation of organizational, small-group, and individual behavior. Many behaviors are unrestricted by laws or rules. This lack of restrictions implicitly shows their social acceptability or a lack of consensus about them. Some of the most significant work for changing the gender system has aimed at changing the *acceptable* to the *unacceptable* and making the taken-for-granted visible and problematic. For example, marital rape and sexual harassment have only recently been formally recognized as phenomena. Marital rape did not exist legally because husbands were defined as always having a right to sex, whether or not their wives wanted sex. Likewise, the kinds of behaviors currently included in sexual harassment were viewed as normal aspects of social life, socially tolerated even if not socially desirable. Historically, the legal institution has given a "green light" to a fundamental vehicle for husbands' domination of wives and male workers' and supervisors' domination of women on the job.

Government programs affecting income transfer also exercise social control, as we saw in Chapter Six. This means that some individuals and groups are defined as deserving tax breaks or subsidies, and others are deemed ineligible. The differential treatment of people who have been put into separate categories and channeled into separate government programs implicitly reflects and enforces dominant gender ideology, punishing those who do not conform. Here, too, significant changes have occurred in the decades since the begining of the second wave of feminism. For example, in the 1970s a widower was not entitled to survivor's benifits from the Social Security Administration if he chose to stay home to take care of a small child, although a widow was so entitled. The law was based on the assumption that widowed women had lost the family breadwinner, but that widowed men had not. It was overturned when Ruth Bader Ginsburg, who later became the second woman appointed to the U.S. Supreme Court, effectively argued in court that a man should not be denied survivor's benefits on the basis of sex.

Both existing formal rules and their enforcement are gendered. Further, the long record of judicial and enforcement agencies shows that apparently similar cases are often treated inconsistently, related to the intersection of gender, class, race, and ethnicity of the parties in question. Inconsistency in treatment is tied to both the social position of the alleged law-breaker(s) and the social position of those who are the object of that behavior. For example, numerous commentators raised questions about the speedy and energetic prosecution of Martha Stewart, contrasted to the prosecutions of a multitude of (almost exclusively male) corporate executives accused of fraud, involving significantly greater amounts of money and numbers of victims, that proceeded extremely slowly.

This inequality in legal treatment has long been recognized in rape cases. For instance, men accused of raping women from their own social class and race are treated far more leniently than those accused of raping women of a higher social class, and than men of color who are accused of raping white women. White men who rape women of color, or women of a lower class than themselves, are treated most leniently.

## POLITICAL LIFE IS DYNAMIC

In saying that government exists to promote and protect the common good, the central role of ideology is made explicit. Ideas and values about what is the common good are represented in the laws and policies of a society. However, these ideas and values may not represent a consensus, because access to political power and influence is not equally distributed. When there is an absence of consensus, those with less power and influence will probably find that their views are not supported governmentally.

Power and influence sometimes appear unexpectedly, when coalitions are formed that put together otherwise powerless individuals and groups. Policies are susceptible to the mobilization of groups eager to change the status quo as well as to competing groups interested in maintaining that status quo. Social and political changes occur despite the edge held by those whose views are supported by government regulation.

Policies also change in more conventional ways through the gradual shifting of legislative, judicial, and executive perspectives influenced by the more institutionalized routes of the ballot box and the purse strings. The low number of women in lawmaking, interpreting, and enforcing agencies has long indicated women's relative political powerlessness. It also helps explain the sexism in traditional law and the slow pace of change relative to changes in public attitudes.

The U.S. Congress has consistently had lower percentages of women than the legislatures of many other industrialized nations. Rather than a simple explanation focused on voter attitudes, analysts emphasize the structure of electoral systems (Norris 1987).

For example, countries differ in the relative power of the "selectorate" (i.e., those who influence the choice of names to come before the electorate). The more power within the *party* to shape the choices given to the voters, the fewer women candidates will be chosen. After Elizabeth Dole ended her historical candidacy for the 2000 Republican presidential nomination, some party strategists explained her lack of support as symptomatic of women's preference for male candidates (Dowd 1999). This presumption by party leaders has been used to justify the underrepresentation of women as candidates.

If the party leadership and potential financial contributors believe that even women voters won't support a woman, a woman candidate will find it more difficult than a man to receive a party's nomination. Thus, the ideological bias (i.e., political strategists' beliefs about what women candidates can accomplish and about how women voters will behave) has an effect because of the social structure of election campaigns (i.e., the way that people are selected to be their party's nominees). In the contemporary United States, the costs of running a successful campaign have skyrocketed, even within a ten-year period. The biases of campaign donors can effectively remove nonconforming candidates from serious consideration. Hillary Clinton's powerful, although ultimately unsuccessful, campaign for president in 2008 showed both the strong streak of sexism in media coverage and popular response, and the willingness of many voters (women and men) to support a woman candidate (Lawless 2009).

The representation of women on the national level in the United States continues to increase slowly (see Table 7.1). As of 2009, the U.S. Congress was only 16.8 percent female. Although women of color comprise almost a quarter of all women in Congress, all seventeen women senators are white. Representative Nancy Pelosi was the first women elected to lead her party in the House of Representatives in 2002.

**Table 7.1  Women in Public Office, 1969–2009**

| | Women as a Percentage of All Office Holders | | | | |
|---|---|---|---|---|---|
| | **1969** | **1979** | **1989** | **1999** | **2009** |
| U.S. House of Representatives | 2% | 3% | 6% | 13% | 17% |
| U.S. Senate | 1% | 1% | 2% | 9% | 17% |
| Statewide Offices | 7% | 11% | 14% | 28% | 24% |
| State Legislatures | 4% | 10% | 17% | 22% | 24% |

**Sources:** Center for the American Woman and Politics, Eagleton Institute of Politics, Rutgers, The State University of New Jersey. Fact Sheets, 2009. Office of the Historian of the United States House of Representatives, *Women in Congress 1917–1990*. Washington, DC: U.S. Government Printing Office, 1991.

Women of color have made their greatest inroads in local and state offices (see, for example, Darling 1998). There are multiple meanings of leadership among women leaders of color. In one interview study of local leaders in New Mexico, Prindeville (2003) found that Hispanic women emphasized a gender, more than an ethnic, self-identification; and Native American women emphasized an ethnic, more than a gender, self-identification. The evidence supports, again, the importance of looking at gender and race-ethnicity simultaneously to better understand the meanings of women's activities.

The trends in Table 7.1 can be interpreted as change at a snail's pace, or they can be seen as showing a slow but inexorable movement (like the tortoise). For example, we can say the female proportion of Congress more than doubled in the 1989–1999 period, or we can say it grew by less than 10 percent. We can say accurately that women state legislators are almost one quarter of all state legislators. We can also say that the rate of increase is now very slow, and if this rate of increase continues to decline, it will be a very long time before women are represented in proportion to their numbers in the population.

Office holding by women increased first at local and state levels, with congressional representation picking up speed only recently. In addition to the smaller financial requirements for running a local or statewide campaign, the practical problems of holding elective office while fulfilling the roles of wife or mother are more manageable without a long-distance commute. As more families have come to expect wives to have a strong commitment to work, the perception of family obligations as an obstacle has probably declined.

Predicting future patterns is a risky venture, because single issues or events may crystallize activities for change or reaction against change. For example, the "March for Women's Lives" brought about 1 million women, men, and children to Washington, DC, in April 2004 (Barr and Williamson 2004). Participation in this event might become the first step of a political career for grass-roots organizers. The demonstration had a dual focus: maintaining and extending reproductive freedoms (such as sex education and access to legal abortion) in the United States and globally, and mobilizing to replace office holders opposed to these goals. If the momentum of that demonstration continues, changes in laws and lawmakers may follow. Obviously, there are a lot of "ifs" here—which is precisely the point. Things happen and have unanticipated consequences, such as the 1991 Hill–Thomas hearings, which undoubtedly help account for the jump in congressional representation of women in the early 1990s. During and soon after President Clinton's impeachment hearings, many political analysts predicted that women candidates would have a future advantage because of the continuing belief in women's superior sexual morality. After the terrorist attacks on September 11, 2001, the growth of militarism in the United States reactivated for many the view of male-as-protector (Young 2003).

In each of these episodes, it is clear that the media do not simply reflect the news, but also influence it. Candidates (and political office holders with plans for future elections) depend in part on media coverage for reaching voters and donors. Politicians trying to develop support for particular policy changes also benefit from appropriate media coverage. Research on reporters' coverage of women candidates and congresswomen indicates, however, that audiences learn about women's actions on "women's" issues but that the involvement and leadership of congresswomen in other areas is underreported (Carroll and Schreiber 1997). Another way in which coverage about women candidates is narrower than that of men was clear in the reporting on the 2007–2008 race for the Democratic presidential nomination. Because of Barack Obama and Hillary Clinton's unusual candidacies, commentators often discussed race or sex. However, the possible candidacy of a person who is nontraditional along both dimensions was never raised (Junn 2009). Similarly, the maleness of Obama and the whiteness of Clinton were not remarked on as factors that might be affecting their campaigns and their reception by the public.

Starting in the early 1990s, talk radio became a significant political force, giving voice to and further encouraging hostility toward a caricatured version of feminism (such as Rush Limbaugh's popularization of the term *feminazi*; Levit 1998). The format, content, and tone of talk radio, rather than the medium of radio itself, has attracted a predominantly male audience (Kohut and Parker 1997). The World Wide Web is the latest, very powerful medium for spreading information and misinformation, and for opening discussion up to many voices. They may choose, however, to listen only to others with similar views. This has become not only a medium for the spread of dangerous information (e.g., related to the construction of bombs and formulae for the "date-rape drug"), but also a place to organize activists for feminist change. Many sites that proclaim themselves vehicles for improving the quality of women's lives, however, merely use the notion of "women's culture" as a way to sell products and services (Prose 2000).

It has been traditional to define political participation narrowly, focusing on party politics and voting behavior. This overlooks grass-roots activity as well as the influence of economic interests on the political process. Formal activities, such as voting in primaries and general elections, and informal activities have contributed to changes in women's and men's opportunities and responsibilities through the enactment of new laws, changes in politics shaping the execution or enforcement of laws, and the taking to court of those practices and laws that have not changed through legislation. Figure 7.1 presents some of the many historical moments that have changed the meaning of gender in the United States.

## FEMINIST ACTIVISM: THE RIGHT TO VOTE

Social movements, broad-based efforts from outside the political institution, have been a significant force for changes throughout U.S. history. The feminist movement itself is a

| 1848 | Seneca Falls Women's Rights Convention. |
|------|------|
| 1855 | FIRST married woman recorded as keeping her own name (Lucy Stone). Others who followed this practice were called "Lucy Stoners." |
| 1866 | FIRST constitutional definition of "citizens" and "voters" as "male," in the 14th Amendment. |
| 1870 | FIRST women served on juries (in the Wyoming Territory). |
| 1888 | New York suffragists won passage of a law requiring women doctors for women patients in mental institutions. |
| 1893 | FIRST state (Colorado) adopted a state amendment enfranchising women. |
| 1900 | Two thirds of divorce cases were initiated by the wife; a century earlier, most had no right to sue for divorce. |
| 1913 | Suffragists parading in Washington, DC, drew people away from President Wilson's arrival in the city. Suffragists were mobbed by abusive crowds. |
| 1917 | FIRST woman elected to the U.S. House of Representatives (Jeannette Rankin of Montana). |
| 1920 | Women receive the right to vote with passage of the 19th Amendment to the U.S. Constitution. However, in most Southern states African American women, like African American men, were denied the vote. |
| 1933 | FIRST woman in a presidential cabinet (Frances Perkins, Secretary of Labor). |
| 1945 | The Equal Pay for Equal Work bill (first introduced in 1872) failed in Congress. It passed in 1963. |
| 1966 | FIRST African American woman appointed to the federal judiciary (Constance Baker Motley). |
| 1968 | EEOC (Equal Employment Opportunity Commission) ruled that unless employers can show a bona fide occupational qualification exists, sex-segregated help wanted newspaper ads are illegal. |
| 1972 | In *Eisenstadt v. Baird* the U.S. Supreme Court rules that the right to privacy encompasses an unmarried person's right to use contraceptives. |
| 1975 | In *Weinberger v. Wiesenfeld* the U.S. Supreme Court ruled that a widower whose wife had paid Social Security taxes is eligible for Social Security survivor benefits to raise a minor child (previously a benefit limited to widows). |
| 1981 | FIRST woman appointed to the U.S. Supreme Court (Sandra Day O'Connor). |
| 1984 | FIRST woman candidate on a major party's presidential slate (Geraldine Ferraro). |
| 1991 | Sexual harassment became a household term, due to Anita Hill's testimony during U.S. Senate confirmation hearings on Justice Thomas' nomination to the Supreme Court. |
| 1993 | The Family and Medical Leave Act was signed into law, giving job protection, under limited circumstances, to men and women who temporarily cannot work because of family care obligations. |
| 1995 | Fourth World Conference on Women sponsored by the United Nations in Beijing, China. |

**Figure 7.1 Pursuing Gender Equity in the U.S. Political and Legal System: Examples of Large and Small Steps and Obstacles**

Sources: The National Women's History Project timeline at: http://www.legacy98.org/timeline.html. Evans, Sara M. 2003. *Tidal Wave.*

leading example of a force effecting basic changes in sociaty. The first wave of feminist action in the United States started before the Civil War, in the mid-nineteeth century. Although best known for its aim to win voting rights, first-wave activists worked for other rights as well, such as the right of married women to own property. The abolitionist challenge to inequalities among people on the basis of race led to challenges of inequalities on the basis of sex. Women's active participation and leadership in the abolition movement itself undermined beliefs about women's nature and the limits in it that justified women's lack of rights under the law. The conditions of enslaved women's lives clearly challenged notions of women's weakness. The momentum of women's rights activism was weakened during and after the Civil War. A resurgence of feminism started in 1890, and the struggle for the vote continued until 1920, when the Nineteenth Amendment to the U.S. Constitution was ratified. The participation of women in the war efforts (World War I) was rewarded with the vote.

Feminist activism decreased after suffrage was achieved. Some supporters saw their goal reached, and lack of consensus among others about the next targets for improving women's rights led to a splintering of movement organizations (see Davidson and Gordon 1979). Though the pace of change slowed considerably, and feminisim seemed to disappear as a collective political position, the values of feminism did not. There were sporadic achievements in the movement toward equality. For example, the first woman cabinet secretary was appointed in 1933, the first woman was appointed to the federal judiciary in 1934, women's service in the military and civilian labor force boomed during World War II, and wives of striking Chicano miners succeeded in putting housing conditions (typically a "woman's issue") on the list of union demands (a struggle depicted in *Salt of the Earth* 1954).

### THE SECOND WAVE

Like the first wave, the "women's movement," or the "second wave" of feminist activism, grew out of women's participation in other political change activities. The civil rights movement of the 1950s and 1960s led to a questioning of the inequities between women and men. Young activist women in the civil rights and then the anti–Vietnam War movements challenged the sexist practices of men in their organizations, especially as some in the antiwar movement embraced "hyper-masculine" rhetoric and strategies (Evans 2003, 23–24). Their feminist activism came to be called "women's liberation" because of its emphasis on freeing women from the many informal and interpersonal, as well as formal, constraints on their achievements of equality.

The political establishment itself contributed to the development of the second wave. President Kennedy, following his 1960 campaign pledge, established a National Commission on the Status of Women. Its report was published in 1963 and helped create momentum for change. The Equal Pay Act of 1963 prohibited unequal pay for people doing the same work, although it did not prohibit discrimination that prevents people from doing the same work. In 1964, the Civil Rights Act was passed, motivated principally to undo race discrimination. Its list of prohibited bases for discrimination also included sex. Ironically, women's rights were in this law as part of a strategy to defeat the legislation in Congress. Introduced in seriousness by one of the few women in the House of Representatives, Martha Griffith of Michigan, it was allowed to remain in the bill when conservative Senator Howard K. Smith of Virginia supported the language. He knew that voting against an antiracial discrimination bill would be too politically dangerous, but expected members of Congress to use the inclusion of women to justify their votes against the proposal. His expectation was wrong, and the bill passed both houses and was signed into law.

One of the many recommendations of the National Commission on the Status of Women was the formation of such commissions in all states. The National Organization for Women (N.O.W.) was formed by a group of prominent women who met while attending a National Conference of State Commissions on the Status of Women. This segment of the second wave, the "women's rights," or equality, branch, focused on changes in political and legal arrangements. This branch was more racially integrated than the liberation branch. This was due in part to the women's rights branch's growth out of existing women's organizations, such as the Y.W.C.A., with long-standing black participation and leadership. In addition, it attracted participation from women active in the network of black women's voluntary associations, like the National Council of Negro Women.

In contrast, the women's liberation adherents were focused on personal change in themselves and the men to whom they were connected. Women of color who chose a women's liberation approach generally found white women unaware of their race privilege or were themselves uncomfortable with the race disloyalty they felt in speaking openly about sexism in front of white women (Evans 2003).

The women's movement quickly gathered momentum with the rapid spread of "consciousness-raising" groups, particularly among younger white women, and the pursuit of changes through legislation and litigation by organizations representing older, and often more organizationally experienced and racially diverse, women. It occurred in a period when activism was regarded as normal and many people believed in the potential for improving people's lives through governmental action. Whether radical or reformist, action took many forms, with multiple targets for change. During the early and mid-1970s, legal obstacles to equality fell rapidly.

On the basis of differences in both the means and the ends advocated by participants in the second wave, Ferree and Hess (1985) described four different perspectives. **Career feminists** envisioned freeing individuals from sexism through personal transformation. Liberal feminists shared the goal of freeing individuals from sexism, but disagreed with career feminists on the means to that end. Liberal feminists believed sociopolitical changes would be the necessary means for achieving individual freedom. Both radical feminists and socialist feminists had new, nonsexist communities as their common goal, but differed on the means to that end. Radical feminists emphasized personal transformation, via cultural transformation. In contrast, socialist feminists, like liberal feminists, considered sociopolitical changes the necessary means, according to Ferree and Hess.

Each variety of feminism made distinctive contributions to the movement's accomplishments and to the positive character of feminism's diversity. Thus, successful career feminists helped develop a base of support for further progress. Liberal feminists led the push toward women's equal participation as politicians, judges, and other policymakers. Radical feminists drew attention to the myriad ways that the culture endorses and reinforces sexist assumptions and behaviors. Socialist feminists emphasized the importance of social class, race, and other dimensions of difference that prevented people from achieving equality.

This way of categorizing feminist activism helps, after the fact, to understand some crucial differences among feminists during the 1970s. It is important, also, to appreciate the intensity of that period, in which approaches and coalitions were evolving rapidly. Feminists were intent on achieving equality, and there were ongoing disputes about what that goal should look like and how it might be reached. People's views were dynamic, changing in response to new ideas and developments.

Starting early in the second wave, feminists aimed at ratification of the proposed Equal Rights Amendment (E.R.A.) to the U.S. Constitution. First proposed in Congress soon after women achieved voting rights, and reintroduced to session after session of Congress, the proposal had never been voted out of committee to the floor. In 1970, Judiciary Committee review was by passed with a petition, signed by a majority of members of the House of Representatives, to bring the bill to the floor. It was quickly ratified in the House and overwhelmingly passed in the Senate, and 30 of the necessary 38 states ratified it within a year of receiving it from the Congress.

### Proposed Equal Rights Amendment to the U.S. Constitution: The Full Text

1. Equality of rights under the law shall not be denied or abridged by the United States or by any State on account of sex.
2. The Congress shall have the power to enforce, by appropriate legislation, the provisions of this article.
3. This amendment shall take effect two years after the date of ratification.

Despite its apparently simple and straightforward language, as time passed a movement against it gathered steam, alleging all sorts of dire results should it be ratified. Thus, it became viewed as increasingly radical as it awaited passage in the states that were the most conservative. Southern and Mormon state legislators were unwilling to support the E.R.A. (Mansbridge 1986).

Gradually, debates over the priority of the E.R.A.'s passage on "the" feminist agenda clarified the existence of different goals among women (and men) who were committed to feminist change. As the struggle to get ratification in the necessary number of states lengthened, increasing numbers of people questioned the use of resources of time and money for its passage (including the campaign for the congressional legislation to extend the deadline for state ratification). Other arenas needed action to improve women's lives, related to different views of both the goals and the means for their achievement. In addition, serious conflict developed about how feminist activism (most notably, by N.O.W.) should be related to the burgeoning, and rapidly changing, movement for lesbian rights (Adam 1995). Presenting their concerns as pragmatically based on the negative effect of public perceptions of feminists as lesbian, some leaders (such as Betty Friedan) argued against incorporating lesbian concerns in feminist action. Certainly, some people taking this position were motivated as well by their own homophobia. The argument that lesbian rights belonged low on the list of N.O.W.'s priorities itself can be interpreted as homophobic.

Combined with a growing awareness of difference within and among feminist organizations, the fight about the E.R.A. was a major source of fragmentation of the second wave. Nonetheless, it had a transforming impact on many aspects of life in the United States. It changed what people take for granted about the relations between the sexes and the use of biologically based categories to limit one's opportunities and responsibilities. The wide-ranging inequalities that remain are undeniable, as is the slow rate of change of the last twenty years. Also undeniable are feminism's many accomplishments. Thus, the *first* woman was elected governor in her own right in 1974; there had been four women governors earlier—widows of two governors, and wives of two governors prevented from reelection by term limits. Attitudes have changed. For example, many people objected to the goal of "equal pay for equal work" in the 1960s, because they assumed that men had greater financial needs and should be paid more. The belief in equal pay for equal work is now widely accepted. A broad range of changes took place in a quarter of a century—in contrast, the women's struggle for suffrage took three quarters of a century to succeed.

Upper-and middle-class white feminists have been more socially and economically secure than women of color, economically marginal women, and lesbians (Christensen 1997). As a result, they tended to focus more or less exclusively on the inequality associated with sex alone. This has led to different priorities for action in the predominantly white groups in the movement and in feminist organizations among women of color. For example, white, middle-class feminist activists may emphasize eliminating the glass ceiling blocking upper-middle- and upper-class women from reaching the very highest professional and managerial positions. Working-class white feminists and feminists of color may emphasize the **sticky floor** that prevents people from moving out of the low-level dead-end jobs into which they were initially hired; or they may make the development of sufficient, affordable, quality child care a high priority.

The media have presented second-wave feminism as a monolithic movement (Huddy 1997; Costain et al. 1997), failing to recognize and report the diversity of feminist issues and the diversity of feminists and feminist organizations. News stories are **framed**: They are put in a particular context, which gives a particular way of making sense of the facts of the story, and they may guide the reporter to exclude other facts that don't make sense within that context (Norris 1997). A "pack" mentality among reporters covering the same story undermines the development of original frames for the story (Vavrus 2002). The choice of frame may be unconscious to the reporter and editor (who see it as the *obvious* way to tell the story). Clearly, what makes sense or is obvious to a person will vary; indeed, some things this book treats as obvious may have struck you as controversial, or incredible.

Stories about feminism and feminists in the media tend to assume that the dominant views of feminism are accurate and relate the facts within those views. Similarly, the news media rely on old-fashioned, often essentialist frames about gender and leadership when reporting on candidates and elected officials (Barnett 2007). Even Internet news sources, which might be expected to be less traditional than print and broadcast news outlets, continue the older sources' pattern of reporting in gender-biased ways. For example, they are more likely to comment on women's than men's appearance and personal lives, while providing less information about women's status and power than on men's (Burke and Mazzarella 2008). With the anticipated integration of news media organizations (along sex, race, and class dimensions), the taken-for-granted views of reporters were expected to change. Although the total number of women in news organizations has increased, parity has not been achieved. In 2001, half of the radio station news staffs still had no women; television stations had a much better representation of women (93.6 percent of stations had at least one woman on staff). A quarter of television stations and almost that proportion of radio stations had women news directors, although in television they were concentrated in stations with smaller staffs. Women were 37 percent of daily newspaper news staffs, and 39 percent of local television newsrooms (RTNDA 2002). Evidence indicates that women's choices of frames have not been significantly different than men's, although their choices of stories have been broader (Mills 1997).

The rate of racial and ethnic integration in media news has been extremely slow; in 2002, people of color were 9 percent of television station news directors, 5 percent of radio station news directors, 21 percent of local television news staffs, and 8 percent of radio station news staffs. The underrepresentation of women of color has contributed to the lack of reporting on feminist consciousness and action among African American, Latina, and Asian American women.

Finally, news staffs actually have become less diverse in social class backgrounds as most reporters now come out of college, rather than working their way up from clerical positions in the organizations. Important white working-class women's activism has also been overlooked in media representations. The different interests common between socially and economically secure women and less privileged women, noted previously, are manifested in the choices of stories and angles made by journalists—who are more likely to be socially and economically secure (Vavrus 2002).

If one takes the multiracial feminist perspective that individuals' oppression results from the multiple systems of domination, the single-minded emphasis on gender issues by many feminists renders them part of the problem of domination. Many women of color and economically marginal women of all racial-ethnic groups have had little interest in white-dominated feminist organizations because of this combination of prioritizing goals according to white middle-class interests and the frequent casting of men in general as the enemy (hooks 1984). Many African American writers and some other feminists have adopted the term **womanist** to describe a perspective that simultaneously focuses on race-ethnicity, class, and gender in the struggle for all people's liberation. A womanist perspective looks at sex inequality but also seeks the improvement of men's lives (Collins 1990). That is, the influence of an oppressive race and class system on men's behavior is emphasized at the same time as the oppressive treatment of women by men of their own class, race, or ethnic group.

Feminist thought and action developed rapidly among Latina and African American women and more slowly among Asian Americans (Chow 1987). Activists developed ideologies that best fit their experiences and concerns. Women from different racial-ethnic groups differed in some of the issues they confronted; further, each category is more heterogeneous than even these umbrella terms suggest. But they all had to deal with the tensions between their feminist views and their racial-ethnic movement. Sometimes they faced accusations of disloyalty for embracing feminist ideas, and generally they faced marginalizing by white feminist activists (García 1989).

## THE THIRD WAVE

Young feminists started calling themselves "the third wave," capturing the centrality of their revisioning of feminism. As described in Chapter One, this generation grew up during the backlash against the women's movement. It confronts challenges opened up by the greater freedoms achieved by the "second wave." For example, with the decrease in overt sex discrimination in response to legal changes and challenges, subtle discrimination has increased. Third-wave feminists are more likely than their second-wave counterparts to focus on concerns about economic, cultural, and sexual inequalities among women of different classes, ethnicities, sexualities, and nationalities.

Many second- and third-wave feminists share an interest in women's oppression globally, such as the effects on women of economic globalization and the AIDS epidemic. Feminist organizations representing women of different generations mobilized against the U.S. invasion of Iraq in 2003, and continued afterwards to mobilize opposition to the Bush administration's foreign policies (Kutz-Flamenbaum 2004). Finally, third-wave feminists are often concerned with issues of sexual exploitation, violence, and the increasing prevalence of health problems stemming from increasingly abnormal cultural demands of thinness for young women (Brumberg 1997).

Third-wave feminists are also more comfortable with cultural symbols that older feminists consider degrading to women. Younger feminists may see themselves sabotaging sexist symbols by taking them over and using them ironically or using them to gain attention for radical messages (*The Righteous Babes* 1998). Approximately one third of a million people under 25 years old participated in the 2004 March for Women's Lives, many wearing tee shirts saying "THIS IS WHAT A FEMINIST LOOKS LIKE."

With the continued media presentation of feminists as man-haters, it is not surprising that many young women do not call themselves feminists even though they are aware of and concerned about sex discrimination (Aronson 2003). Most young feminists are not hostile toward men. In one large and racial-ethnically diverse survey of college students, women who self-identified as feminist were even less likely than other women to express hostility toward males (Anderson, Kanner, and Elsayegh 2009).

## MEN'S ACTIVISM

Many men have engaged in confronting sexism in U.S. society. Early in the second wave of the women's movement, the men's movement consisted of groups aimed at helping to eliminate sexism (see, for example, Farrell 1975). More recently, men's activism has come to include profeminist and antifeminist branches. Some groups focus on protecting men from antimale practices perceived as flowing from feminist action.

Featured in cover stories in major news magazines, Susan Faludi's 1999 book, *Stiffed*, reports on the tough position in which working men in the contemporary United States find themselves. Regardless of political standpoint, analysts of men's positions agree that masculinity is in crisis. However, though it is popular to blame the crisis on women's growing equality, leading socialist feminist and multiracial feminist social scientists (e.g., Michael Kimmel and R. W. Connell) highlight the changing political economy, including the erosion of U.S. political and economic hegemony internationally. Thus, as we saw in Chapter Six, it is largely the erosion of working men's economic conditions that has brought them closer to women's situation, rather than enormous gains in women's circumstances.

Consistent with distortions in media coverage of other gender-related issues, the media have also underreported the economic and social factors eroding men's situations. Indeed, although Faludi's book was widely reported, most reviews and discussions coming out of its publication largely ignored her assessment of the importance of the changing economy. Instead, the media focused more or less exclusively on women's advances as causing men's loss of status.

Some men's rights activists have also focused on eliminating traditional arrangements that are unfair to men, such as the almost automatic granting of custody to mothers in contested divorces through the mid- to late twentieth century. Other groups focus on men's psychological pain, most prominently with weekend retreats to the woods to facilitate getting in touch with one's real self. The antistate orientation of the father's rights movement is more commonly reported, with its focus on custody, child support orders, and the frequently uncritical acceptance of allegations of men's violence. Less frequently noted is the positive impact of the movement on many participants' attention to their relationships with their children (Crowley 2008).

The Promise Keepers, a Christian organization, flourished in the late 1990s (Kimmel 1997). It used large rallies around the United States to create a sense of brotherhood and renewal. It is the largest and most publicized of the organizations aimed at individual men's redemption through a more responsible performance of traditional family roles. However, it is doubtful that much transformation actually occurs among men who attend the rallies. According to Kimmel, "Current men's movements are often like psychological first aid, applying a salve to the wounds and then sending the men back out into the fray" (1996, 331).

In contrast to movements led by and for men in dominant class and racial-ethnic positions, marginal groups are more apt to include a political agenda in their organizations. Organized by religious leaders, the Million Man March combined macro- and micro-social agendas for African American men. Speakers called on men to examine their failures to fulfill traditional masculine responsibilities in the family. They also called on men to build together organizations for the improvement of their communities. Numerous local Million Man organizations were started around the country to foster economic and social initiatives for community improvement. While addressing economic and racial marginality, leaders nonetheless presumed a heterosexual audience, underscoring the marginal position of gay and bisexual men within African American communities (Cole and Guy-Sheftall 2003).

Women in general, and feminists in particular, have had mixed views of these organizations and events. Some organizations, like the Promise Keepers, have clear statements embracing patriarchy in the family (although these statements are selectively publicized). Other have provided an umbrella under which men with varied views of women's rights gather. Thus, the Million Man March—rather than the Million People March—was seen by some as a call to men's taking leadership in the African American community, and by others as simply a call to men's sharing the work of the community and the family more fairly with women. For communities in economic and political crisis, the increased participation of men is welcome and may be worth the cost of an ambiguous message about patriarchy.

## AFFIRMATIVE ACTION: LEGAL CHANGE AND SOCIAL RESISTANCE

Affirmative action, developed under Republican President Richard Nixon, has had a long and controversial history. Despite the fact that white women have been the largest group benefiting from affirmative action policy, the popular conception among white men has been that affirmative action is largely about race, rather than sex. Similarly, evidence that shows the importance of affirmative action policy in creating and enforcing nondiscriminatory corporate practices tends to be disregarded. Instead, the myth persists that affirmative action leads to the employment of unqualified individuals. Numerous other myths continue to survive, partly because of the lack of coverage of the contrary evidence, but also because many people refuse to believe the facts that contradict strongly held beliefs they already have (Valian 1998). For example, many whites believe (inaccurately) that *qualified* people of color generally oppose affirmative action, on the presumption that they will be considered unqualified employees who have merely been hired or promoted to meet corporate goals.

These very different perceptions among white men, white women, and women and men of various racial and ethnic minority groups stem from multiple causes. With a lack of media attention to evidence, individuals rely on reports from friends and family—typically racially and ethnically homogeneous groups. Individuals with relationships across racial-ethnic lines may carefully avoid discussing such a charged topic, and discussions about race-related topics are often taboo. In U.S. culture, individuals who disagree with racist comments or jokes generally believe it would be uncivil to challenge the speaker. To do so, they fear, would be to challenge the very survival of the group in which they are participating (Eliasoph 1999). Thus, people with nonracist attitudes and beliefs suffer from **pluralistic ignorance**, unaware that others share their views because no one speaks up. Those who make racist comments are also unaware of the different views among those taking part in the conversation. Stories of discrimination and reverse discrimination are repeated, distorted, and credited or discredited on the basis of group membership.

Attitudes about affirmative action, and their sources, are complex. Although individual prejudice helps explain rejection of affirmative action policies (specifically those focused on race), Williams and his colleagues (1999) found that even prejudiced individuals approved of affirmative action if they also believed in basic American values of equal opportunity. This complexity of public sentiment helps explain the relative stability of affirmative action despite numerous announcements by politicians in the late 1990s that they would dismantle it.

Congressional and presidential elections and appointments to the federal judiciary, and the selection of employees and supervisors in federal agencies, will continue to affect the ongoing struggle over evolving affirmative action policies and their enforcement. We have come full circle to the question of the composition of elected and appointed governmental positions and agencies with which the chapter began.

## ACTIVISM AROUND SEXUALITIES AND SEX IDENTIFICATION

In the 1960s, accompanying the growth of the civil rights, women's rights, and the anti–Vietnam War movements, gay men and lesbian women started to organize for their rights. Early efforts preceded the night in June 1969 when police encountered full-scale resistance to their raid on the Stonewall, a homosexual bar in New York City's Greenwich Village. The movement, gaining strength during the rapidly evolving second wave of feminism, was characterized by rifts between and among homosexual men and women as well as by solidarity as they worked to overcome legal and informal homophobic practices and beliefs.

Just as women in the civil rights and antiwar movements criticized their male fellow activists, lesbians criticized gay leaders and organizations for their masculinist biases. Organizing strategies and goals often did not reflect patterned differences in the lifestyles of female and male homosexuals as well as differences related to their experiences of societal sexism. The selection of leaders, the dynamics of organizations, and the goals of homosexual activism sometimes reproduced the patriarchal behaviors and values of the heterosexual majority.

Similarly, reformist and radical tendencies among activists have frequently been the basis of conflict within the movement. Some gay rights activists have adopted radical strategies (such as ACT UP's and Queer Nation's "in your face" demonstrations). Others have worked through the system to try to change the laws regarding partner and parental rights of gay men and lesbians, membership in the military, and hate-motivated violence (Jenness 1999). Movement organizations and activists have also been affected by opposing activists on the religious right, in some ways being reshaped and becoming stronger in response to the right's attacks (Fetner 2008).

In one of his earliest actions as president in 1993, Bill Clinton ordered a new policy for the military: "Don't Ask, Don't Tell." Homosexual men and lesbians are permitted to serve in the military, as long as their sexual orientation does not become known. If they (or anyone else) reveal their orientation, they will be dishonorably discharged from the service. This compromise has been an uneasy one since its inception. There is increasing pressure (from many military leaders as well as others) to simply make sexual orientation irrelevant to military service.

Two events of the late 1990s influenced public perceptions and beliefs about sexualities and their place in U.S. social life. In 1998, Matthew Shepard, a young gay college student, was beaten to death by two men he met in a Laramie, Wyoming, bar. The public outrage, focused on the event and reawakened a year later by the trials, brought awareness of and concern about homophobic violence to the fore. At about the same time as the trials, the film *Boys Don't Cry* was released, based on the true story of a rape and murder of a young woman who was living as a young man. Its star won the Academy Award for best actress in 1999. A changing cultural environment led to extensive media coverage about the Shepard murder and the marketing of a feature film sympathetic to a transgendered person. Subsequently, the coverage and the film contributed to further changes in cultural beliefs about sexualities as well as awareness of the extent of homophobic violence. In 2009 the U.S. Congress passed and President Obama signed the Matthew Shepard Act, broadening existing hate crime legislation to extend to those based on the sexuality of the victim.

With the growing controversy about same-sex marriage, previous levels of acceptance of gay and lesbian people may be threatened. While some opponents of same-sex marriage appear to base their position very specifically on religious meanings of marriage, others may be using the controversy to undo previously achieved increases in public acceptance of homosexuality and same-sex relationships. Shortly after endorsing a proposed constitutional amendment that would ban same-sex marriage, President Bush's

Days after the unanimous ruling by the Iowa Supreme Court allowing same-sex marriage (April 2009) thousands of supporters rallied in Des Moines.
Photo credit: Tracy E.Ore.

administration announced a change in its interpretation of a regulation formerly used to provide equal employment protection to nonheterosexual federal employees (FederalTimes.com 2004). After his inauguration, President Obama announced a change in federal policy, extending benefits to the same-sex partners of federal employees.

Recently, activism has grown around the social construction of the biologically marked sexes. People who consider themselves neither male nor female are calling for a reshaping of arrangements that currently presume all people fit into one of these two sexes. Dormitories and athletic teams, for example, are the focus of student activism by and on the behalf of transgendered people on campuses (F. Bernstein 2004).

The inadequacies of the two-sex categorization are also challenged by people whose bodies do not fit the unnaturally narrow expectations for their sex. For example, a large-framed woman customer wearing jeans, a sweatshirt, and short hair may be called "sir" by a salesperson. Her misclassification is due to the inadequate conceptions of femaleness and maleness. She is certainly dressed like many other women, with a hairstyle and absence of makeup that many other women also practice; she defines herself as a woman. If she chooses to disrupt the interaction by identifying herself as a woman, she will also disrupt the gendered expectations held by the salesperson, even if only temporarily (Lucal 1999). Others, with more recognizable sex identities, may choose gender bending as a strategy to destabilize the gender system.

### THINKING ABOUT POLITICAL ACTION

Feminist scholars have drawn attention to the essential contributions of rank-and-file members and sympathizers of organization and movement activities: An exclusive focus on public leadership distorts any picture of the process of political change. This distortion systematically understates the ways in which women and socially disadvantaged men have been political actors in the history of this society. Thus, photographs of the formal leaders of many organizations suggest that the organization is male-led.

Women have had leading roles and performed essential rank-and-file work in many obviously political campaigns, such as labor strikes (Fonow 1998) and antilynching activism. In addition, by creating and maintaining a healthy infrastructure of community organizations, working-class women and women of color have been crucial in sustaining communities during particularly oppressive periods and in mobilizing the communities during periods of seeking expanded rights. The civil rights movement of the 1950s and 1960s was able to develop quickly largely because of the strong tradition of women's activism within African American communities. With the high visibility of the clergy as the leadership of the more reformist branch of the civil rights movement, however, the important roles of churchwomen and other African American women remained invisible at worst and seriously underestimated at best. The contributions of women in the more radical organizations within the civil rights movement were also undervalued (Barnett 1993). The intersection of race and gender had significant implications in the civil rights movement. Black and white women traveled different paths to activism and participated in different ways once recruited (Irons 1998).

In addition to the many modes that political action can take, apparently apolitical activity also has significant political ramifications. On the basis of their study of a rape crisis center, Schmitt and Martin (1999) conclude that many individual members of mainstream organizations and agencies may work toward feminist goals by using knowledge and persuasion during interactions that are a normal part of organizational and interorganizational contacts. Similarly, when community activists got jobs in public agencies, they tried to use those jobs to create change (Naples 1991).

From this perspective, most estimates of the magnitude of feminist activism will be fatally flawed, underestimating the actual impact of the feminist movement. One example of the broader influence of the feminist movement is the increased availability of "couples' groups" that many churches offer to help married couples learn to communicate better, with the goals of strengthening marriages and reducing the likelihood of divorce. More generally, feminist action has contributed to the increased variety of family forms and the growing irrelevance of the concept of a "normal" family (Lempert and DeVault 2000).

### ECONOMICS AND POLITICS

Focusing on public leadership can also underestimate the role played by interested economically powerful groups. Involved behind the scenes, groups with the power to make significant financial contributions, promises, or threats might stain the reputation of a social movement or an organization. Thus, in their cross-national review of antifeminist movements past and present, Chafetz and Dworkin (1987) reveal a pattern of the quiet financial support from groups with a vested interest in maintaining the gender status quo. For example, fearing that enfranchised women would support antiliquor policies, liquor industry organizations were the primary financial backers of antisuffrage activism in some locales.

Protective legislation, by which women were excluded from full economic opportunity, was initially passed for the good of those women. Most advocates of women's rights supported laws prohibiting employers from exposing women and children to dangerous working conditions. However, when the conditions deemed harmful to women were known also to be harmful to men, men were often left unprotected or with less protection by these laws. Corporations chose the least costly alternative. Thus, a particularly high-risk group (women, especially those of childbearing age) was excluded, and the company avoided the costs of removing or reducing the unsafe workplace conditions to protect all workers. Through Supreme Court action, exclusion based on sex was ruled illegal in 1991.

If regulations or lawsuits change the cost–benefit equation through the imposition of fines or payments to injured workers, workplace conditions may improve. Alternatively, corporations will move to locations with weaker regulations or enforcement or both. Men often refrain from demanding workplace cleanup because they fear that employers would shut down or move their operations, rather than spend money to comply with government regulations. As long as men have the primary responsibility for wage earning, this pattern persists.

Men therefore often work in hazardous settings, perhaps fearing unemployment, and women are often deprived of employment opportunity because of previously formal, currently habitual patriarchal policy to protect them from hazards. Protective legislation worked against each sex in different ways.

## GENDER IDEOLOGY AND SOCIAL CONTROL

Several themes in this culture's traditional version of patriarchy help explain the "logic" underlying the gendering of public policies and civil and criminal law. Patriarchy itself defines maleness as a necessary condition for authority, though not a sufficient one. Being female, in contrast, means being childlike, powerless, and incapable of surviving independently of a man. In this view, women, by their nature, are vulnerable to victimization and in need of protection. The power that comes with being male implies the potential for violence, the abuse of male power (Levit 1998).

Patterns of social control are also influenced by a related set of themes about sexuality: Women are seen as having a malevolent and usually sexual power that makes them dangerous to men. Women's menacing sexuality is aggravated by men's vulnerability, due to their presumed uncontrollably strong, biological sexual drives. Although women's enjoyment of sexuality is currently viewed as normal, women are still perceived as able to control their sexual energies when men cannot. Therefore, a woman cannot use her sexuality as a defense for unacceptable social behavior as a man might for rape and other acts of violence.

Thus, cultural views of the essentially male and essentially female include gender-specific versions of goodness and evil. Women are treated alternatively as childlike and wicked creatures. For example, there is a legal tradition that suggests that females are temptresses, whether or not they are conscious of their role. Two of the ways in which the legal institution has given a message that females are likely to be evil in a sexualized, seductive, manipulative way have been the legal treatment of rape cases and the construction of "incorrigible" adolescent girls.

Sexual assault is increasingly understood among social scientists to be an assertion of power, rather than an act of uncontrollable sexual desire. Indeed, some men who commit homosexual rape are quite clear that they are not homosexual; their assault was a way to establish dominance. Conversely, male rape victims have reported that they feel stigmatized by others, perhaps more because they have been dominated than because they might be presumed to be homosexual.

Rape and other forms of sexual violence provide the most extreme examples of legal sexism and the clearest examples of legal ideology that defines females as seductive. The victim's appearance and personal history are sometimes formally used to justify her rape. Even rapes of very young girls are sometimes attributed to the seductive behavior of the victim. Officials have been notoriously unresponsive to reports of rape and attempted rape from women in the U.S. service academies and in the military itself (Schmitt 2004).

The double standard is clear if we think of alternative situations: Could a bank robbery be justified by the presence of an irresistible amount of money? While women are blamed if they are attacked in places they should have avoided, no one blames the victims of drunk drivers for driving near taverns (Fuentes 1997, cited in Feltey 2001).

Parents are more likely to call the police when a girl disappears; if she is picked up as a runaway, she will be charged. If a boy doesn't come home, his parents are less likely to notify the police (Chesney-Lind and Belknap 2004). Legal minors whose offenses do not break any laws are "status offenders"; what they do is considered wrong only because of their minor status. They may be defined as stubborn, labeled incorrigible, and treated as juvenile offenders. This legal label is more often applied to adolescent girls than boys when a family has trouble dealing with an uncooperative teenager. Girls are expected to be rather compliant, docile people, but difficult boys are understandable ("boys will be boys"). Girls who are violent, even if in response to violent victimization, are punished for violating gender-specific norms (Schaffner 2006).

### JUSTICE AND GENDER

The law as written, interpreted, and enforced demonstrates institutionalized beliefs about gender (Bumiller 1990). Although the last thirty-five years have seen major changes in legal views of gender, significant problems remain. As discussed in Chapter Two, people have come to believe that problems of gender inequality have been solved (Rhode 1997). Those problems that clearly remain are often justified as resulting from women's own choices and characteristics. For those injustices related to gender that are undeniable, like injustices related to race, many people take no responsibility for working toward change, because they themselves did not create the injustices. These views contribute to the slow rate of change in the legal system and the ways in which it treats people of different racial-gender categories differently.

*The law*, a commonly used term, disguises great variation within the legal system. In the United States, legislation is enacted on local, county, state, and federal levels. As long as the U.S. Constitution, Congress, or the federal court system does not override legislative or executive acts, local governments are free to enact their own formal rules. Likewise, judges may make decisions that differ by legal jurisdiction. This possibility creates many different, coexisting legal realities that impinge on people's lives, when inconsistencies remain among rulings (Haney 2000). For example, the 1989

Supreme Court ruling in the case of *Webster v. Reproductive Health Services* returned to states the authority to restrict abortion that had been removed in 1973, when the Court ruled that such laws violated a woman's constitutional right to privacy. The Violence Against Women Act (V.A.W.A.), passed in 1994, states that "all persons shall have the right to be free from crimes motivated by gender" (quoted in Jenness 1999). By the enactment of this law, and the early 1990s group of anti-hate-crimes laws, Congress sought a level of protection for people throughout the United States. In 2000, much of V.A.W.A.'s protection was eliminated when the Supreme Court ruled that it interfered with constitutionally based states' rights. Activists must work in each state for the passage of such protective legislation.

In one state, gender may be irrelevant to the limitations imposed on people or the rights granted to them, but in another state, gender may be legally linked to opportunities or obstacles. The states vary in their granting of rights to the same-sex stepparent of a partner's biological child. States and indeed judges may differ in their decision to remove custody from a parent simply because of that parent's homosexuality. In some states, forced sex by a husband is rape only if the wife is living apart from the husband, although in most states it is rape if it is forced even if they live together. Young women who seek abortions are required to inform a parent in some states and not in others. In some states requiring notification, judges are empowered to waive the requirement at their own discretion. Judges who believe abortion is immoral are free to deny a waiver. Women who can afford to will travel from states with restrictive abortion laws or a scarcity of abortion providers to states that support reproductive choice. Women with fewer economic resources, however, must abide by local restrictions; they are less able to afford travel to less restrictive locations.

There is certainly a gendered, punitive dimension to the treatment of expectant parents. Despite rhetoric about protecting the unborn, men and women are not pressured equally to behave in ways known to improve the chances of fetal health. For example, court rulings increasingly punish alcohol abuse by pregnant mothers (resulting in fetal alcohol syndrome). In contrast, fathers' alcohol abuse goes unregulated, even though violence against pregnant wives or partners is strongly related to men's alcohol abuse. Making abortion access difficult is seen as a lesson for irresponsible or immoral teenage girls, but no lessons are directed to the adult men who are the sexual partners in the majority of such pregnancies.

The judiciary continues to be disproportionately male, but the rate of change, especially on lower levels of the system, has been rapid. Research on attorneys' and judges' awareness of gender bias found a significant difference between the sexes, with women much more likely than men to have a feminist consciousness (Martin, Reynolds, and Keith 2002). This difference is even more marked between women of color and all men.

The first woman was appointed to the federal bench in 1934, but she was followed by very small numbers until the impact of the women's movement was felt. Judges have typically been white men. When an African American woman plaintiff appeared before Constance Baker Motley (the first African American woman on the federal bench) defense attorneys asked that she recuse herself. She pointed out, in response, that white male judges regularly heard cases involving white males with no such expectation of recusal (reported in Hill 2007). In a similar "logic," during the 2009 review of Sonia Sotomayor's nomination to the Supreme Court, some commentators expressed concern that, as a Latina, she might be biased in cases involving people of color. There was no concern expressed that white male justices would suffer from bias in cases with white men.

In the early 1970s, the proportion of law students who were women began to increase rapidly. Thus, the pipeline now provides large numbers of women attorneys with the years of experience expected for judicial appointments. By 1997, 284 women held more than 15 percent of federal judgeships (varying slightly by type of court; Costello et al. 1998). Nonetheless, a 1999 study by Citizens for Independent Courts, a nonpartisan research group, found a significantly longer delay in Senate actions on female nominees than on male nominees, and a comparable inequity in the review process regarding nominees of color compared with whites. Although the impact of a more integrated judiciary is debated, there is an expectation that women jurists will contribute to the end of sexism in the courtroom.

States that have called for reviews of sexism in the legal system have found it to be widespread (see Crites and Hepperle 1987). Although legislatures have been quite responsive to calls for less biased rape laws, in numerous instances judicial decisions have enforced a more traditional view of female sexuality. In these cases, the victim is blamed for provoking a male, who is supposedly always potentially uncontrollable by his nature (Spencer 1987). This independent ability to undo or ignore legislative decisions exemplifies the importance of judicial appointments. In recent years, however, the power of grass-roots activism has been demonstrated regarding these issues, and the goal of changing the rules of evidence has been achieved in many jurisdictions.

### SEX, RACE, AND INEQUITY

It is distorting to discuss the importance of gender without referring to its interaction with race and class in criminal justice treatment (Chasin 2004). Being male or female is only one of the socially fateful categories for people in contact with the criminal justice system. The race or ethnicity of the accused has been shown to be pertinent at the many decision points in the criminal justice system. A long series of research projects, conducted in many jurisdictions, finds a disparity in treatment depending on the race, ethnicity, and gender of the individual. For example, Spohn, Gruhl, and Welch (1990) found that the cases against white *men* were less likely than those against either African American or Latina *women* to reach trial. The race-ethnicity of the victim is also associated with the level of punishment. Research has repeatedly found that when whites are victimized, offenders receive harsher punishments than when the victim is not white.

Additional complexity is gained by looking at both the racial-ethnic category of the accused and of the victim of that crime. For example, African American men who are convicted of raping white women get harsher sentences than white men convicted or raping white women or African American men convicted of raping African American women. African American women, it should be added, have a higher rate of victimization than white women (Feltey 2001).

Although the daily work of corrections officers is not violent and does not involve the use of force, their training is designed to prepare them for the prisons organized around male criminals. When corrections officers are assigned to women's prisons, they have not been trained to exercise authority with this population and to function within the different set of norms common to facilities designed for nonviolent inmates (Britton 2003).

In the 1990s, prison populations swelled, and the construction and running of prisons has become one of the costliest parts of government. In response to the economic downturn of 2008, policymakers have developed a fiscally motivated interest in reversing this trend (Steinhauer 2009).

A major component of the increase comes from the drug laws that removed discretion from the hands of federal judges. State laws against drug offenders generally allow more discretion in sentencing than federal laws have done. However, research indicates that people of color are far more likely than whites accused of drug crimes to be charged in federal, rather than state, court. Thus, the incarceration rates and lengths of sentences are far more racially disproportionate than is the commission of drug-related crimes (Russell 1998). Most dramatic, perhaps, are the discrepancies between penalties for possession of crack cocaine (very long punishments) and powder cocaine (much shorter punishments). The former is more likely to be used among people of color and poorer people, and the latter is more likely to be used by whites and higher-income people. This disparity was a campaign issue for Barack Obama; within a few months of his inauguration a high-ranking Justice Department representative testified before Congress in support of reducing crack cocaine sentences (Moore 2009).

The female population soared even more than the male in the 1990s. Mandatory sentencing prevented prosecutors and judges from agreeing to probation for first-time or minor offenses, or to take into account the pressure on impoverished single mothers that might have led previously law-abiding women to engage in drug-related crime. Because women's involvement in drugs is low in the hierarchy, women are unlikely to have information to trade for a lesser sentence (Chesney-Lind 2002).

The majority of women inmates, in contrast to men, have been convicted of nonviolent (especially low-level drug-related) crimes. Among women convicted of violent crimes, a large proportion are against abusive family members. Men and women in prison, like male and female juvenile offenders, have very different personal histories. The women are far more likely than the men to have been victims of physical and sexual abuse in both childhood and adulthood. Of those men who were abuse victims, much smaller proportions went on to experience further abuse in adulthood. Girls who are incarcerated are more likely than their male peers to be incarcerated because of "status offenses," such as running away from (an often abusive) home (Chesney-Lind and Belknap 2004).

The long-standing practice of "racial profiling" (which is typically simultaneously gendered) became an important political issue in the late 1990s. On the basis of stereotypes, law enforcement personnel often treat men of color, particularly African American men, more harshly than other members of the public. Relying on white Americans' exaggerated fears of African American men (fed by distorted media representations), police were allowed to exercise more forceful, often violent strategies (Russell 1998). The best-publicized of these is the practice of stopping drivers without adequate cause (informally referred to as being stopped for DWB, or driving while black). This practice was based on unfounded beliefs in higher rates of transporting contraband (e.g., illegal drugs or weapons) among drivers of color. However, several studies of the actual rate of success (that is, stops resulting in the discovery of contraband) have discovered that white drivers are as likely, or even more likely, to be carrying illegal materials as African American or Latino drivers (Russell 1998).

Although African American and Latino men are disproportionately stopped for street searches (of people not in vehicles) and targeted for traffic stops, "flying while black" has been a problem for both women and men, who are disproportionately singled out for searches by U.S. Customs officers. In 2000, this problem became publicized with the filing of a class action suit on behalf of African American women returning to the United States from locations in the Caribbean.

After the attacks of September 11, the public sentiment that had been growing against profiling abruptly changed. Concern about safety from terrorism led to violations of the constitutional rights of American men of Arab and Middle Eastern backgrounds, as well as Islamic men (categories that, as we saw in Chapter Two, are overlapping but not identical). Women in these groups have not been objects of official profiling concern, although they have experienced harassment from others.

### TECHNOLOGY AND PUBLIC POLICY

Changes in reproductive and birth-control technologies exemplify the complex relationship between public policies and technological change. For example, medical researchers have developed a "morning after" combination of drugs that in effect brings on an early abortion and enables women to avoid visiting an abortion clinic. Avoiding this public, often hostile, experience or the trip to a less limiting jurisdiction, women are able to make their decisions more freely when the drug is available to them. Although a panel of experts reporting to the Food and Drug Administration recommended in 2005 that the "morning after" pill (or "Plan B") be made available to women as an over-the-counter drug, political pressure delayed action (Kaufman 2005). In 2006 approval was given to selling Plan B to women 18 and older. It was not until a federal judge ordered (in 2009) compliance with the original recommendation that Plan B became available to 17-year-olds.

Another pharmaceutical approach to ending pregnancy, RU486, was widely used in other countries, but its production was long delayed in the United States because of pressure from antiabortion groups. This drug has proven beneficial for a variety of other conditions (such as advanced rheumatoid arthritis), whose sufferers were also prevented from using the drug in the United States because of the antiabortion activism. Arrangements for the limited availability of abortion, worked out through political conflict and compromise, are rendered obsolete when new technologies become available.

### SUMMARY

Changes are being made in the gender ideology emanating from the political and legal arenas. However, the political and legal system, with its multiplicity of jurisdictions, is still characterized by mixed messages about gender. Different courts and legislative bodies pass laws and make judgments that reflect multiple ideologies of gender. Simply put, we have moved from a long-standing systemwide acceptance of the presumably fundamental differences between females and males (and thus from a limit to their automatically common responsibilities and rights) to an inconsistent stance within the political and legal institution that makes each possible right or limitation problematic. Changes in national or state leadership sometime result in an about-face in rights and regulations (Finlay 2006).

Though a radical feminist perspective directs attention to the importance of cultural beliefs about the sexes, a multiracial perspective highlights the fateful differences in treatment of people of the same sex but different class or racial-ethnic groups, whether they are victims or perpetrators of crime.

Groups that routinely experience less than equal treatment continue to push for change. State referenda and legislation have been proposed to grant antidiscrimination protections based on sexual preference and to extend the privileges and responsibilities of legal marriage to same-sex couples. Lawsuits, boycotts, and demonstrations are used by those fighting the practice of racial profiling.

Those whose immediate intimate environment suits them, and who have autonomy and adequate income from their work, underestimate the importance of political life. However, as inroads into reproductive rights increasingly threaten heterosexual couples' control over their family planning and as the relationship between government policies and the economic status of workers changes, more individuals are becoming aware of the crucial role of the political institution in defining, facilitating, or removing aspects of the gender system.

Enormous resources were devoted to the goal of passing the Equal Rights Amendment. Indeed, the persistent pursuit of its ratification was a major source of conflict within the feminist movement because of the consequent lack of attention to and resources for other issues. We can understand arguments for giving the proposed amendment a high priority when we realize that it could have produced consistency among jurisdictions. Instead, people and organizations continue to struggle, issue by issue and jurisdiction by jurisdiction, for equal rights.

### DISCUSSION QUESTIONS

1. Review the timeline (Figure 7.1). Make a list of five additional historical events or trends that you think help in understanding the evolving U.S. gender system. Insert them in the appropriate places on the figure, and consider how their occurrence might have affected, and been affected by, the other events nearby in time.
2. Select two or three current realities of gender you would like to see changed, and sketch a strategy for achieving the changes. How does your strategy draw on what has been effective in making change in the past?
3. Working with each of the various feminist perspectives in turn, explore how it helps make sense of the patterns between gender and crime, and what questions it seems to leave unanswered. ✦

# CHAPTER 8

# The Changing Gender System

How can we predict the future meanings and systems of gender in this society? What will it mean to "do gender" in everyday life? How central will gender be in determining quality of life, and how extensively will the economic system reflect and reinforce differences in status for males and females?

## A CHANGING ECONOMY AND A CHANGING CULTURE

The rapid economic changes described in Chapter Six have had an enormous impact on the gender system. Cultural and political changes occur more slowly than the remarkable change in labor market participation and the subsequent arrangements called for at home. The everyday lives of many people have changed and are continuing to do so, with many wives earning more than their husbands, and couples working different shifts so that parents rather than strangers can provide child care. Even without a particular commitment to or identification with feminism, women and men increasingly cross lines that seemed impermeable forty years ago.

Like the continuing, but weakened, linkage of occupational distribution to sex, most people have not given up conceptions of gender-appropriate guidelines for living, but now often treat norms of feminine and masculine behavior as general suggestions rather than hard-and-fast rules. At the same time, some people who have moved away from traditional norms in one aspect of their lives (such as wage-earning) have chosen to embrace traditional behaviors in others.

Power, especially political and economic power, is at the center of most explanations of the gender system. The economy is continuing its rapid changes, with increasing globalization and increasing concentration of ownership (fewer and fewer corporations controlling larger markets and more industries). The shapes of hegemonic masculinity have changed over hundreds of years to better suit the changing dominant political-economic forces (Connell 1995; Connell and Wood 2005). As those forces continue shaping change in the future, we can expect masculinities and feminities—their content and the extent of their salience—to shift.

To foster creative thinking about the future, Acker (1999) offers one metaphor for contemporary capitalism: It is a monster that mutates, with changes in technologies and social organization. How it changes is uncertain but she maintains that "as the mutations continue, classes change, as do the forms of gender and racial oppression" (63). The continuing pattern of street demonstrations during meetings of international political and economic leaders illustrates that people organize against what they consider destructive mutations. Labor groups in the United States work with organized labor abroad to stop the practices by which corporations remove or degrade jobs (Clawson 2003). Ignorance about these developments reflects mass media programming decisions that undermine public discussion of major policy questions.

In the area of gender, as in other areas of U.S. cultural life, disagreement is rife about where we are and where we should go. The rapid changes, including widespread loss of homes and double-digit unemployment rates in some areas of the United States that began in late 2008, have brought an opportunity to consider future directions. During the Great Depression of the 1930s and in the period of rising unemployment after World War II, a dominant assumption was that women should not be taking "men's jobs"—if there were not enough jobs for all the men, women should stop participating in the labor force. This point of view is unlikely to return to dominance, but there are likely to be more conflicts both in workplaces and in homes as diverse views of gender are mobilized to support different divisions of scarce opportunities and resources. The coming years will likely not be smooth, regardless of where they take us.

Rather than attempting the impossible by trying to predict the future meanings and salience of gender in this society, let us summarize the basic premises of this book. They will help as we try to understand and explain shifting social realities in the future.

## PEOPLE CAN CHANGE IN IMPORTANT WAYS

They can do so more quickly than is implicit in studies of socialization and of differences between women and men. The impact of opportunity structures and social constraints on people's behaviors are separate and distinct from the differential socialization of males and females. Social arrangements influence what an individual does, whether or not that individual approves of such arrangements. Changes in the norms of socialization and gender need not originate from internalized values. Change can be initiated from external sources. It is possible to create obstacles to discourage now unacceptable behaviors, and rewards to encourage desirable ones.

Just as some people conform to traditional gender-related norms because of social pressure and despite their own beliefs, people may change their patterned responses as new definitions of gender-appropriate behavior emerge. Employers who fear a stiff financial penalty if they discriminate are likely to avoid discrimination, despite prejudices they may have. As part of the efforts to revitalize one labor union, immigrant activists loosened up the previous gendered division of tasks and responsibilities in the organization (Cranford 2007). People who are not pleased with new norms nonetheless often conform to them. Meanwhile, a new generation is socialized by models of newly accepted behavior.

Finally, pragmatic conformity to new social constraints may lead people to realize that previous constructions of reality were inaccurate. People who are pushed into what they consider gender-inappropriate situations (e.g., newly integrated workplaces) may see that their previous beliefs about men's or women's capabilities were actually invalid (Gray 1984). This change in viewpoint is happening as the idea spreads that sex alone is not an adequate basis for different opportunities or limitations. This view is replacing the assumption that males and females are so different that there is no reason to expect their treatment to be comparable.

### CULTURE AND SOCIAL STRUCTURE ARE INTERDEPENDENT

Changes in one influence changes in another; the initiation of social change is not restricted to one or the other (Ridgeway and Correll 2004). For example, beliefs changed among the Catholic laity in recognition of the successful integration of women into low-level leadership positions: the structure influenced culture. Now the laity are an important source of pressure on the church for further changes in arrangements: The cultural views led people to press for structural change (Wallace 1988). The developing impact and implications of the Internet also illustrate the intertwined ways in which changes in one area of social activity are significantly shaped by and shapers of previously existing social and cultural arrangements (DiMaggio et al. 2001). Similarly, the lack of change in one of these spheres will affect the rate and direction of change in the other. Thus, many women who work part time continue to explain their difficulties by focusing on individual circumstances rather than organizational shortcomings (Webber and Williams 2008). As long as this social construction of the problem persists, employing organizations can continue to ignore the need to adapt to the patterned constraints and needs of their part-time workforce.

### SOCIAL INSTITUTIONS ARE HIGHLY INTERDEPENDENT

This has implications in assessing strategies for social change (regardless of the direction of change) as well as for the maintenance of current arrangements. It also directs attention to the particular ways in which a change (whether or not gender-focused) in one area of social life may impinge on other areas—because of the effects on resources or worldviews of people, who simultaneously participate in multiple institutions. For example, many families revised their gendered household arrangements because men's earnings declined with the export or automation of well-paid manufacturing jobs and the expansion of less well-paid service jobs. Women's earnings have become more important in those homes, and women's childrearing time outside the labor force, or in part-time rather than full-time employment has shrunk (see Chapter Four). This reduction in the degree of inequality in financial contributions of women and men has also led many women to be less interested in marrying (Edin 2000). Nevertheless, marriage continues to provide more economical stability than divorce for most women (Smock, Manning, and Gupta 1999).

## MULTIPLE LEVELS OF SOCIAL STRUCTURE INFLUENCE ONE ANOTHER, AND THE INDIVIDUAL

People have ideas about their lives; they conduct their daily lives within small groups, formal organizations, and local, regional, and national social systems. Characteristics of those contexts combine to have an impact on how people act. For example, earning a patent (one indicator of a scientist or engineer's productivity) is more common for women who work in settings that are less hierarchically organized than the traditional university or corporation (Whittington and Smith-Doerr 2008). This greater productivity results at least in part from the difference in organizational cultures that accompanies the difference in structures.

There will be reactions at other levels when changes originate at the individual, micro, middle, or macro social levels. These reactions are not likely to simply follow along with the initiating changes; they may be reactions *against* the changes, or accept them selectively. People exercise agency when faced with changes, actively exploring alternative responses and complying where necessary. For example, participants in court-mandated therapy for domestic batterers were selective about adopting changes in behaviors and beliefs (Schrock and Padavic 2007). They integrated a less violent approach to conflict, but they retained a patriarchal view of the privilege that should accompany wage-earning.

The concept of an **inequality regime**, the "interrelated practices, processes, actions, and meanings that result in and maintain . . . inequalities within particular organizations" (Acker 2006, 443) captures the complexity of organizational arrangements that are involved when organizational participants or external groups work to decrease inequality.

## GENDERED REALITIES CANNOT BE UNDERSTOOD SEPARATELY FROM MEMBERSHIPS IN SOCIALLY SIGNIFICANT CATEGORIES OF RACE, CLASS, AGE, AND SEXUALITY

First, being male or female has different implications for people depending on their access to resources. That is, access to economic power or social prestige offers some protection from general disadvantages in a sexist society. Conversely, any promise of "male privilege" is much less significant for economically or ethnically marginal men than for men with economic power. Clearly, the erosion of privilege is experienced differently because it was not possessed equally (Pfeil 1995). The individual's construction of a sense of masculinity or femininity is designed using available opportunities. People's ideas of where their interests lie reflect their combined race, gender, and class memberships (Talwar 2004). The form and extent of future activism will be influenced by the changing meanings of these intersecting positions, particularly in the changing economy.

Historically, economic factors have been important prerequisities to social change. In addition to the impact of changing economic conditions, such as the development of industrialization and its removal of men's work from their homes, stability or relative affluence on the societal level has been associated with major changes in gender stratification, particularly in the definition of male family roles. Feminist activism and other human rights movements have occurred in periods of relative economic affluence in the society as a whole. It is easier to share resources in new ways in a time of abundance; social protest is also easier to sustain in times of greater affluence.

How will previously observed relationships between periods of economic well-being and human rights activism apply to new economic patterns? As more women are employed in upper-tier positions than in the past, they may be the foundation of continued or increased feminist activism. However, women in the lower tier, which is more and more characterized by economic hardship, may not be activist. Alternatively, economically marginal women may focus their activism on the struggles they share with men of their racial-ethnic and economic positions. When "retirement age" workers decided to postpone their retirement because their pensions had decreased in value, younger participants in the labor force saw expected job openings disappear. How will age (a dimension of difference that has typically been ignored by scholars of gender) intersect with other social statuses to shape the gender system?

Culturally, stereotypes that rationalize discrimination are based on beliefs about the intersection of gender, race-ethnicity, and class. Researchers have started to examine the more complex typing that people do, and how it varies with their own characteristics (Glick and Fiske 1999). More complex research will be required to add an understanding of the impact of perceptions and expectations related to age and sexuality.

## ECONOMICALLY AND POLITICALLY DOMINANT GROUPS HAVE MORE CONTROL THAN OTHERS OVER THE NATURE OF THE STRATIFICATION SYSTEM, INCLUDING THE WAYS IN WHICH IT IS GENDERED

This applies at the macro-social, public policy level with the establishment of such policies as the welfare "reform" that requires mothers with toddlers to work outside the home. In activity more explicitly aimed at gender stratification, it applies to participation in feminist and antifeminist movements. Economically and politically powerful groups have played important, although often covert, economic and planning roles in antifeminist movements in various societies throughout history (Chafetz and Dworkin 1987).

In organizations (the middle level of social analysis), power affects the ability to change or maintain existing arrangements. Coalitions form and re-form, creating a power base through their combination of resources (Hall 1999). At the micro-social level, individuals in small groups affect the significance of gender; for example, wives whose earnings are essential may insist that money go to buy services that they would otherwise be expected to perform.

Making change requires an appreciation of the power of a nation's **policy regime**, the complex of "policies and regulations enacted over time . . . reflect[ing ]a broader philosophical orientation that transcends any individual [political] administration" (Bird and Rieker 2008, 78) The gender policy regime is complex and effecting change will require attention to its overarching character.

## THROUGH INDIVIDUAL AGENCY, PEOPLE MAKE CHANGE

Although agency is often limited to finding ways to adapt to existing conditions, it is the route to social change. Individuals also exercise agency to reinstitute or retain old practices (Reskin 2000). For example, in organizations with formal policies endorsing equal opportunity, people with traditional, or stereotypical, views of gender may influence coworkers' perceptions of jobs as male- or female-appropriate, and their perceptions of what their occupational choices realistically are (Ridgeway 1997).

Whether affecting the practices of small groups to which one belongs (Sullivan 2006; Kennelly 2002), or organizations, or working through coalition to create full-scale social movements, the individual has a role in shaping social life, moving change forward or protecting gains already made. Some people whose actions are gender atypical may defend their gender identity by drawing distinctions between themselves and others who they allege are truly gender transgressive (for example, women rugby players studied by Ezzell, 2009).

In analyzing the complex interplay of individual and social factors to understand people's health behavior and health outcomes, Bird and Rieker (2008) provide a model of "constrained choice" (Figure 8.1). We will come closer to understanding why an individual follows a lifestyle with particular health implications if we pay attention to all the sources of influence represented in the model. Similarly, paying attention to multiple sources of influence or constraints will contribute to our explaining the variability of people's behavior and gendered outcomes.

Understanding and actively applying these ideas should lead to more sophisticated inquiry in the future: When a change in the social world catches our attention, we should try to imagine ways in which it may be connected to the gendering of social life. By integrating these premises into our views of how things happen, we may be more alert for subtle repercussions of that change. We may produce another "generation" of questions that will help develop a more accurate and complex understanding of reality.

## AN ONGOING ENDEAVOR: STUDYING THE SOCIOLOGY OF GENDER

The study of gender is itself dynamic, framing and addressing questions with increasing complexity and an appreciation for the need to learn from the standpoints of previously unheard or underappreciated voices (Olesen and Clarke 1999). As the world and the society change quickly, in predictable and unanticipated ways, we are challenged to keep up, rethinking old ideas as we see new realities unfold, or as we see a lack of change that had seemed inevitable.

An intersectional approach is one of the most promising perspectives for increasing our understanding. With its fundamental emphasis on how the particular identities of race and ethnicity, class, and sex intersect, it demands a broad research program. A wider appreciation of the dimensions of sexuality and age will add to the complexity of this understanding. By studying lived realities, we see how people develop their ideas and their actions related to the gender system. We will be better able to predict what may happen in the future as agency is exercised to adjust to or rebel against existing gender demands. At the same time, the culture of sociology itself values the ultimate development of more generalized propositions, models, or even theories. Theories are abstract, and are judged by their success at explaining wide-ranging observations. The challenge for the sociology of gender will be to collect observations at the many different points of lived experience, without losing sight of the goal of developing more generalized explanations of gender in social life.

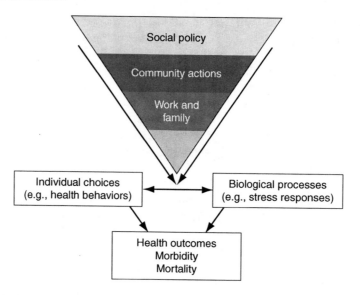

**Figure 8.1  Conceptualization of Constrained Choice**
Source: Bird CE and Rieker PP, *Gender and Health: The Effects of Constrained Choices and Social Policies*, New York: Cambridge University Press, 2008.

DISCUSSION QUESTIONS

1. Identify a current gender-related controversy in the news. Use ideas from this chapter to predict what will happen next, and in the long run, with the controversy.
2. Use the "constrained choice" framework to develop an explanation for one area of gendered behavior (such as occupational selection).
3. Rhode (1997) identifies three obstacles to reducing gender inequality: the denial that it still exists, the belief that people are generally content with current (even unequal) arrangements, and the view that even though inequality is undesirable, a person has no responsibility for it or for working toward its elimination. How would you respond to each of these ideas? ✦

**affirmative action** The policy of proactively working to improve the representation of women and racial-ethnic minority group members in employment and in educational institutions.

**agency** An individual's capacity to actively pursue ways to participate in, adapt to, or change her or his circumstances.

**biculturalism** The practice of moving between the design for living of one's ethnic group and that of the dominant culture; belonging to and participating in both cultures.

**capitalism** The economic system of private ownership of production, with the paramount value of maximizing profit.

**career feminism** The viewpoint, during the second wave, that envisioned freeing individuals from sexism through personal transformation.

**commodification** The process of transforming women's bodies into objects of economic value.

**culture** A people's established beliefs and practices; their design for living.

**difference feminism** A perspective that highlights women's sexual and procreative oppression, and celebrates women's procreative, sexual, and nurturance characteristics; maximalist feminism. This position contrasts with equality, or minimalist, feminism.

**"doing gender"** An individual behaving in a particular way to conform to a broadly applicable set of rules for acting like a male or a female in that society.

**downsizing** The process of cutting the size of a corporation's workforce, although not its profits.

**epistemology** Ways of knowing. Traditionally a matter for philosophers. Since the late 1980s, feminist epistemology has been an increasingly important area where scholars of disciplines across the humanities and the social sciences draw on one another's work.

**equality feminism** A perspective advocating equality based on a minimization of gender differences; minimalist feminism. This position contrasts with difference, or maximalist, feminism.

**essentialism** The belief that many gender differences are actually biologically shaped.

**family** A group whose members are linked by ties of blood, marriage, or adoption.

**feminism** The view that women are oppressed in significant ways and that this oppression should be ended.

**frame** To place a report in a particular context that gives a particular way to make sense of the facts of the story and implicitly guides the reporter to exclude facts that aren't relevant within that context.

**gender** The totality of meanings that are attached to the sexes within a particular social system.

**gender appropriate** Those attitudes or behaviors that conform to the norms for the person's sex.

**gender identity** The belief that an individual has about the relation between her or his sex and its social meanings.

**gender system** A system of meaning and differentiation among people, linked to the sexes through social arrangements.

**gender transgression** Choices of self-presentation (through clothing, grooming, and verbal and nonverbal behaviors) that underscore the instability of the sex–gender binary.

**glass ceiling** The barrier, in many organizations, limiting women's promotion beyond certain levels.

**global feminism** The study of gender across national and regional boundaries.

**hegemony** Domination, particularly cultural domination.

**heteronormativity** The structuring of "social life so that heterosexuality is always assumed, expected, ordinary, and privileged" (Martin and Kazyak 2009, 316).

**homophobia** The fear or hatred, or both, of homosexuality (or other departures from heterosexuality).

**ideology** Belief system or worldview.

**index of dissimilarity** A measure of the extent of segregation.

**inequality regime** The "interrelated practices, processes, actions, and meanings that result in and maintain . . . inequalities within particular organizations" (Acker 2006, 443).

**intersectionalism** A perspective that emphasizes the simultaneous importance of race, class, and gender (and, sometimes, additional dimensions, such as age and sexuality) in formulating questions and looking for answers about gender.

**job segregation** Restriction of employment (usually by sex or race-ethnicity, or both) in an occupation within a given employment setting.

**labor force participation rate** The proportion of people (in a specified category) who are either employed or actively seeking work.

**liberal feminism** The perspective that social change can be achieved through reformist rather than extreme efforts.

**macro-social** The largest scale of social life, such as national, multinational, and international levels.

**marginal** The characteristic of being less than a full member of a social category because one is simultaneously a member of another category, when the two categories are socially constructed as mutually incompatible.

**maximalist feminism** A perspective that highlights women's sexual and procreative oppression, and celebrates women's procreative, sexual, and nurturance characteristics; difference feminism. This position contrasts with equality, or minimalist, feminism.

**micro-social** The scale of social life that focuses on small groups of people.

**middle level** Social life among larger numbers of people, such as a school, corporation, government agency, or neighborhood.

**minimalist feminism** A view that equality should be based on a minimization of gender differences; equality feminism. Contrasts with maximalist, or difference, feminism.

**mommy track** A career ladder with limited prospects because the loyalties of women on it are presumed to be greater to family than to job.

**multiracial feminism** The perspective that focuses simultaneously on the intersecting importance of race, class, and gender (and, sometimes, additional dimensions, such as age and sexuality) in formulating questions and looking for answers about gender.

**norm** A social rule (which may or may not be official or even articulated).

**normative** Following a social rule or *norm* for behavior.

**opportunity structure** The patterned access an individual or group has to particular social positions, including the expected ease or difficulty of access to each of the positions.

**patriarchy** The social system of male domination over females.

**pluralistic ignorance** The condition of thinking that one's views or behaviors are unusual, although they actually are not.

**policy regime** The complex of "policies and regulations enacted over time . . . reflect [ing] a broader philosophical orientation that transcends any individual [political] administration" (Bird and Rieker 2008, 78).

**postfeminism** A perspective that embraces individual equality but asserts that systemic discrimination is in the past, making collective political action outmoded and unnecessary.

**postmodern feminism** The view that challenges (seeking to unsettle or destabilize) existing assumptions about how the world works, particularly with reference to dimensions of sex and gender.

**poststructuralism** The perspective that, like postmodernism, rejects the possibility of discovering underlying rules of social reality, but emphasizes the distribution of power in society as a shaper of the forms social constructions take.

**racism** The system of prejudicial beliefs and discriminatory behaviors toward people because of their race.

**radical feminism** The view that emphasizes gender as the crucial dimension dividing people, and focuses on how males dominate females through a system of supporting beliefs and social structures.

**role** The set of responsibilities, privileges, and obligations that are connected to a particular social position, or *status.*

**schema theory** A view of gender development in which the person constructs two schema (one about each gender) that are normally evolving as the person is exposed to different or more complex aspects of reality.

**separate spheres** A doctrine or ideology holding that the sexes should participate in segregated arenas of social life, with males predominantly in public arenas and females in private ones.

**sex identity** A perception of a person as being male or being female, or being transgendered, and the sense that this is a permanent trait of the person.

**sexes** The categories that most contemporary societies define as physically based, despite the existence of many people whose bodies (genitally or genetically, or both) do not fit neatly into either a female or male category.

**sexism** The system of prejudicial beliefs and discriminatory behaviors toward people because of their sex.

**sexual identity** The sense that one is homosexual, bisexual, or heterosexual.

**significant others** People with whom a child has frequent and regular contact, who have control over rewards and punishments for the child, and who have some image of what the child should become.

**social construction** The perspective that aspects of reality are created by social factors rather than preexisting in nature.

**social control** The use of rewards and punishments to enforce social norms.

**social institution** A constellation of activities and ideas that addresses a major area of basic human needs in a particular society.

**social stratification** The differentiation among people based on their membership in categories socially defined as significant and the accompanying differences in their access to resources and in their obligations.

**social structure** The pattern of social relationships and behaviors in a group, organization, or society.

**socialist feminism** The view that patriarchy and capitalism are equally important forces in explaining the inequalities in society and between females and males.

**socialization** The process of learning the rules of the social group or culture to which we belong or hope to belong, and learning to define ourselves and others within that setting.

**stagflation** A state in which an economy has a low growth rate but a high inflation rate.

**stalking** Following another person with whom one is (typically sexually) obsessed.

**standpoint** The position from which one observes and experiences the world.

**status** A particular social position within a given social structure.

**sticky floor** A combination of obstacles that prevents people from moving out of the low-level dead-end jobs into which they were initially hired.

**subcultures** Designs for living, sets of beliefs, and practices that are transmitted from one generation to another within a subgroup of the population, usually defined by membership in a particular racial, ethnic, immigrant, or sectarian religious group.

**telecommuting** Performing employment-related activities at home while using communications technologies.

**transgendered** Sex identities including people who have completely or partially changed themselves physically into the "other" sex, through either medical or surgical procedures or both, as well as people categorized as intersexual because of an inborn mix of physical characteristics, and people who subjectively experience themselves as fitting into neither of the hegemonic sex categories.

**womanism** A perspective that simultaneously focuses on race-ethnicity, class, and gender in the struggle for all people's liberation. ✦

# REFERENCES

Acker, Joan. 1999. "Rewriting Class, Race, and Gender: Problems in Feminist Thinking." In *Revisioning Gender*, edited by M. M. Ferree, B. B. Hess, and J. Lorber. Thousand Oaks, CA: Sage Publications, 44–69.

—— 2006. "Inequality Regimes." *Gender & Society* 20:441–464.

Acosta, Katie L. 2008. "Lesbianas in the Borderlands." *Gender & Society* 22:639–660.

Adam, Barry D. 1995. *The Rise of a Gay and Lesbian Movement*. New York: Simon & Schuster.

Adams, Jimi. 2007. "Stained Glass Makes the Ceiling Visible." *Gender & Society* 21:80–105.

Adams, Natalie, and Pamela Bettis. 2003. "Commanding the Room in Short Skirts: Cheering as the Embodiment of Ideal Girlhood." *Gender & Society* 17:73–91.

Ahmed, Leila. 1993. *Women and Gender in Islam*. New Haven, CT: Yale University Press.

Albert, Alexa A., and Judith R. Porter. 1988. "Children's Gender-Role Stereotypes." *Sociological Forum* 3:184–210.

Alessio, John C., and Julie Andrzejewski. 2000. "Unveiling the Hidden Glass Ceiling: An Analysis of the Cohort Effect Claim." *American Sociological Review* 65:311–315.

Allen, Sarah M., and Alan J. Hawkins. 1999. "Maternal Gatekeeping: Mothers' Beliefs and Behaviors That Inhibit Greater Father Involvement in Family Work." *Journal of Marriage and the Family* 61:199–212.

Allen, Susan M., and Pamela S. Webster. 2001. "When Wives Get Sick: Gender Role Attitudes, Marital Happiness, and Husbands' Contribution to Household Labor." *Gender & Society* 15:898–916.

Altman, Dennis. 1987. *AIDS in the Mind of America*. Garden City, NY: Anchor Books.

Altman, Lawrence K. 2004a. "Action Urged on Diseases With Dangers for Women." *New York Times*, February 28, A13.

—— 2004b. "Study Finds That Teenage Virginity Pledges Are Rarely Kept." *New York Times*, March 10, A20.

Amato, Paul R., David R. Johnson, Alan Booth, and Stacy J. Rogers. 2003. "Continuity and Change in Marital Quality Between 1980 and 2000." *Journal of Marriage and the Family* 65:1–22.

American Civil Liberties Union. 1999. "ACLU Announces Settlement of Lawsuit Against Healthcare Providers Who Discriminated Against Lesbian Patient." Press release, August 31.

Amott, Teresa L., and Julie A. Matthaei. 1991. *Race, Gender, & Work*. Boston: South End Press.

Anderson, Eric. 2002. "Openly Gay Athletes: Contesting Hegemonic Masculinity in a Homophobic Environment." *Gender & Society* 16:860–877.

Anderson, Kristin J., Melinda Kanner, and Nisreen Elsayegh. 2009. "Are Feminists Man Haters?" *Psychology of Women Quarterly* 33:216–224.

Anderson, Kristin L., and Debra Umberson. 2001. "Gendering Violence: Masculinity and Power in Men's Accounts of Domestic Violence." *Gender & Society* 15:358–380.

Angier, Natalie. 1999. *Woman: An Intimate Geography*. New York: Houghton Mifflin.

Appelbaum, Eileen, Annette Bernhardt, and Richard J. Murnane. 2003. "Low-wage America: An Overview." In *Low-Wage America: How Employers Are Reshaping Opportunity in the Workplace*, edited by Eileen Appelbaum, Annette

Bernhardt, and Richard J. Murnane. New York: Russell Sage Foundation, 1–29.

Arenson, Karen W. 2003. "Colleges Struggle to Help Black Men Stay Enrolled." *New York Times*, December 30, A1, B9.

Armstrong, Elisabeth. 2002. *The Retreat From Organization: U.S. Feminism Reconceptualized.* Albany: State University of New York Press.

Aronson, Pamela. 2003. "Feminists or 'Postfeminists'? Young Women's Attitudes Toward Gender and Gender Relations." *Gender & Society* 17:903–922.

Artis, Julie E., and Eliza K. Pavalko. 2003. "Explaining the Decline in Women's Household Labor." *Journal of Marriage and the Family* 65:746–761.

Barajas, Heidi L., and Jennifer L. Pierce. 2001. "The Significance of Race and Gender in School Success Among Latinas and Latinos in College." *Gender & Society* 15:859–878.

Barnes, Brooks. 2009. "What Do Boys Want? She Digs Into Minds and Closets to See." *New York Times*, April 14, A1, A14.

Barnett, Bernice McNair. 1993. "Invisible Southern Black Women Leaders in the Civil Rights Movement." *Gender & Society* 7:162–182.

Barnett, Rosalind Chait. 2007. "Women, Leadership, and the Natural Order." In *Women & Leadership*, edited by B. Kellerman and D. L. Rhode. San Francisco: Jossey-Bass, 149–173.

Barr, Cameron W., and Elizabeth Williamson. 2004. "Women's Rally Draws Vast Crowd." *Washington Post*, April 26, A1.

Barstow, David, Remy Gerstein, and Robin Stein. 2003. "U.S. Rarely Seeks Charges for Deaths in Workplace." *New York Times*, December 22, A1, 28.

Beattie, Irenee R. 2002. "Are All 'Adolescent Econometricians' Created Equal? Racial, Class, and Gender Differences in College Enrollment." *Sociology of Education* 75:19–43.

Beauboeuf-Lafontant, Tamara. 2003. "Strong and Large Black Women? Exploring Relationships Between Deviant Womanhood and Weight." *Gender & Society* 17:111–121.

Bellafante, Ginia. 2004. "Two Fathers, With One Happy to Stay at Home." *New York Times*, January 12, A1, A12.

Bendick, Marc and Mary Lou Egan. 2009. "Research Perspectives on Race and Employment in the Advertising Industry." Washington, D.C.: Bendick and Egan Economic Consultants. Accessed at http://www.bendickegan.com/pdf/2009/Bendick%20Egan%20Advertising%20Industry%20Report%20Jan%2009.pdf.

Benitez, Margarita. 1998. "Hispanic Women in the United States." In *The American Woman 1999–2000*, edited by C. B. Costello, S. Miles, and A. J. Stone. New York: W. W. Norton, 133–150.

Benokraitis, Nijole V., and Joe R. Feagin. 1994. *Modern Sexism*. Englewood Cliffs, NJ: Prentice-Hall.

Benokraitis, Nijole V., and Yoku Shaw-Taylor (eds.). 2001. *Contemporary Ethnic Families in the United States*. Englewood Cliffs, NJ: Prentice-Hall.

Benston, Margaret. 1969. "The Political Economy of Women's Liberation." *Monthly Review* 21:13–27.

Bergvall, Victoria, Janet Bing, and Alice Freed (eds.). 1996. *Rethinking Language and Gender Research: Theory and Practice*. London: Longman.

Berns, Nancy. 2001. "Degendering the Problem and Gendering the Blame: Political Discourse on Women and Violence." *Gender & Society* 15:262–281.

Bernstein, Fred A. 2004: "On Campus, Rethinking Biology 101." *New York Times*, March 7, Styles 1, 6.

Bernstein, Jared, and Lawrence Mishel. 1997. "Has Wage Inequality Stopped Growing?" *Monthly Labor Review* 120 (December):3–16.

Bernstein, Nina. 2004. "Behind Fall in Pregnancy, a New Teenage Culture of Restraint." *New York Times*, March 7, A1, A36.

Bettie, Julie. 2000. "Women Without Class: *Chicas, Cholas*, Trash, and the Presence/Absence of Class Identity." *Signs* 26:1–35.

Bettis, Pamela J., and Natalie G. Adams. 2003. "The Power of the Preps and a Cheerleading Equity Policy." *Sociology of Education* 76:128–142.

Bianchi, Suzanne M., John P. Robinson, and Melissa A. Milkie. 2006. *Changing Rhythms of American Family Life*. New York: Russell Sage.

Bird, Chloe E. 1999. "Gender, Household Labor, and Psychological Distress: The Impact of the Amount and Division of Housework." *Journal of Health & Social Behavior* 40:32–44.

Bird, Chloe E., and Patricia P. Rieker. 2008. *Gender and Health*. New York: Cambridge University Press.

Blair-Loy, Mary. 2001. "Cultural Constructions of Family Schemas: The Case of Women Finance Executives." *Gender & Society* 15:687–709.

Blau, Joel. 1992. *The Visible Poor*. New York: Oxford University Press.

Blee, Kathleen M. 2004. "Women and Organized Racism." In *Home-Grown Hate: Gender and Organized Racism*, edited by Abby L. Ferber. New York: Routledge, 49–74.

Blow, Charles M. 2008. "The Demise of Dating." *New York Times*, December 13, A21.

Blum, Linda M., and Theresa Deussen. 1996. "Negotiating Independent Motherhood: Working-Class African American Women Talk About Marriage and Motherhood." *Gender & Society* 10:199–211.

Blumstein, Philip, and Pepper Schwartz. 1990. "Intimate Relationships and the Creation of Sexuality." In *Homosexuality/Heterosexuality: Concepts of Sexual Orientation*, edited by D. P. McWhirter, S. A. Sanders, and J. M. Reinisch. New York: Oxford University Press.

Bodine, Ann. 1975. "Androcentrism in Prescriptive Grammar." *Language and Society* 4:129–146.

Booth, Cathryn L., K. Alison Clarke-Stewart, Deborah Lowe Vandell, Kathleen McCarney, and Margaret Tresch Owen. 2002. "Child-Care Usage and Mother–Infant 'Quality Time.'" *Journal of Marriage and the Family* 64:16–26.

Boraas, Stephanie, and William M. Rodgers III. 2003. "How Does Gender Play a Role in the Earnings Gap? An Update." *Monthly Labor Review* 126 (March), 9–15.

Bowen, William G., and Sarah A. Levin. 2003. *Reclaiming the Game: College Sports and Educational Values*. Princeton, NJ: Princeton University Press.

Brewster, Karin L., and Irene Padavic. 2000. "Change in Gender-Ideology, 1977–1996: The Contributions of Intracohort Change and Population Turnover." *Journal of Marriage and the Family* 62:477–487.

Britton, Dana M. 2003. *At Work in the Iron Cage: The Prison as Gendered Organization*. New York: New York University Press.

Brodkin, Karen. 1998. *How Jews Become White Folks & What That Says About Race in America*. New Brunswick, NJ: Rutgers University Press.

Brody, Leslie. 1999. *Gender, Emotion, and the Family*. Cambridge, MA: Harvard University Press.

Broughton, Chad. 2008. "Migration as Engendered Practice: Mexican Men, Masculinity, and Northward Migration." *Gender & Society* 22:568–589.

Browne, Irene, and Joya Misra. 2003. "The Intersection of Gender and Race in the Labor Market." *Annual Review of Sociology* 29:487–513.

Brubaker, Sarah Jane. 2007. "Denying, Embracing, and Resisting Medicalization." *Gender & Society* 21:528–552.

Brumberg, Joan Jacobs. 1997. *The Body Project: An Intimate History of American Girls*. New York: Vintage Books.

Bumiller, Kristin. 1990. "Fallen Angels: The Representation of Violence Against Women in Legal Culture." *International Journal of the Sociology of Law* 18:125–142.

Burke, Cindy, and Sharon R. Mazzarella. 2008. "A Slightly New Shade of Lipstick." *Women's Studies in Communication* 31:395–418.

Calasanti, Toni M. 2006. "Gender and Old Age: Lessons from Spousal Care Work." In *Age Matters*, edited by T. Calasanti and K. Slevin. New York: Routledge, 269–294.

Calasanti, Toni, and Neal King. 2005. "Firming the Floppy Penis: Age, Class, and Gender Relations in the Lives of Old Men." *Men and Masculinities* 8:3–23.

Calasanti, Toni M., and Kathleen F. Slevin. 2006. "Introduction." In *Age Matters*, edited by T. M. Calasanti and K. F. Slevin. New York: Routledge, 1–17.

Cameron, Deborah. 1998. "Gender, Language, and Discourse: A Review Essay." *Signs* 23:945–973.

——. 2008. *The Myth of Mars and Venus*. New York: Oxford University Press.

Campbell, Lori D., and Michael P. Carroll. 2007. "The Incomplete Revolution: Theorizing Gender When Studying Men Who Provide Care to Aging Parents." *Men and Masculinities* 9:491–508.

Cancian, Francesca M. 1985. "Gender Politics: Love and Power in the Private and Public Spheres." In *Gender and the Life Course*, edited by A. S. Rossi. Washington, DC: American Sociological Association, 253–264.

Cannuscio, Carol C., Graham A. Colditz, Eric B. Rimm, Lisa F. Berkman, Camara P. Jones, and Ichiro Kawachi. 2004. "Employment Status, Social Ties, and Caregivers' Mental Health." *Social Science & Medicine* 58:1247–1258.

Caputi, Jane. 1989. "The Sexual Politics of Murder." *Gender & Society* 3:437–456.

Carolan, Marsha T. 1999. "Contemporary Muslim Women and the Family." In *Family Ethnicity*, edited by H. P. McAdoo. Thousand Oaks, CA: Sage, 213–221.

Carroll, Susan J., and Ronnee Schreiber. 1997. "Media Coverage of Women in the 103rd Congress." In *Women, Media, and Politics*, edited by P. Norris. New York: Oxford University Press, 131–148.

Casper, Monica J. 1998. *The Making of the Unborn Patient: A Social Anatomy of Fetal Surgery*. New Brunswick, NJ: Rutgers University Press.

Center for American Women and Politics, Eagleton Institute of Politics, Rutgers, The State University of New Jersey. 2009. *Fact Sheets*. Accessed April 20, 2009, at http://www.cawp.rutgers.edu/fast_facts/.

Cha, Youngjoo, and Sarah Thebaud. 2009. "Labor Markets, Breadwinning, and Beliefs." *Gender & Society* 23:215–243.

Chafetz, Janet Saltzman, and Anthony Gary Dworkin. 1987. "In the Face of Threat: Organized Antifeminism in Comparative Perspective." *Gender and Society* 1:33–60.

Chan, Jachinson W. 2000. "Bruce Lee's Fictional Models of Masculinity." *Men and Masculinities* 2:371–387.

Chasin, Barbara. 2004. *Inequality and Violence in the United States: Casualities of Capitalism*. Atlantic Highlands, NJ: Humanities Press.

Chen, Anthony S. 1999. "Lives at the Center of the Periphery, Lives at the Periphery of the Center: Chinese American Masculinities and Bargaining with Hegemony." *Gender & Society* 13:584–607.

Chesney-Lind, Meda. 2002. "Imprisoning Women: The Unintended Victims of Mass Imprisonment." In *Invisible Punishment: The Collateral Consequences of Mass Imprisonment*, edited by Marc Mauer and Meda Chesney-Lind. New York: New Press, 79–94.

Chesney-Lind, Meda, and Joanne Belknap. 2004. "Trends in Delinquent Girls' Aggression and Violent Behavior: A Review of the Evidence." In *Aggression, Antisocial Behavior and Violence Among Girls: A Developmental Perspective*, edited by Martha Putallaz and Karen L. Bierman. New York: Guilford, 203–222.

*Chore Wars*, New York, NY: First Run/Icarus Films, distributor, 1995, 48 minutes.

Chow, Esther Ngan-Ling. 1987. "The Development of Feminist Consciousness Among Asian American Women." *Gender & Society* 1:284–299.

Christensen, Kimberly. 1997. "With Whom Do You Believe Your Lot Is Cast? White Feminists and Racism." *Signs* 22:617–649.

Citizens for Independent Courts, Task Force on Federal Judicial Selection. 1999. "Justice Held Hostage: Politics and Selecting Federal Judges." Washington, DC: The Constitution Project.

Clarke, Adele E., and Virginia L. Olesen (eds.). 1999. *Revisioning Women, Health, and Healing: Feminist, Cultural, and Technoscience Perspectives*. New York: Routledge.

Clarke, Lee. 1988. "Explaining Choices Among Technological Risks." *Social Problems* 35:22–35.

Clawson, Dan. 2003. *The Next Upsurge: Labor and the New Social Movements*. Ithaca, NY: Cornell University Press.

Cohen, Philip N. 2004. "The Gender Division of Labor: 'Keeping House' and Occupational Segregation in the United States." *Gender & Society* 18:239–252.

Cohn, Carol, and Cynthia Enloe. 2003. "A Conversation With Cynthia Enloe: Feminists Look at Masculinity and the Men Who Wage War." *Signs* 28:1187–1207.

Cole, Elizabeth R., and Andrea L. Press. 1999. *Speaking of Abortion*. Chicago: University of Chicago Press.

Cole, Johnnetta Betsch, and Beverly Guy-Sheftall. 2003. *Gender Talk: The Struggle for Women's Equality in African American Communities.* New York: One World.

Collins, Patricia Hill. 1990. *Black Feminist Thought.* Boston: Unwin Hyman.

——. 1999. "Moving Beyond Gender: Intersectionality and Scientific Knowledge." In *Revisioning Gender,* edited by M. M. Ferree, B. B. Hess, and J. Lorber. Thousand Oaks, CA: Sage, 261–284.

Coltrane, Scott. 1996. *Family Man.* New York: Oxford University Press.

Connell, R. W. 1995. *Masculinities.* Los Angeles: University of California Press.

——. 1999. "Making Gendered People: Bodies, Identities, Sexualities." In *Revisioning Gender,* edited by M. M. Ferree, B. B. Hess, and J. Lorber. Thousand Oaks, CA: Sage, 449–471.

Connell, R. W., and James Messerschmidt. 2005. "Hegemonic Masculinity." *Gender & Society* 19:829–859.

Connell, R. W., and Julian Wood. 2005. "Globalization and Business Masculinities." *Men and Masculinities* 7:347–364.

Corcoran, Mary, Sandra K. Danziger, Ariel Kalil, and Kristin S. Seefeldt. 2000. "How Welfare Reform Is Affecting Women's Work." *Annual Review of Sociology* 26:241–269.

Corsaro, William A., and Laura Fingerson. 2003. "Development and Socialization in Childhood." In *Handbook of Social Psychology,* edited by John Delamater. New York: Kluwer Academic/Plenum Publishers, 125–155.

Costain, Anne N., Richard Braunstein, and Heidi Berggren. 1997. "Framing the Women's Movement." In *Women, Media, and Politics,* edited by P. Norris. New York: Oxford University Press, 205–220.

Costello, Cynthia B., Shari Miles, and Anne J. Stone (eds.). 1998. *The American Woman, 1999–2000: A Century of Change—What's Next?* New York: W. W. Norton.

Cowan, Ruth Schwartz. 1983. *More Work for Mother.* New York: Basic Books.

Cranford, Cynthia J. 2007. "It's Time to Leave Machismo Behind!" *Gender & Society* 21:409–438.

Crenshaw, Kimberle. 1989. "Demarginalizing the Intersection of Race and Sex." *University of Chicago Legal Forum* 139:139–167.

Crites, Laura L., and Winifred L. Hepperle (eds.). 1987. *Women, the Courts, and Equality.* Newbury Park, CA: Sage.

Crowley, Jocelyn Elise. 2008. *Defiant Dads.* Ithaca, NY: Cornell University Press.

Cunningham, Mick. 2001. "The Influence of Parental Attitudes and Behaviors on Children's Attitudes Toward Gender and Household Labor in Early Adulthood." *Journal of Marriage and the Family* 63:111–122.

Curcio, Williams. 1999. "Domestic Abuse, Sexual Trauma, and Welfare Receipt." Ph.D. Dissertation, Department of Sociology, Rutgers University.

Curran, Laura, and Laura S. Abrams. 2000. "Making Men Into Dads: Fatherhood, the State, and Welfare Reform." *Gender & Society* 14:662–678.

Dalton, Susan E., and Denise D. Bielby. 2000. "That's Our Kind of Constellation: Lesbian Mothers Negotiate Institutionalized Understandings of Gender Within the Family." *Gender & Society* 14:36–61.

Daniels, Jessie. 2008. "Beyond Separate Silos: Andersen Symposium Introduction." *Gender & Society* 22:83–87.

Darling, Marsha J. 1998. "African-American Women in State Office in the South." In *Women and Elective Office,* edited by S. Thomas and C. Wilcox. New York: Oxford University Press, 150–162.

David, Deborah S., and Robert Brannon. 1976. "The Male Sex Role: Our Culture's Blueprint of Manhood, and What It's Done for Us Lately." In *The Forty-Nine Percent Majority,* edited by D. David and R. Brannon. Reading, MA: Addison-Wesley, 1–45.

Davidson, Laurie, and Laura Kramer Gordon. 1979. *The Sociology of Gender.* Chicago: Rand McNally College Publishing.

Davison, Kevin G. 2007. "Methodological Instability and the Disruption of Masculinities." *Men and Masculinities* 9:379–391.

De Beauvoir, Simone. 1952. *The Second Sex.* New York: Knopf.

Delgado, Richard, and Jean Stefancic. 1995. "Minority Men, Misery, and the Marketplace of Ideas." In *Constructing Masculinity*, edited by M. Berger, B. Wallis, and S. Watson. New York: Routledge, 211–220.

Dentinger, Emma, and Marin Clarkberg. 2002. "Informal Caregiving and Retirement Timing Among Men and Women: Gender and Caregiving Relationships in Late Midlife." *Journal of Family Issues* 23:857–879.

Deutsch, Francine M. 2007. "Undoing Gender." *Gender & Society* 21:106–127.

DiMaggio, Paul, Eszter Hargittai, W. Russell Neuman, and John P. Robinson. 2001. "Social Implications of the Internet." *Annual Review of Sociology* 27:307–336.

Dobratz, Betty A., and Stephanie L. Shanks-Meile. 2004. "The White Separatist Movement: Worldviews on Gender, Feminism, Nature, and Change." In *Home-Grown Hate: Gender and Organized Racism*, edited by Abby L. Ferber. New York: Routledge, 113–141.

Dow, Bonnie J. 1996. *Prime-Time Feminism: Television, Media Culture, and the Women's Movement Since 1970*. Philadelphia: University of Pennsylvania Press.

Dowd, Maureen. 1999. "Why Can't a Woman . . ." *New York Times*, October 24, WK, 15.

Dunne, Gillian A. 2000. "Opting Into Motherhood: Lesbians Blurring the Boundaries and Transforming the Meaning of Parenthood and Kinship." *Gender & Society* 14:11–35.

Dworkin, Shari L., and Michael A. Messner. 1999. "Just Do . . What? Sport, Bodies, Gender." In *Revisioning Gender*, edited by M. M. Ferree, B. B. Hess, and J. Lorber. Thousand Oaks, CA: Sage, 341–361.

Eckholm, Erik. 2009. " '07 U.S. Births Break Baby Boom Record." *New York Times*, March 19, A14.

Edin, Kathryn, 2000. "What Do Low-Income Single Mothers Say About Marriage?" *Social Problems* 47:112–133.

Edin, Kathryn, and Laura Lein. 1997. "Work, Welfare, and Single Mothers' Economic Survival Strategies." *American Sociological Review* 62:253–266.

Edwards, Linda N., and Elizabeth Field-Hendley. 1996. "Home-Based Workers: Data from the 1990 Census of Population." *Monthly Labor Review* 119 (November):26–34.

Edwards, Mark E. 2001. "Uncertainty and the Rise of the Work-Family Dilemma." *Journal of Marriage and the Family* 63:183–196.

Egan, Timothy. 2002. "Body-Conscious Boys Adopt Athletes' Taste for Steroids." *New York Times*, November 22, A1, 24.

Eliasoph, Nina. 1999. "Everyday Racism in a Culture of Political Avoidance: Civil Society, Speech, and Taboo." *Social Problems* 46:479–502.

Ellis, Deborah. 1999. Personal communication.

Elson, Jean. 2003. "Hormonal Hierarchy: Hysterectomy and Stratified Stigma." *Gender & Society* 17:750–770.

Elvira, Marta M., and Ishak Saporta. 2001. "How Does Collective Bargaining Affect the Gender Pay Gap?" *Work and Occupations* 28:469–490.

Emerson, Rana A. 2002. " 'Where My Girls At?' Negotiating Black Womanhood in Music Videos." *Gender & Society* 16:115–135.

England, Paula. 1999. "The Impact of Feminist Thought on Sociology." *Contemporary Sociology* 28:263–268.

England, Paula, Carmen Garcia-Beaulieu, and Mary Ross. 2004. "Women's Employment Among Blacks, Whites, and Three Groups of Latinas." *Gender & Society* 18:494–509.

England, Paula, and Su Li. 2006. "Desegregation Stalled." *Gender & Society* 20:657–677.

Epstein, Cynthia Fuchs. 1999. "Similarity and Difference." In *Handbook of the Sociology of Gender*, edited by Janet Saltzman Chafetz. New York: Kluwer Academic/Plenum Publishers, 45–61.

Epstein, Debbie, Mary Kehily, Mairtin Macan Ghaill, and Peter Redman. 2001. "Boys and Girls Come Out to Play: Making Masculinities and Femininities in School Playgrounds." *Men and Masculinities* 4:158–172.

Eriksen, Shelley, and Naomi Gerstel. 2002. "A Labor of Love or Labor Itself: Care Work Among Adult Brothers and Sisters." *Journal of Family Issues*. Cited in Garey, Anita Ilta, Karen V. Hansen,

Rosanna Hertz, and Cameron Macdonald. 2002. "Care and Kinship: An Introduction." *Journal of Family Issues* 23:703–715.

Espiritu, Yen Le. 2001. "'We Don't Sleep Around Like White Girls Do': Family, Culture, and Gender in Filipina American Lives." *Signs* 26:415–440.

Evans, Sara M. 2003. *Tidal Wave: How Women Changed America at Century's End.* New York: Free Press.

Ezzell, Matthew B. 2009. "'Barbie Dolls' on the Pitch." *Social Problems* 56:111–131.

Faludi, Susan. 1999. *Stiffed.* New York: William Morrow.

Farrell, Warren. 1975. *The Liberated Man.* New York: Bantam.

Fausto-Sterling, Anne, 1995. "How to Build a Man." In *Constructing Masculinity,* edited by M. Berger, B. Wallis, and S. Watson. New York: Routledge, 127–134.

Featherstone, Brid. 1996. "Victims or Villains? Women Who Physically Abuse Their Children." In *Violence and Gender Relations: Theories and Interventions,* edited by B. Fawcett, B. Featherstone, J. Hearn, and C. Toft. London: Sage, 178–189.

*Federal Times.* 2004. "OSC to Study Whether Bias Law Covers Gays." March 15. Accessed April 2004, at www.federaltimes.com/index.php?S=272718S.

Feltey, Kathryn M. 2001. "Gender Violence: Rape and Sexual Assault." In *Gender Mosaics: Social Perspectives,* edited by D. Vannoy. Los Angeles: Roxbury, Chapter 35.

Ferber, Abby L., and Michael S. Kimmel 2004. "'White Men Are This Nation': Right-Wing Militias and the Restoration of Rural American Masculinity." In *Home-Grown Hate: Gender and Organized Racism,* edited by Abby L. Ferber. New York: Routledge, 143–160.

Ferguson, Ann Arnett. 2000. *Bad Boys: Public Schools in the Making of Black Masculinity.* Ann Arbor: University of Michigan Press.

Ferguson, Susan J. 2000. "Challenging Traditional Marriage: Never-Married Chinese American and Japanese American Women." *Gender and Society* 14:136–159.

Ferree, Myra Marx, and Beth B. Hess. 1985. *Controversy and Coalition.* Boston: Twayne.

Ferree, Myra Marx, Beth B. Hess, and Judith Lorber (eds.). 1999. *Revisioning Gender.* Thousand Oaks, CA: Sage.

Fetner, Tina. 2008. *How the Religious Right Shaped Lesbian and Gay Activism.* Minneapolis: University of Minnesota Press.

Fine, Michelle. 1989. "The Politics of Research and Activism: Violence Against Women." *Gender & Society* 3:549–558.

Fine, Michelle, Lois Weis, Judi Addelston, and Julia Marusza. 1997. "Constructing White Working-Class Masculinities in the Late 20th Century." *Gender & Society* 11:52–68.

Fingerson, Laura. 1999. "Active Viewing." *Journal of Contemporary Ethnography* 28:389–418.

Finlay, Barbara. 2006. *George W. Bush and the War on Women.* London: Zed Books.

Fischer, Claude S., Michael Hout, Martin Sanchez-Jankowski, Samuel R. Lucas, Ann Swidler, and Kim Voss. 1996. *Inequality by Design: Cracking the Bell Curve Myth.* Princeton NJ: Princeton University Press.

Fong-Torres, Ben. 1986. "Why Are There No Male Asian Anchor *Men* on TV?" *San Francisco Chronicle,* "Datebook," July 13. Reprinted 2000 in *Reconstructing Gender,* edited by E. Disch. Mountain View, CA: Mayfield, 383–388.

Fonow, Mary Margaret. 1998. "Protest Engendered: The Participation of Women Steelworkers in the Wheeling–Pittsburgh Steel Strike of 1985." *Gender and Society* 12:710–728.

Fox, Mary Frank. 2001. "Women, Science, and Academia: Graduate Education and Careers." *Gender & Society* 15:654–666.

Fox, Mary Frank, Gerhard Sonnert, and Irina Nikiforova. 2009. "Successful Programs for Undergraduate Women in Science and Engineering." *Research in Higher Education* 50:333–353.

Frankenberg, Ruth. 1993. *The Social Construction of Whiteness: White Women, Race Matters.* Minneapolis: University of Minnesota Press.

Frankfort, Ellen. 1972. *Vaginal Politics.* New York: Bantam.

Freed, Alice F. 1995. "Language and Gender." *Annual Review of Applied Linguistics* 15:3–22.

—— 2003. "Epilogue: Reflections on Language and Gender Research." In *The Handbook of Language and Gender,* edited by Janet Holmes and Miriam Meyerhoff. Oxford, UK: Blackwell, 699–721.

Freedman, Audrey. 1989. "Those Costly 'Good Old Boys.'" *New York Times,* July 12, 1 23.

Freund, Peter, and George Martin. 1993. *The Ecology of the Automobile.* Montreal: Black Rose Books.

Friedan, Betty. 1963. *The Feminine Mystique.* New York: Norton.

Frisco, Michelle L., and Kristi Williams. 2003. "Perceived Housework Equity, Marital Happiness, and Divorce in Dual-Earner Households." *Journal of Family Issues* 24:51–73.

Fuentes, Annette. 1997. "Crime Rates Are Down . . . But What About Rape?" *Ms.* 8:19–22.

Gagne, Patricia, and Deanna McGaughey. 2002. "Designing Women: Cultural Hegemony and the Exercise of Power Among Women Who Have Undergone Elective Mammoplasty." *Gender & Society* 16:814–838.

Gallagher, Sally K. 2004. "Where Are the Antifeminist Evangelicals?" *Gender & Society* 18:451–472.

García, Alma M. 1989. "The Development of Chicana Feminist Discourse, 1970–1980." *Gender & Society* 3:217–238.

García-Lopez, Gladys. 2008. " 'Nunca Te Toman En Cuenta' [They Never Take You into Account]." *Gender & Society* 22:590–612.

Gardiner, Judith Kegan. 2000. "*South Park,* Blue Men, Anality, and Market Masculinity." *Men and Masculinities* 2:251–271.

Garey, Anita Ilta, Karen V. Hansen, Rosanna Hertz, and Cameron Macdonald. 2002. "Care and Kinship: An Introduction." *Journal of Family Issues* 23:703–715.

Garfinkel, Perry. 1985. *In a Man's World.* New York: Penguin Books.

Gerson, Kathleen. 1993. *No Man's Land: Men's Changing Commitments to Family and Work.* New York: Basic Books.

——. 2002. "Moral Dilemmas, Moral Strategies, and the Transformation of Gender: Lessons From Two Generations of Work and Family Change." *Gender & Society* 16:8–28.

Gerstel, Naomi, and Sally K. Gallagher. 2001. "Men's Caregiving." *Gender & Society* 15:197–217.

Giannarelli, Linda, and James Barsimantov. 2000. "Child Care Expenses of America's Families." Occasional paper. New York: Urban Institute. Accessed August 30, 2009 at http://www.urban.org/url.cfm?ID=310028.

Gilbert, Richard, and Kristin Constantine. 2005. "When Strength Can't Last a Lifetime." *Men and Masculinities* 7:424–433.

Gilligan, Carol. 1982. *In a Different Voice.* Cambridge, MA: Harvard University Press.

Gilmore, Stephanie (ed.). 2008. *Feminist Coalitions.* Champaign: University of Illinois Press.

Gimenez, Martha. 2004. "Recent Developments in Contemporary Feminist Theory." In *Issues in Contemporary Sociological Theory,* edited by Berch Berberoglu. New York: Rowman & Littlefield (forthcoming).

Giordano, Peggy C. 2003. "Relationships in Adolescence." *Annual Review of Sociology* 29:257–281.

Giuffre, Patti A., and Christine L. Williams. 2000. "Not Just Bodies: Strategies for Desexualizing the Physical Examination of Patients." *Gender & Society* 14:457–482.

Glenn, Evelyn Nakano. 2008. "Yearning for Lightness." *Gender & Society* 22:281–302.

Glick, Peter, and Susan T. Fiske. 1999. "Gender, Power Dynamics, and Social Interaction." In *Revisioning Gender,* edited by M. M. Ferree, B. B. Hess, and J. Lorber. Thousand Oaks, CA: Sage, 365–398.

Goffman, Erving. 1962. *Asylums: Essays on the Social Situation of Mental Patients and Other Intimates.* Chicago: Aldine.

Goldin, Claudia, and Lawrence F. Kartz. 2000. The Power of the Pill: Oral Contraceptives and Women's Career and Marriage Decisions. Cambridge, MA: Harvard University and National Bureau of Economic Research.

Gossett, Jennifer Lynn, and Sarah Byrne. 2002. " 'Click Here': A Content Analysis of Internet Rape Sites." *Gender & Society* 16:689–709.

Grant, Linda. 1994. "Helpers, Enforcers, and Go-Betweens: Black Females in Elementary School Classrooms." In *Women of Color in U.S. Society*, edited by M. Baca Zinn and B. T. Dill. Philadelphia: Temple University Press, 43–64.

Grauerholz, Liz, and Lori Baker-Sperry. 2003. "The Pervasiveness and Persistence of the Feminine Beauty Ideal in Children's Fairy Tales." *Gender & Society* 17:711–726.

Gray, Stan. 1984. "Sharing the Shop Floor." *Canadian Dimension*, June 18. Reprinted 2000 in *Reconstructing Gender*, edited by E. Disch. Mountain View, CA: Mayfield, 388–401.

Greenhouse, Steven. 1999. "Priest vs. 'Big Chicken' in Fight for Labor Rights." *New York Times*, October 6, A16.

——. 2000. "Poll of Working Women Finds Them Stressed." *New York Times*, March 10, A15.

Greenstein, Theodore N. 2000. "Economic Dependence, Gender, and the Division of Labor in the Home: A Replication and Extension." *Journal of Marriage and the Family* 62:322–335.

Gremillion, Helen. 2001. "In Fitness and in Health: Crafting Bodies in the Treatment of Anorexia Nervosa." *Signs* 27:381–414.

Grindstaff, Laura, and Emily West. 2006. "Cheerleading and the Gendered Politics of Sport." *Social Problems* 53:500–518.

Gross, Jane. 2004. "Older Women Team Up to Face Future Together." *New York Times*, February 27, A1, A22.

Gupta, Sanjiv. 1999. "Effects of Transitions in Marital Status on Men's Performance of Housework." *Journal of Marriage and the Family* 61:700–711.

Gurevich, Maria, Scott Bishop, Jo Bower, Monika Malka, and Joyce Nyhof-Young. 2004. "(Dis)-embodying Gender and Sexuality in Testicular Cancer." *Social Science & Medicine* 58:1597–1607.

Guthrie, Doug, and Louise Marie Roth. 1999. "The State, Courts, and Maternity Policies in U.S. Organizations." *American Sociological Review*. 64:41–63.

Hacker, Andrew. 2003. "How the B. A. Gap Widens the Chasm Between Men and Women." *Chronicle of Higher Education*, June 20, B10–11.

Hall, Elaine J., and Marine Salupo Rodriguez. 2003. "The Myth of Postfeminism." *Gender & Society* 17:878–902.

Hall, Kira, and Mary Bucholtz (eds.). 1995. *Gender Articulated: Language and the Socially Constructed Self*. New York: Routledge.

Hall, Richard H. 1999. *Organizations*. Upper Saddle River, NJ: Prentice-Hall.

Hammonds, Evelynn, and Baanu Subramaniam. 2003. "A Conversation on Feminist Science Studies." *Signs* 28:923–944.

Hand, Jeanne Z., and Laura Sanchez. 2000. "Badgering or Bantering? Gender Differences in, Experience of, and Reactions to, Sexual Harassment Among U.S. High School Students." *Gender & Society* 4:718–746.

Haney, Lynne A. 2000. "Feminist State Theory: Applications to Jurisprudence, Criminology, and the Welfare State." *Annual Review of Sociology* 26:641–666.

Hannerz, Ulf. 1969. *Soulside: Inquiries in Ghetto Culture and Community*. New York: Columbia University Press.

Harding, Sandra. 1987. *Feminism and Methodology*. Bloomington: Indiana University Press.

Harris, Gardiner. 2003. "If Shoe Won't Fit, Fix the Foot? Popular Surgery Raises Concern." *New York Times*, December 7, A1, A36.

——. 2004. "Pfizer Gives Up Testing Viagra on Women." *New York Times*, February 28, C1.

Harris, Judith. 1998. *The Nurture Assumption*. New York: Free Press.

Harrison, Kristen, and Joanne Cantor. 1997. "The Relationship Between Media Consumption and Eating Disorders." *Journal of Communication* 47:40–68.

Hartmann, Heidi. 1976. "Capitalism, Patriarchy, and Job Segregation by Sex." *Signs* 1:137–169.

Hasbrook, Cynthia A., and Othello Harris. 2000. "Wrestling With Gender." In *Masculinities, Gender Relations, and Sport*, edited by Jim McKay, Michael A. Messner, and Don Sabo. Thousands Oaks, CA: Sage, 13–30.

Haskell, Kari. 2002. "Sizing Up Teenagers." *New York Times*, October 13, WK6.

Hatchett, Shirley J., and James S. Jackson. 1999. "African American Extended Kin Systems." In *Family Ethnicity*, edited by H. P. McAdoo. Thousand Oaks, CA: Sage, 171–190.

Haubeggar, Christy. 1994. "I'm Not Fat, I'm Latina." In *Essence*, December. Reprinted 2000 in *Reconstructing Gender: A Multicultural Anthology*, edited by E. Disch. Mountain View: CA: Mayfield, 181–182.

Hays, Sharon, 1996. *The Cultural Contradictions of Motherhood*. New Haven, CT: Yale University Press.

Headlam, Bruce. 2000. "Barbie PC: Fashion Over Logic." *New York Times*, January 20, G4.

Hecker, Daniel E. 1998. "Earnings of College Graduates: Women Compared with Men." *Monthly Labor Review* 121 (March):62–71.

Heinecken, Dawn. 2004. "No Cage Can Hold Her Rage? Gender, Transgression, and the World Wrestling Federation's Chyna." In *Action Chicks: New Images of Tough Women in Popular Culture*, edited by Sherrie A. Inness. New York: Palgrave Macmillan, 181–206.

Henley, Nancy. 1995. "Ethnicity and Gender Issues in Language." In *Bringing Cultural Diversity to Feminist Psychology*, edited by H. Landrine, Washington, DC: American Psychological Association.

Henson, Kevin D., and Jackie Krasas Rogers. 2001. "'Why Marcia You've Changed!' Male Clerical Temporary Workers Doing Masculinity in a Feminized Occupation." *Gender & Society* 15:218–238.

Hequembourg, Amy L., and Michael P. Farrell. 1999. "Lesbian Motherhood: Negotiating Marginal–Mainstream Identities." *Gender & Society* 13:540–557.

Herd, Pamela, and Madonna Harrington Meyer. 2002. "Care Work: Invisible Civic Engagement." *Gender & Society* 16:665–688.

Hesse-Biber, Sharlene. 2007. *Am I Thin Enough Yet?* New York: Oxford University Press.

Hill, Anita. 2007. "What Difference Will Women Judges Make?" In *Women & Leadership*, edited by B. Kellerman and D. L. Rhode. San Francisco: Jossey-Bass, 175–194.

Hill, Shirley A., and Joey Sprague. 1999. "Parenting in Black and White Families: The Interaction of Gender With Race and Class." *Gender & Society* 13:480–502.

Hinze, Susan Waldoch. 2000. "Inside Medical Marriages: The Effect of Gender on Income." *Work and Occupations* 27:464–499.

Hochschild, Arlie. 1989. *The Second Shift*. New York: Viking.

Holson, Laura M. 2004. "And the Winner Is . . . the Older Woman." *New York Times*, January 18, WK 12.

Hondagneu-Sotelo, Pierrette. 2001. *Doméstica: Immigrant Workers Cleaning and Caring in the Shadows of Affluence*. Berkeley: University of California Press.

hooks, bell. 1984. *Feminist Theory: From Margin to Center*. Boston: South End Press.

Hooyman, Nancy R., and Judith Gonyea. 1997. *Feminist Perspectives on Family Care*. Thousand Oaks, CA: Sage.

Horvat, Erin McNamara, and Kristine S. Lewis. 2003. "Reassessing the 'Burden of "Acting White"': The Importance of Peer Groups in Managing Academic Success." *Sociology of Education* 76:265–280.

Huddy, Leonie. 1997. "Feminists and Feminism in the Newsroom." In *Women, Media, and Politics*, edited by P. Norris. New York: Oxford University Press, 183–203.

Hulett, Denise M., Marc Bendick, Jr., Sheila Y. Thomas, and Francine Moccio. 2008. "Enhancing Women's Inclusion in Firefighting in the USA." *International Journal of Diversity in Organisations, Communities & Nations* 8:189–207.

Hyde, Janet S., and Janet E. Mertz. 2009. "Gender, Culture, and Mathematics Performance." *Proceedings of the National Academy of Sciences* 106:8801–8807.

Inness, Sherrie A. 2004. "It's a Girl Thing': Tough Female Action Figures in the Toy Store." In *Action Chicks: New Images of Tough Women in Popular Culture*, edited by Sherrie A. Inness. New York: Palgrave Macmillan, 75–94.

Institute for Women's Policy Research. 2008. Data Tables on the Economic Status of Women of Color in the United States, Key Data Points. Washington, DC: Institute for Women's Policy Research. Accessed June 11, 2009, at http://www.iwpr.org/femstats/wocdata.html.

Irons, Jenny. 1998. "The Shaping of Activist Recruitment and Participation: A Study of Women in the Mississippi Civil Rights Movement." *Gender & Society* 12:692–709.

Isaacs, Susan. 1999. *Brave Dames and Wimpettes: What Women Are Really Doing on Page and Screen.* New York: Ballantine.

Isaksen, Lise Widding. 2002. "Toward a Sociology of (Gendered) Disgust: Images of Bodily Decay and the Social Organization of Care Work." *Journal of Family Issues* 23:791–811.

Jacobs, Eva E. (ed.). 1997. *Handbook of U.S. Labor Statistics.* Lanham, MD: Bernan Press.

Jacobs, Eva E., and Mary Meghan Ryan (eds.) 2003. *Handbook of U.S. Labor Statistics.* Sixth edition. Lanham, MD: Bernan Press.

Jagannathan, Radha, and Michael J. Camasso. 2003. "Family Cap and Nonmarital Fertility: The Racial Conditioning of Policy Effects." *Journal of Marriage and the Family* 65:52–71.

James, Deborah, and Janice Drakich. 1993. "Understanding Gender Differences in Amount of Talk." In *Gender and Conversational Interaction*, edited by D. Tannen. New York: Oxford University Press, 281–312.

Jenness, Valerie. 1998. "Managing Differences and Making Legislation: Social Movements and the Racialization, Sexualization, and Gendering of Federal Hate Crime Law in the U.S., 1985–1998." *Social Problems* 46:548–571.

Jenson, Jennifer, and Chloe Brushwood Rose. 2003. "Women@Work: Listening to Gendered Relations of Power in Teachers' Talk About New Technologies." *Gender & Education* 15:169–181.

Johnson, Earl S., Ann Levine, and Fred C. Doolittle. 1999. *Fathers' Fair Share.* New York: Russell Sage Foundation.

Johnson, Michael P. 1995. "Patriarchal Terrorism and Common Couple Violence: Two Forms of Violence Against Women." *Journal of Marriage and the Family* 57:283–294.

——. 2008. *A Typology of Domestic Violence.* Boston: Northeastern University Press.

Johnson, Michael P., and Kathleen J. Ferraro. 2000. "Research on Domestic Violence in the 1990s: Making Distinctions." *Journal of Marriage and the Family* 62:948–963.

Junn, Jane. 2009. "Making Room for Women of Color." *Politics & Gender* 5:105–110.

Kalof, Linda, Kimberly K. Eby, Jennifer L. Matheson, and Rob J. Kroska. 2001. "The Influence of Race and Gender on Student Self-Reports of Sexual Harassment by College Professors." *Gender & Society* 15:282–302.

Kane, Emily W. 2000. "Racial and Ethnic Variations in Gender Related Attitudes." *Annual Review of Sociology* 26:419–439.

Kane, Emily W., and Else K. Kyyro. 2001. "For Whom Does Education Enlighten? Race, Gender, Education, and Beliefs About Social Inequality." *Gender & Society* 15:710–733.

Kang, Miliann. 2003. "The Managed Hand: The Commercialization of Bodies and Emotions in Korean Immigrant-Owned Nail Salons." *Gender & Society* 17:820–839.

Kaufman, Leslie. 2003. "Are Those Leaving Welfare Better Off Now? Yes and No." *New York Times*, October 20, B1, B3.

Kaufman, Marc. 2005. "FDA Official Quits Over Delay on Plan B." *Washington Post*, September 1, A08.

Kempner, Joanna. 2006. "Uncovering the Man in Medicine." *Gender & Society* 20: 632–656.

Kendall, Lori. 2000. "Oh No! I'm a Nerd! Hegemonic Masculinity on an Online Forum." *Gender & Society* 14:256–274.

Kennelly, Ivy. 2002. " 'I Would Never Be a Secretary': Reinforcing Gender in Segregated and Integrated Occupations." *Gender & Society* 16:603–624.

Kilborn, Peter T., and Lynette Clemetson. 2002. "Gains of 90's Did Not Lift All, Census Shows." *New York Times*, June 5, A1, A20.

Kimmel, Michael S. 1996. *Manhood in America.* New York: Free Press.

———. 1997. "Promise Keepers: Patriarchy's Second Coming as Masculine Renewal." *Tikkun* 12 (March/April): 46–50.

———. 2000. "Saving the Males: The Sociological Implications of the Virginia Military Institute and the Citadel." *Gender & Society* 14:494–516.

King, Leslie, and Madonna Harrington Meyer. 1997. "The Politics of Reproductive Benefits: U.S. Insurance Coverage of Contraceptive and Infertility Treatments." *Gender & Society* 11: 8–30.

King, Neal. 2008. "Generic Womanhood." *Gender & Society* 22:238–260.

Klass, Perri. 2009. "At Last, Facing Down Bullies (and Their Enablers)." *New York Times*, June 9, D5.

Klein, Patricia Vawter. 1987. "'For the Good of the Race': Reproductive Hazards From Lead and the Persistence of Exclusionary Policies Toward Women." In *Women, Work, and Technology*, edited by B. Wright. Ann Arbor: University of Michigan Press, 101–117.

Kleinman, Sherryl. 1996. *Opposing Ambitions.* Chicago: University of Chicago Press.

Kmec, Julie A. 2003. "Minority Job Concentration and Wages." *Social Problems* 50:38–59.

Kocieniewski, David. 1999. "Study Finds Mixed Results in Reducing Welfare Rolls." *New York Times*, October 22, B6.

Kohut, Andrew, and Kimberly Parker. 1997. "Talk Radio and Gender Politics." In *Women, Media, and Politics*, edited by P. Norris. New York: Oxford University Press, 221–234.

Kolata, Gina. 1992. "Track Federation Urges End to Gene Test for Femaleness." *New York Times*, February 2, A1, B11.

———. 2003. "A Sexual Subtext to the Debate Over Breast Implants." *New York Times*, October 19, WK4.

Kramer, Laura. 1991. "Social Class and Occupational Sex Desegregation." In *The Sociology of Gender: A Text-Reader*, edited by L. Kramer. New York: St. Martin's Press, 288–300.

Kramer, Laura, and Alice Freed. 1991. "Gender and Language." In *The Sociology of Gender: A Text-Reader*, edited by L. Kramer. New York: St. Martin's Press, 23–28.

Kristof, Nicholas D. 2002. "Shaming Young Mothers." *New York Times*, August 23, A17.

———. 2009. "Is Rape Serious." *New York Times*, April 30, A27.

Kulczycki, Andrezej, and Arun P. Lobo. 2002. "Patterns, Determinants, and Implications of Intermarriage Among Arab Families." *Journal of Marriage and Family* 64:202–210.

Kuperberg, Arielle, and Pamela Stone. 2008. "The Media Depiction of Women Who Opt Out." *Gender & Society* 22:497–517.

Kurz, Demine. 2001. "Violence Against Women by Intimate Partners." *In Gender Mosaics: Social Perspectives*, edited by D. Vannoy. Los Angeles: Roxbury Publishing, Chapter 20.

Kutz-Flamenbaum, Rachel V. 2004. "Feminist and Women's Organizing in the 2002–2003 Anti-War Movement." Unpublished paper. Stony Brook, NY: S.U.N.Y. Stony Brook, Department of Sociology.

Lamb, Michael E., Joseph H. Pleck, and James A. Levine 1986. "Effects of Increased Parental Involvement on Children in Two-Parent Families." In *Men in Families,* edited by R. A. Lewis and R. E. Salt. Beverly Hills, CA: Sage, 169–180.

Lauzen, Martha M. 2003. "Boxed In: Women on Screen and Behind the Scenes in the 2002–03 Prime-time Season." Executive summary. Unpublished report. San Diego, CA: San Diego State University.

———. 2008. "Boxed In." San Diego State University Center for the Study of Women in Television and Film. Accessed May 7, 2009, at http://womenintvfilm.sdsu.edu/files/Boxed%20In%202007-08%20Report.pdf.

———. 2009. "The Celluloid Ceiling." San Diego State University Center for the Study of Women in Television and Film. Accessed May 7, 2009, at http://womenintvfilm.sdsu.edu/files/2998_celluloid_ceiling.pdf.

Law, Jules. 2000. "The Politics of Breastfeeding: Assessing Risk, Dividing Labor." *Signs* 25: 407–450.

Lawless, Jennifer L. 2009. "Sexism and Gender Bias in Election 2008." *Politics & Gender* 5: 70–80.

Lee, Felicia. 2003. "Networking on TV: A Feminine Touch." *New York Times*, November 29, B9, 11.

Lee, James Daniel. 2002. "More Than Ability: Gender and Personal Relationships Influence Science and Technology Involvement." *Sociology of Education* 75:349–373.

Leland, John. 2004. "He's Retired, She's Working, They're Not Happy." *New York Times*, March 23, A1, A20.

Lempert, Lora Bex, and Marjorie L. DeVault. 2000. "Guest Editors' Introduction: Special Issues on Emergent and Reconfigured Forms of Family Life." *Gender & Society* 14:6–10.

Levit, Nancy. 1998. *The Gender Line: Men, Women, and the Law*. New York: New York University Press.

Lewin, Tamar. 2000. "Insurance Should Cover Cost of Contraceptives, Suit Says." *New York Times*, July 20, A16.

——. 2004. "Despite Gain in Degrees, Women Lag in Tenure in 2 Main Fields." *New York Times*, A23, January 15.

Liberman, Mark. 2006. "Sex on the Brain." Boston Globe, September 24. Accessed on May 7, 2009, at http://www.boston.com/news/globe/ideas/articles/2006/09/24/sex_on_the_brain/.

Lichter, Daniel T., Deborah Roempke Graefe, and J. Brain Brown. 2003. "Is Marriage a Panacea? Union Formation Among Economically Disadvantaged Unwed Mothers." *Social Problems* 50:60–86.

Liebow, Elliot. 1993. *Tell Them Who I Am*. New York: Free Press.

*The Life and Times of Rosie the Riveter*. Los Angeles: Direct Cinema Ltd., 1987, 65 minutes.

Lim, In-Sook. 1997. "Korean Immigrant Women's Challenge to Gender Inequality at Home: The Interplay of Economic Resources, Gender, and Family." *Gender & Society* 11:31–51.

Lorber, Judith. 1989. "From the Editor." *Gender & Society* 3:157–159.

——. 1994. *Paradoxes of Gender*. New Haven, CT: Yale University Press.

——. 1999. "Embattled Terrain: Gender and Sexuality." In *Revisioning Gender*, edited by M. M. Ferree, B. B. Hess, and J. Lorber. Thousand Oaks, CA: Sage, 416–448.

——. 2001a. "Gender Hierarchies in Health Professions." In *Gender Mosaics: Social Perspectives*, edited by D. Vannoy. Los Angeles: Roxbury Publishing, Chapter 42.

——. 2001b. *Gender Inequality: Feminist Theories and Politics*. Los Angeles: Roxbury Publishing.

Lovejoy, Meg. 2001. "Disturbances in the Social Body: Differences in Body Image and Eating Problems Among African American and White Women." *Gender & Society* 15:239–261.

Lucal, Betsy, 1999. "What It Means to Be Gendered Me: Life on the Boundaries of a Dichotomous Gender System." *Gender & Society* 13:781–797.

Lyall, Sarah. 2004. "In Europe, Lovers Now Propose: Marry Me, a Little." *New York Times*, February 15, 3.

MacFarquhar, Neil. 2003. "Saudi Women Find a New Ally: Muhammad's Wife." *New York Times*, December 24, A4.

Malacrida, Claudia. 2002. "Alternative Therapies and Attention Deficit Disorder: Discourses of Maternal Responsibility and Risk." *Gender & Society* 16:366–385.

Manning, Wendy D., and Pamela J. Smock. 2002. "First Comes Cohabitation Then Comes Marriage." *Journal of Family Issues* 23:1065–1087.

Mansbridge, Jane. J. 1986. *Why We Lost the ERA*. Chicago: University of Chicago Press.

Marin, Rick. 2000. "At-Home Dads Step Out to Find They Are Not Alone." *New York Times, January* 2, 1, 17.

Martin, Emily 1991. "The Egg and the Sperm: How Science Has Constructed a Romance Based on Stereotypical Male-Female Roles." *Signs* 16:485–501.

Martin, Joyce A., Brady E. Hamilton, Paul D. Sutton, Stephanie J. Ventura, Fay Menacker, and Martha L. Munson. 2003. "Births: Final Data for 2002." *National Vital Statistics Reports* 52, no. 10 (December 17).

Martin, Karin. 2003. "Giving Birth Like a Girl." *Gender & Society* 17:54–72.

Martin, Karin A., and Emily Kazyak. 2009. "Hetero-Romantic Love and Heterosexiness in Children's G-Rated Films." *Gender & Society* 23:315–336.

Martin, Patricia Yancey, and David L. Collinson. 1999. "Gender and Sexuality in Organizations." In *Revisioning Gender*, edited by M. M. Ferree, B. B. Hess, and J. Lorber. Thousand Oaks, CA: Sage, 285–310.

Martin, Patricia Y., John R. Reynolds, and Shelley Keith. 2002. "Gender Bias and Feminist Consciousness Among Judges and Attorneys." *Signs* 27:665–701.

Martinez, Estella. 1999. "Mexican American/Chicano Families." In *Family Ethnicity*, edited by H. P. McAdoo. Thousand Oaks, CA: Sage, 121–134.

Mason, Karen Oppenheim, John L. Czajka, and Sara Arber. 1976. "Change in U.S. Women's Sex-Role Attitudes, 1964–1974." *American Sociological Review* 41:573–596.

McCall, Leslie. 2005. "The Complexity of Intersectionality." *Signs* 30:1771–1800.

McCaughey, Martha. 2007. *The Caveman Mystique.* New York: Routledge.

McCloskey, Laura Ann. 1996. "Socioeconomic and Coercive Power Within the Family." *Gender & Society* 10:449–463.

McGuffey, Shawn C., and B. Lindsay Rich. 1999. "Playing in the Gender Transgression Zone: Race, Class, and Hegemonic Masculinity in Middle Childhood." *Gender & Society* 13:608–627.

McGuire, Gail M. 2002. "Gender, Race, and the Shadow Structure: A Study of Informal Networks and Inequality in a Work Organization." *Gender & Society* 16:303–322.

McIntosh, Peggy. 1988. "White Privilege and Male Privilege: A Personal Account of Coming to See Correspondences Through Work in Women's Studies." Working Paper 189. Wellesley, MA: Wellesley College Center for Research on Women.

McPherson, Miller, Lynn Smith-Lovin, and James M. Cook. 2001. "Birds of a Feather: Homophily in Social Networks." *Annual Review of Sociology* 27:415–444.

McQuillan, Julia, Arthur L. Greil, Karina M. Shreffler, and Veronica Tichenor. 2008. "The Importance of Motherhood Among Women in the Contemporary United States." *Gender & Society* 22:477–496.

Media Women—New York. 1970. "How to Name a Baby—A Vocabulary Guide for Working Women." In *Sisterhood Is Powerful*, edited by R. Morgen. New York: Vintage Books, 526–527.

Medina, Jennifer. 2009. "Boys and Girls Together, Taught Separately in School." *New York Times*, March 11, A24, A28.

Messerschmidt, James. 1993. *Masculinities and Crime.* Lanham, MD: Rowman & Littlefield.

Messner, Michael A. 1989. "Masculinities and Athletic Careers." *Gender & Society*, 3:71–88.

——. 2000. "Barbie Girls Versus Sea Monsters: Children Constructing Gender." *Gender & Society* 14:765–784.

Mickelson, Roslyn Arlin. 2003. "Gender, Bourdieu, and the Anomaly of Women's Achievement Redux." *Sociology of Education* 76:373–375.

Mihelich, John, and Debbie Storrs. 2003. "Higher Education and the Negotiated Process of Hegemony." *Gender & Society* 17:404–422.

Milkie, Melissa A. 2002. "Contested Images of Femininity: An Analysis of Cultural Gatekeepers' Struggles With the 'Real Girl' Critique." *Gender & Society* 16:839–859.

Miller, Casey, and Kate Swift. 1996. "Reclaiming Language." In *Women Transforming Communication: Global Intersections*, edited by D. Allen, R. R. Rush, and S. J. Kaufman, Thousand Oaks, CA: Sage, 243–248.

Miller, Susan L., Kay B. Forest, and Nancy C. Jurik. 2003. "Diversity in Blue: Lesbian and Gay Police Officers in a Masculine Occupations." *Men and Masculinities* 5:355–385.

Miller, Tina. 2007. "Is This What Motherhood Is All About?" *Gender & Society* 21:337–358.

Miller-Bernal, Leslie. 2000. *Separate by Degree.* New York: Peter Lang.

Mills, Kay. 1997. "What Difference Do Women Journalists Make?" In *Women, Media, and Politics*, edited by P. Norris. New York: Oxford University Press, 41–55.

Moghadam, Valentine M. 2002. "Islamic Feminism and its Discontents: Toward a Resolution of the Debate." *Signs* 27:1135–1171.

Moore, Solomon 2009. "Justice Dept. Seeks Equity in Sentences for Cocaine." *New York Times*, April 30, A17.

Moore, Valerie A. 2001. "'Doing' Racialized and Gendered Age to Organize Peer Relations: Observing Kids in Summer Camp." *Gender & Society* 15:835–858.

Morris, Edward W. 2008. "'Rednecks,' 'Rutters,' and 'Rithmetic'." *Gender & Society* 22:728–751.

Mosisa, Abraham T. 2003. "The Working Poor in 2001." *Monthly Labor Review* 126 (November/December): 13–19.

Moss, Philip, and Chris Tilly. 2001. *Stories Employers Tell: Race, Skill, and Hiring in America.* New York: Russell Sage Foundation.

Mueller, Charles W., Stacy De Coster, and Sarah Beth Estes. 2001. "Sexual Harassment in the Workplace: Unanticipated Consequences of Modern Social Control in Organizations." *Work and Occupations* 28:411–446.

Mullings, Leith. 1997. *On Our Own Terms: Race, Class, and Gender in the Lives of African American Women.* New York: Routledge.

Nanda, Serena. 2000. "Multiple Genders Among North American Indians." In *Gender Diversity: Crosscultural Variations*, Waveland Press. Reprinted in *Kaleidoscope of Gender*, edited by Joan Z. Spade and Catherine G. Valentine. Belmont, CA: Thomson Wadsworth, 2003, 64–70.

Naples, Nancy A. 1991. "Contradictions in the Gender Subtext of the War on Poverty." *Social Problems* 38:316–332.

——. 2003. *Feminism and Method: Ethonography, Discourse Analysis, and Activist Research.* New York: Taylor & Francis.

Nasar, Sylvia, and Kirsten B. Mitchell. 1999. "Booming Job Market Draws Young Black Men Into Fold." *New York Times*, May 23, A1, 24.

National Center for Education Statistics. 2002. *The Condition of Education.* Washington, DC: U.S. Department of Education.

National Coalition for the Homeless. 2008. "How Many People Experience Homelessness?" Accessed June 16, 2009, at http://www.nationalhomeless.org/factsheets/How_Many.html.

N.E.A. Research. 2003. *Status of the American Public School Teacher 2000–2001.* Washington, DC: National Education Association.

*National Law Journal.* 1995. "Regional Reports: New York, Dad Sues for a Change." January 9, A10.

National Women's History Project Timeline, Accessed August 30, 2009 at: http://www.legacy98.org/timelline.html.

Nelkin, Dorothy. 1987. *Selling Science.* New York: W. H. Freeman.

*New York Times.* 1999. "As G.I. Joe Bulks Up, Concern for the 98-Pound Weaking." May 30, IV 2.

Norris, Pippa. 1987. *Politics and Sexual Equality: The Comparative Position of Women in Western Democracies.* Boulder, CO: Rienner, 1–18.

——. 1997. "Introduction." In *Women, Media, and Politics*, edited by P. Norris. New York: Oxford University Press.

*Not Without My Veil: Women in Oman.* New York: Filmmakers Library, Distributor, 1993, 29 minutes.

Office of the Historian of the United States House of Representatives. 1991. *Women in Congress 1917–1990.* Washington, DC: U.S. Government Printing Office.

Olesen, Virginia L., and Adele E. Clarke. 1999. "Resisting Closure, Embracing Uncertainties, Creating Agendas." In *Revisioning Women, Health, and Healing: Feminist, Cultural, and Technoscience Perspectives*, edited by Adele E. Clarke and Virginia L. Olesen. New York: Routledge, 355–357.

Olson, Elizabeth. 2009. "Though Many Are Stalked, Few Report It, Study Finds." *New York Times*, February 15, 22, 24.

Olson, Laura Katz. 2003. *The Not-So-Golden Years: Caregiving, the Frail Elderly, and the Long-Term Care Establishment.* Lanham, MD: Rowman & Littlefield.

Orr, Amy J. 2003. "Black–White Differences in Achievement: The Importance of Wealth." *Sociology of Education* 76:281–304.

Oswald, Ramona F. 2002. "Resilience Within the Family Networks of Lesbians and Gay Men: Intentionality and Redefinition." *Journal of Marriage and Family* 64:374–383.

Oudshoorn, Nelly. 2003. *The Male Pill: A Biography of a Technology in the Making.* Durham, NC: Duke University Press.

Palkovitz, Rob, Marcella A. Copes, and Tara N. Woolfolk. 2001. "'It's Like ... You Discover a New Sense of Being': Involved Fathering as an Evoker of Adult Development." *Men and Masculinities* 4:49–69.

Parelius, Ann P. 1991. "Mathematics and Science Majors: Gender Differences in Selection and Persistence." In *The Sociology of Gender*, edited by L. Kramer. New York: St. Martin's Press, 140–160.

Pascoe, C. J. 2007. *Dude, You're a Fag.* Berkeley: University of California Press.

Patterson, Charlotte. 1995. "Lesbian and Gay Parenthood." In *Handbook of Parenting, Vol. 3: Status and Social Conditions of Parenting*, edited by M. H. Bornstein. Mahwah, NJ: Lawrence Erlbaum Associates, 255–274.

——. 2000. "Family Relationships of Lesbians and Gay men." *Journal of Marriage and Family* 62:1052–1069.

Pauwels, Anne. 1998. *Women Changing Language.* London: Longman.

Payne, Kenneth W., and Stephen J. Risch. 1984. "The Politics of AIDS." *Science for the People* 16 (September/October): 17–24.

Pear, Robert. 2004. "Despite Sluggish Economy, Welfare Rolls Actually Fell." *New York Times*, March 22, A21.

Pearson, A. Fiona. 2007. "The New Welfare Trap." *Gender & Society* 21:723–748.

Pelak, Cynthia F. 2002. "Women's Collective Identity Formation in Sports: A Case Study from Women's Ice Hockey." *Gender & Society* 16:93–114.

Perkins, H. Wesley, and Debra K. DeMies. 1996. "Gender and Family Effects on the Second Shift Domestic Activity of College-Educated Young Adults." *Gender & Society* 10:78–93.

Perkins, Linda M. 1997. "For the Good of the Race: Married African-American Academics—A Historical Perspective." In *Academic Couples: Problems and Promises*, edited by Marianne A. Ferber and Jane W. Loeb. Urbana: University of Illinois Press, 80–103.

Petersen, Alan. 2003. "Research on Men and Masculinities." *Men and Masculinities* 6:54–69.

Pfeil, Fred. 1995. *White Guys.* London: Verso.

Pope, Harrison G., Jr., Roberto Olivardia, Amanda Gruber, and John Borowiecki. 1999. "Evolving Ideals of Male Body Image as Seen Through Action Toys." *International Journal of Eating Disorders* 26:65–72.

Postrel, Virginia. 2004. "Economic Scene." *New York Times*, March 25, C2.

Press, Julie E., and Eleanor Townsley. 1998. "Wives' and Husbands' Housework Reporting." *Gender & Society* 12:188–218.

Presser, Harriet B. 2003. *Working in a 24/7 Economy: Challenges for American Families.* New York: Russell Sage Foundation.

Preves, Sharon E. 2001. "Sexing the Intersexed: An Analysis of Sociocultural Responses to Intersexuality." *Signs* 27:523–556.

Prindeville, Diane-Michele. 2003. "Identity and the Politics of American Indian and Hispanic Women Leaders." *Gender & Society* 17:591–608.

Pronger, Brian. 2000. "Wrestling With Gender." In *Masculinities, Gender Relations, and Sport*, edited by Jim McKay, Michael A. Messner, and Don Sabo. Thousand Oaks, CA: Sage, 222–244.

Prose, Francine, 2000. "A Wasteland of One's Own." *New York Times*, March 13, Section 6, 66–71.

Pyke, Karen D., and Denise L. Johnson. 2003. "Asian American Women and Racialized Feminities: 'Doing Gender' Across Cultural Worlds." *Gender & Society* 17:33–53.

Queneau, Herve. 2006. "Is the Long-Term Reduction in Occupational Sex Segregation Still Continuing in the United States?" *The Social Science Journal* 43:681–688.

Quinn, Beth A. 2002. "Sexual Harassment and Masculinity: The Power and Meaning of 'Girl Watching.'" *Gender & Society* 16:386–402.

Radford-Hill, Sheila. 2002. "Keepin' It Real: A Generational Commentary on Kimberly

Springer's 'Third Wave Black Feminism?'" *Signs* 27:1083–1089.

Ranson, Gillian. 2001. "Men at Work: Change—or No Change?—in the Era of the 'New Father.'" *Men and Masculinities* 4:3–26.

Ratcliff, Kathryn Strother, and Janet Bogdan. 1988. "Unemployed Women: When Social Support Is Not Supportive." *Social Problems* 35:54–63.

Read, Jen'nan Ghazal, and John P. Bartkowski. 2000. "To Veil or Not to Veil." *Gender & Society* 14:395–417.

Reid, Lori L. 2002. "Occupational Segregation, Human Capital, and Motherhood: Black Women's Higher Exit Rates From Full-Time Employment." *Gender & Society* 16:728–747.

Reskin, Barbara F. 1998. *The Realities of Affirmative Action in Employment.* Washington, DC: American Sociological Association.

——. 2000. "The Proximate Causes of Employment Discrimination." *Contemporary Sociology* 29:310–328.

——. 2002. "Rethinking Employment Discrimination and Its Remedies." In *The New Economic Sociology*, edited by M. F. Guillen, R. Collins, P. England, and M. Meyer. New York: Russell Sage Foundation. Cited in Browne, Irene, and Joya Misra. 2003. "The Intersection of Gender and Race in the Labor Market." *Annual Review of Sociology* 29:501.

Reskin, Barbara F., and Debra Branch McBrier. 2000. "Why Not Ascription? Organizations' Employment of Male and Female Managers." *American Sociological Review* 65:210–233.

Reskin, Barbara F., and Irene Padavic. 1994. *Women and Men at Work.* Thousand Oaks, CA: Pine Forge Press.

——. 1999, "Sex. Race, and Ethnic Inequality in United States Workplaces." In *Handbook of Sociology of Gender*, edited by Janet Saltzman Chafetz. New York: Kluwer Academic/Plenum Publishers, 343–374.

Rhode, Deborah L. 1997. *Speaking of Sex: The Daniel of Gender Equality.* Cambridge, MA: Harvard University Press.

Richie, Beth E. 1999. "The Social Construction of the 'Immoral' Black Mother." In *Revisioning Women, Health, and Healing: Feminist, Cultural, and Technoscience Perspectives*, edited by Adele E. Clarke and Virginia L. Olesen. New York: Routledge, 283–299.

Ridd, Rosemary, and H. Calloway (eds.). 1987. *Women and Political Conflict: Portraits of Struggle in Times of Crisis.* New York: New York University Press.

Ridgeway, Cecilia. 1997. "Interaction and the Conservation of Gender Inequality." *American Sociological Review* 62:218–235.

——. 2009. "Framed Before We Know It." *Gender & Society* 23:145–160.

Ridgeway, Cecilia L., and Shelley J. Correll. 2004. "Unpacking the Gender System." *Gender & Society* 18:494–509.

Ridgeway, Cecilia L., and Lynn Smith-Lovin. 1999. "The Gender System and Interaction." *Annual Review of Sociology* 25:191–216.

*The Righteous Babes.* New York: Women Make Movies, distributor, 1998, 50 minutes.

Riley, Lisa A., and Jennifer L. Glass. 2002. "You Can't Always Get What You Want—Infant Care Preferences and Use Among Employed Mothers." *Journal of Marriage and the Family* 64:2–15.

Rimer, Sara. 2004. "Unruly Students Facing Arrest, Not Detention." *New York Times*, January 14, A1, A17.

Risman, Barbara J. 1998. *Gender Vertigo.* New Haven, CT: Yale University Press.

——. 2009. "From Doing to Undoing." *Gender & Society* 23: 81–84.

Robinson, John P., and Melissa A. Milkie. 1998. "Back to the Basics: Trends in and Role Determinants of Women's Attitudes Toward Housework." *Journal of Marriage and the Family* 60:205–218.

Rockquemore, Kerry A. 2002. "Negotiating the Color Line." *Gender & Society* 16:485–503.

Roschelle, Anne R. 1999. "Gender, Family Structure, and Social Structure: Racial Ethnic Families in the United States." In *Revisioning Gender*, edited by M. M. Ferree, B.B. Hess, and J. Lorber. Thousand Oaks, CA: Sage, 311–340.

Rosen, Ellen Israel. 1987. *Bitter Choices.* Chicago: University of Chicago Press.

Rosenfield, Dana, and Christopher Faircloth. 2006. "Introduction." In *Medicalized Masculinities*, edited by D. Rosenfield and C. Faircloth. Philadelphia: Temple University Press, 1–20.

Roth, Louise Marie. 2006. *Selling Women Short.* Princeton, NJ: Princeton University Press.

Rothman, Barbara Katz. 1987. "Reproduction." In *Analyzing Gender*, edited by B. B. Hess and M. M. Ferree. Newbury Park, CA: Sage, 154–170.

RTNDA/F Research. 2003. "2002 Women & Minorities Survey." Accessed February 2004, at www.rtndf.org/research/womin.html.

Rushing, Wanda. 2002. "'Sin, Sex, and Segregation': Social Control and the Education of Southern Women." *Gender & Education* 14:167–179.

Russell, Katheryn K. 1998. *The Color of Crime.* New York: New York University Press.

Russell, Richard. 2007. "The Work of Elderly Men Caregivers: From Public Careers to an Unseen World." *Men and Masculinities* 9:298–314.

Rust, Paula C. 1996. "The Impact of Multiple Marginalization." In *Bisexuality: The Psychology and Politics of an Invisible Minority*, edited by B. A. Firestein. Thousand Oaks, CA: Sage, 248–255. Reprinted in *Reconstructing Gender: A Multicultural Anthology*, edited by E. Disch, 2000. Mountain View, CA: Mayfield, 248–255.

Sacks, Karen Brodkin. 1988. *Caring by the Hour.* Urbana: University of Illinois Press.

Sadker, Myra, and David Sadker. 1994. *Failing at Fairness.* New York: Charles Scribner's Sons.

Salazar Parrenas, Rhacel. 2000. "Migrant Filipina Domestic Workers and the International Division of Reproductive Labor." *Gender & Society* 14:560–581.

*Salt of the Earth.* Oak Park, IL: MPI Home Videos, distributor, 1954, 94 minutes.

Sandler, Bernice, 1999. "Ways in Which Men and Women May Be Treated Differently." *About Women on Campus* 8 (Summer).

Sargent, Paul. 2001. *Real Men or Real Teachers? Contradictions in the Lives of Men Elementary School Teachers.* Harriman, TN: Men's Studies Press.

Sassler, Sharon, and Robert Schoen. 1999. "The Effect of Attitudes and Economic Activity on Marriage." *Journal of Marriage and the Family* 61: 147–159.

Savage, Ann M. 2003. *They're Playing Our Songs: Women Talk About Feminist Rock Music.* Westport, CT: Praeger.

Schaffner, Laurie. 2006. *Girls in Trouble With the Law.* New Brunswick, NJ: Rutgers University Press.

Schiebinger, Londa. 2003. "Introduction: Feminism Inside the Sciences." *Signs* 28:859–866.

Schippers, Mimi. 2000. "The Social Organization of Sexuality and Gender in Alternative Hard Rock: An Analysis of Intersectionality." *Gender & Society* 14:747–764.

Schlosser, Eric. 2001. *Fast Food Nation.* Boston: Houghton Mifflin.

Schmitt, Eric. 2004. "Reports of Rape in Pacific Spur Air Force Steps." *New York Times*, March 9, A1, A18.

Schmitt, Frederika E., and Patricia Yancey Martin. 1999. "Unobtrusive Mobilization by an Institutionalized Rape Crisis Center." *Gender & Society* 13:364–384.

Schneider, Joseph W., and Sally L. Hacker. 1973. "Sex Role Imagery and Use of the Generic 'Man' in Introductory Texts." *American Sociologist* 8:12–18.

Schorr, Lisbeth B. 1998. *Common Purpose: Strengthening Families and Neighborhoods to Rebuild America.* New York: Anchor Books,

Schrock, Douglas P., and Irene Padavic. 2007. "Negotiating Hegemonic Masculinity in a Batterer Intervention Program." *Gender & Society* 21:625–649.

Schwartz, Pepper, and Amy E. Singer. 2001. "Equity in Heterosexual and Homosexual Relationships." In *Gender Mosaics: Social Perspectives*, edited by D. Vannoy. Los Angeles: Roxbury Publishing, Chapter 18.

Scott, Ellen K., Andrew S. London, and Nancy A. Myers. 2002. "Dangerous Dependencies: The Intersection of Welfare Reform and Domestic Violence." *Gender & Society* 16:878–897.

Scott, Janny. 2004. "Nearly Half of Black Men Found Jobless: Group Is Hardest Hit by Recession in City." *New York: Times*, February 28, B1, B4.

Seaman, Barbara. 2003. *The Greatest Experiment Ever Performed on Women: Exploding the Estrogen Myth*. New York: Hyperion.

Seccombe, Karen. 1999. *"So You Think I Drive a Cadillac?": Welfare Recipients' Perspectives on the System and Its Reform*. Boston: Allyn & Bacon.

Seigel, Jessica 2004. "The Cups Runneth Over." *New York Times*, February 13, A31.

Sengupta, Somini. 1999. "Openings Go Unfilled as City Officials Plan How to Spend Day-Care Money." *New York Times*, October 30, B1, B6.

Sered, Susan Starr. 1999. "'Woman' as Symbol and Women as Agents: Gendered Religious Discourses and Practices." In *Revisioning Gender*, edited by M. M. Ferree, B. B. Hess, and J. Lorber. Thousand Oaks, CA: Sage, 193–221.

Shows, Carla, and Naomi Gerstel. 2009. "Fathering, Class, and Gender." *Gender & Society* 23:161–187.

Smallwood, Scott. 2003. "American Women Surpass Men in Earning Doctorates." *Chronicle of Higher Education*, December 12, A10.

Smith, Barbara Ellen. 1999. "The Social Relations of Southern Women." In *Neither Separate Nor Equal*, edited by B. E. Smith. Philadelphia: Temple University Press, 13–31.

Smith, Ruth Bayard. 2000. "Listen to the Radio and Get an Earful." *New York Times*, July 22, A15.

Smith, Ryan A. 2002. "Race, Gender, and Authority in the Workplace: Theory and Research." *Annual Review of Sociology* 28:509–542.

Smith-Shomade, Beretta E. 2002. *Shaded Lives: African-American Women and Television*. New Brunswick, NJ: Rutgers University Press.

Smock, Pamela J. 2000. "Cohabitation in the United States: An Appraisal of Research Themes, Findings, and Implications." *Annual Review of Sociology* 26:1–20.

Smock, Pamela J., Wendy D. Manning, and Sanjiv Gupta. 1999. "The Effect of Marriage and Divorce on Women's Economic Well-Being." *American Sociological Review* 64:794–812.

Snyder, R. Claire. 2008. "What Is Third-Wave Feminism? A New Essay." *Signs* 34:175–196.

Sokoloff, Natalie J. 1980. *Between Money and Love: The Dialectics of Women's Home and Market Work*. New York: Praeger.

Spencer, Cassie C. 1987. "Sexual Assault: The Second Victimization." In *Women, The Courts, and Equality* edited by L.L. Crites and W. L. Hepperle. Newbury Park, CA: Sage, 54–73.

Spohn, Cassia, John Gruhl, and Susan Welch. 1990. *Criminal Behavior*, edited by H. Kelley Delos, New York: St. Martin's Press, 425–473.

Sprague, Joey. 1997. "Holy Men and Big Guns: The Can[n]on in Social Theory." *Gender & Society* 11:88–107.

Sprague, Joey, and Diane Kobrynowicz. 1999. "A Feminist Epistemology." In *Handbook of Sociology of Gender*, edited by Janet Saltzman Chafetz. New York: Kluwer Academic/Plenum Publishers, 25–43.

Sprague, Joey, and Mary K. Zimmerman. 1989. "Quality and Quantity: Reconstructing Feminist Methodology." *American Sociologist* 20:71–86.

Springer, Kimberly. 2002. "Third Wave Black Feminism?" *Signs* 27:1059–1082.

Springer, Kristen W. 2007. "Research or Rhetoric?" *Sociological Forum* 22:111–116.

Stanley, Alessandra. 2004. "L'Affaire Bodice: Why We Are Shocked, Shocked." *New York Times*, February 8, WK 16.

Steinberg, Ronnie J. 2001. "How Sex Gets Into Your Paycheck and How to Get It Out: The Gender Gap in Pay and Comparable Worth." In *Gender Mosaics: Social Perspectives*, edited by D. Vannoy. Los Angeles: Roxbury Publishing, Chapter 25.

Steinhauer, Jennifer. 2009. "To Trim Costs, States Relax Hard Line on Prisons." *New York Times*, March 25 A1, A22.

Stevens, Daphne, Gary Kiger, and Pamela J. Riley. 2001. "Working Hard and Hardly Working: Domestic Labor and Marital Satisfaction Among Dual-Earner Couples." *Journal of Marriage and the Family* 63:514–526.

Stevens, Patricia E. 1996. "Lesbians and Doctors: Experiences of Solidarity and Domination in Health Care Settings." *Gender & Society* 10:24–41.

Stewart, Abigail J., and Andrea Dottolo. 2006. "Feminist Psychology." *Signs* 31:493–509.

Stockard, Jean. 1999. "Gender Socialization." In *Handbook of the Sociology of Gender*, edited by

Janet Saltzman Chafetz. New York: Kluwer Academic/Plenum Publishers, 215–227.

Stoltenberg, John. 1990. *Refusing to Be a Man: Essay on Sex and Justice.* New York: Meridian.

Stolzenberg, Ross M. 2001. "It's About Time and Gender: Spousal Employment and Health." *American Journal of Sociology* 107:61–100.

Stratta, Terese M. Peretto. 2003. "Cultural Expressions of African American Female Athletes in Intercollegiate Sport." In *Athletic Intruders: Ethnographic Research on Women, Culture, and Exercise,* edited by Anne Bolin and Jane Granskog. Albany: State University of New York Press, 79–106.

Suárez, Zulerma E. 1999. "Islamic Family Ideals." In *Family Ethnicity,* edited by H. P. McAdoo. Thousand Oaks, CA: Sage, 213–221.

Sudarkasa, Niara. 1999. "African American Females as Primary Parents." In *Family Ethnicity,* edited by H. P. McAdoo. Thousand Oaks, CA: Sage, 191–200.

Sullivan, Maureen. 1996. "Rozzie and Harriet? Gender and Family Patterns of Lesbian Couples." *Gender & Society* 10:747–767.

Sullivan, Oriel. 2006. *Changing Gender Relations, Changing Families.* Lanham, MD: Rowman & Littlefield.

Talwar, Jennifer Parker. 2004. *Fast Food, Fast Track: Immigrants, Big Business, and the American Dream.* Boulder, CO: Westview Press.

Tavris, Carol. 1992. *The Mismeasure of Woman.* New York: Touchstone.

Taylor, Verta. 1996. *Rock-a-by Baby: Feminism, Self-Help, and Postpartum Depression.* New York: Routledge.

Tester, Griff. 2008. "An Intersectional Analysis of Sexual Harassment in Housing." *Gender & Society* 22:349–366.

Thierry Texeira, Mary. 2002. " 'Who Protects and Serves Me?' A Case Study of Sexual Harassment of African American Women in One U.S. Law Enforcement Agency." *Gender & Society* 16:524–545.

Thompson, Becky W. 1992. " 'A Way Outta No Way': Eating Problems Among African-American, Latina, and White Women." *Gender & Society* 6:546–561.

Thompson, Maxine S., and Verna M. Keith. 2001. "The Blacker the Berry: Gender, Skin Tone, Self-Esteem, and Self-Efficacy." *Gender & Society* 15:336–357.

Thorne, Barrie. 1993. *Gender Play: Girls and Boys in School.* New Brunswick, NJ: Rutgers University Press.

Thornton, Arland, and Linda Young-DeMarco. 2001. "Four Decades of Trends in Attitudes Toward Family Issues in the United States: The 1960s Through the 1990s." *Journal of Marriage and the Family* 63:1009–1037.

Tichenor, Veronica Jaris. 1999. "Status and Income as Gendered Resources: The Case of Marital Power." *Journal of Marriage and the Family* 61:638–650.

Tidball, M. Elizabeth, Daryl G. Smith, Charles S. Tidball, and Lisa E. Wolf-Wendel. 1998. *Taking Women Seriously.* Phoenix, AZ: Oryx Press.

Toner, Robin. 2004. "The Culture Wars, Part II." *New York Times,* February 29, WK 1,3.

Treichler, Paula A. 1988. "Biomedical Discourse: An Epidemic of Signification." In *AIDS: Cultural Analysis/Cultural Activism,* edited by D. Crimp. Cambridge, MA: MIT Press, 31–70.

Tyson, Karolyn. 2003. "Notes From the Back of the Room: Problems and Paradoxes in the Schooling of Young Black Students." *Sociology of Education* 76:326–343.

United Food and Commercial Workers. 2004. "Fact Sheets and Backgrounders Perdue Farms: Overview." Accessed at http://www.ufcw.org/press_room/fact_sheets_and_backgrounder/perduefacts.cfm.

U.S. Census Bureau. 2009. FactFinder. "United States and States. Median Age at First Marriage for Women." Accessed June 9, 2009, at http://factfinder.census.gov/servlet/GRTTable?_bm=y&-box_head_nbr=R1205&-ds_name=ACS_2007_1YR_G00_&-format=US-30. Also "United States and States Median Age at First Marriage for Men." Accessed June 9, 2009, at http://factfinder.census.gov/servlet/GRTTable?_bm=y&-geo_id=01000US&-_box_head_nbr=R1204&-ds_name=ACS_2007_1YR_G00_&-redoLog=false&-=US-30&-mt_name=ACS_2007_1YR_G00_R1205_US30.

U.S. Department of Commerce, Bureau of the Census. 1976. *A Statistical Portrait of Women in the U.S.* Current Population Reports. Series P-23, No.58. Washington, DC.

—— 2009. *The 2009 Statistical Abstract.* Accessed April 23, 2009, at http://www.census.gov/compendia/statab/tables/09s0058.pdf.

U.S. Department of Education. 2009. *Mini Digest of Education Statistics, 2008.* Washington, DC: U.S. Government Printing Office.

U.S. Department of Education, National Center for Educational Statistics. 2009. *Digest of Educational Statistics 2008.* Washington, DC: U. S. Government Printing Office.

U.S. Department of Justice, Bureau of Justice Statistics. 2009. "Homicide Trends in the U.S.: Intimate Homicide." Accessed August 30, 2009 at http://www.ojp.usdoj.gov/bjs/homicide/intimates.htm.

U.S. Department of Labor, Bureau of Labor Statistics. 2001. *Working in the 21ˢᵗ Century.* Accessed June 8, 2009, at http://www.bls.gov/opub/working/chart16.pdf.

——. 2003. "Women at Work: A Visual Essay." *Monthly Labor Review* 126 (October): 45–50. Accessed April 10, 2004 at http://www.bls.gov/opub/mlr/2003/10/ressum3.pdf.

——. 2008a. *Labor Force Characteristics by Race and Ethnicity, 2007.* Accessed June 9, 2009, at http://www.bls.gov/cps/cpsrace2007.pdf.

——. 2008b. *Women in the Labor Force: A Databook (2008 Edition).* Accessed June 8, 2009, at http://www.bls.gov/cps/wlf-databook2008.htm.

——. 2009a. Current Population Survey. *Household Data Annual Averages.* Accessed August 30, 2009 at http://www.bls.gov/cps.

——. 2009b. "The Editor's Desk: Wives Earning More Than Their Husbands, 1987–2006." Accessed June 8, 2009, at http://www.bls.gov/opub/ted/2009/jan/wkl/art05/htm.

U.S. Selective Service System. n.d. "Men 18–25 Years You Can Handle This: Read It. Fill It. Mail It." Distributed in U.S. Post Office, 2004.

Valian, Virginia. 1998. *Why So Slow?* Cambridge, MA: MIT Press.

Vavrus, Mary Douglas. 2002. *Postfeminist News: Political Women in Media Culture.* Albany: State University of New York Press.

Verbrugge, Lois M., and Deborah L. Wingard. 1987. "Sex Differentials in Health and Mortality." *Women & Health* 12(2). Reprinted 1991 in *The Sociology of Gender: A Text-Reader,* edited by L. Kramer. New York: St. Martin's Press, 447–458.

Vespa, Jonathan. 2009. "Gender Ideology Construction." *Gender & Society* 23:363–387.

Villarosa, Linda. 2003. "More Teenagers Say No to Sex, and Experts Aren't Sure Why." *New York Times,* December 23, F6, 8.

Wachs, Faye Linda. 2003. "'I Was There . . .': Gendered Limitations, Expectations, and Strategic Assumptions in the World of Co-ed Softball." In *Athletic Intruders: Ethnographic Research on Women, Culture, and Exercise,* edited by Anne Bolin and Jane Granskog. Albany: State University of New York Press, 177–199.

Wajcman, Judy. 1991. *Feminism Confronts Technology.* University Park: Pennsylvania State University Press.

Walk, Stephan R. 2000. "Moms, Sisters, and Ladies." In *Masculinities, Gender Relations, and Sport,* edited by Jim McKay, Michael A. Messner, and Don Sabo. Thousand Oaks, CA: Sage, 31–46.

Wallace, Ruth A. 1988. "Catholic Women and the Creation of a New Social Reality." *Gender & Society* 2:24–38.

Walters, Suzanna Danuta. 1999. "Sex, Text, and Context: (In) Between Feminism and Cultural Studies." In *Revisioning Gender,* edited by M. M. Ferree, B. B. Hess, and J. Lorber. Thousand Oaks, CA: Sage, 222–257.

Warner, Rebecca L., and Brent S. Steel. 1999. "Child Rearing as a Mechanism for Social Change: The Relationship of Child Gender to Parents' Commitment to Gender Equity." *Gender & Society* 13:503–517.

Webber, Gretchen, and Christine Williams. 2008. "Mothers in 'Good' and 'Bad' Part-Time Jobs." *Gender & Society* 22: 752–777.

Weis, Lois. 2006. "Masculinity, Whiteness, and the New Economy: An Exploration of Privilege and Loss." *Men and Masculinities* 8:262–272.

Weitz, Rose. 2001. "Women and Their Hair: Seeking Power Through Resistance and Accommodation." *Gender & Society* 15:667–686.

Weitzer, Ronald, and Charis E. Kubrin. 2009. "Misogyny in Rap Music." *Men and Masculinities* 11:3–29.

Welsh, Sandy. 1999. "Gender and Sexual Harassment." *Annual Review of Sociology* 25:169–190.

West, Candace, and Don H. Zimmerman. 1987. "Doing Gender." *Gender & Society* 1:125–151.

Whittaker, Terri. 1996. "Violence, Gender and Elder Abuse." In *Violence and Gender Relations: Theories and Interventions*, edited by B. Fawcett, B. Featherstone, J. Hearn, and C. Toft. London: Sage, 147–159.

Whittington, Kjersten Bunker, and Laurel Smith-Doerr. 2008. "Women Inventors in Context." *Gender & Society* 22:194–218.

Wilkins, Amy C. 2008. *Wannabes, Goths, and Christians*. Chicago: University of Chicago Press.

Williams, Christine L. 1992. "The Glass Elevator." *Social Problems* 39:253–267.

Williams, David R., James S. Jackson, Tony N. Brown, Myriam Torres, Tyrone A. Forman, and Kendrick Brown. 1999. "Traditional and Contemporary Prejudice and Urban Whites' Support for Affirmative Action and Government Help." *Social Problems* 46:503–527.

Williams, L. Susan. 2002. "Trying on Gender, Gender Regimes, and the Process of Becoming Women." *Gender & Society* 16:29–52.

Winkler, Anne E. 1998. "Earning of Husbands and Wives in Dual-Earner Families." *Monthly Labor Review* 121 (April):42–48.

Winterich, Julie A. 2003. "Sex, Menopause, and Culture: Sexual Orientation and the Meaning of Menopause for Women's Sex Lives." *Gender & Society* 17:627–642.

Wollstonecraft, Mary. 1787. *Thought on the Education of Daughters*. London: Johnson.

Woodrow Wilson School of Public and International Affairs at Princeton University and the Brookings Institution. *The Future of Children*. Accessed March 22, 2004, at http://www.futureofchildren. org/information2826/information_show.htm?doc_id=73254.

Woods, Nancy Fugate. 1999. "Midlife Women's Health: Conflicting Perspectives of Health Care Providers and Midlife Women and Consequences for Health." In *Revisioning Women, Health, and Healing: Feminist, Cultural, and Technoscience Perspectives*, edited by Adele E. Clarke and Virginia L. Olesen. New York: Routledge, 343–353.

Wootton, Barbara H. 1997. "Gender Differences in Occupational Employment." *Monthly Labor Review* 120 (April): 15–24.

Wu, Zheng, Margaret J. Penning, Michael S. Pollard, and Randy Hart. "'In Sickness and in Health': Does Cohabitation Count?" *Journal of Family Issues* 24:811–838.

Yeung, W. Jean, John F. Sandberg, Pamela E. Davis-Kean, and Sandra Hofferth. 2001. "Children's Time With Fathers in Intact Families." *Journal of Marriage and the Family* 63:136–154.

Young, Iris M. 2003. "The Logic of Masculinist Protection: Reflections on the Current Security State." *Signs* 29:1–25.

Zavella, Patricia. 1991. "Mujeres in Factories: Race and Class Perspectives on Women, Work, and Family." In *Gender at the Crosswords of Knowledge: Feminist Anthropology in the Postmodern Era*, edited by M. Di Leonardo. Berkeley: University of California Press, 312–336.

Zeisler, Andi. 2008. *Feminism and Pop Culture*. Berkeley, CA: Seal Press.

Zicklin, Gilbert. 1997. "Media, Science, and Sexual Ideology: The Promotion of Sexual Stability." In *A Queer World*, edited by M. Duberman. New York: New York University Press, 381–394.

Zimbalist, Andrew. 2000. "Backlash Against Title IX: An End Run Around Female Athletes." *Chronicle of Higher Education*, March 3, B9.

Zippel, Kathrin S. 2006. *The Politics of Sexual Harassment*. New York: Cambridge University Press.

# AUTHOR INDEX

# SUBJECT INDEX

CPSIA information can be obtained at www.ICGtesting.com

233735LV00004B/2/P